THE HOME
WORKSHOP

Other Publications:

THE EPIC OF FLIGHT
THE GOOD COOK
THE SEAFARERS
THE ENCYCLOPEDIA OF COLLECTIBLES
THE GREAT CITIES
WORLD WAR II
THE WORLD'S WILD PLACES
THE TIME-LIFE LIBRARY OF BOATING
HUMAN BEHAVIOR
THE ART OF SEWING
THE OLD WEST
THE EMERGENCE OF MAN
THE AMERICAN WILDERNESS
THE TIME-LIFE ENCYCLOPEDIA OF GARDENING
LIFE LIBRARY OF PHOTOGRAPHY
THIS FABULOUS CENTURY
FOODS OF THE WORLD
TIME-LIFE LIBRARY OF AMERICA
TIME-LIFE LIBRARY OF ART
GREAT AGES OF MAN
LIFE SCIENCE LIBRARY
THE LIFE HISTORY OF THE UNITED STATES
TIME READING PROGRAM
LIFE NATURE LIBRARY
LIFE WORLD LIBRARY
FAMILY LIBRARY:
  HOW THINGS WORK IN YOUR HOME
  THE TIME-LIFE BOOK OF THE FAMILY CAR
  THE TIME-LIFE FAMILY LEGAL GUIDE
  THE TIME-LIFE BOOK OF FAMILY FINANCE

HOME REPAIR
AND IMPROVEMENT

THE HOME
WORKSHOP

BY THE EDITORS OF
TIME-LIFE BOOKS

TIME-LIFE BOOKS
ALEXANDRIA, VIRGINIA

HOME REPAIR AND IMPROVEMENT

Editorial Staff for Home Workshop

Editor Robert M. Jones
Assistant Editors Betsy Frankel, Leslie Marshall
Designer Edward Frank
Chief Researcher Oobie Gleysteen
Picture Editor Neil Kagan
Associate Designer Kenneth E. Hancock
Text Editors William C. Banks, Katherine Miller, Brooke Stoddard,
William Worsley
Staff Writers Lynn R. Addison, Patricia Bangs, Michael Blumenthal,
Jan Leslie Cook, Robert A. Doyle, Steven J. Forbis,
Kathleen M. Kiely, Victoria Monks, Peter Pocock,
Mary-Sherman Willis
Art Associates George Bell, Fred Holz, Lorraine D. Rivard
Editorial Assistant Susan Larson

Editorial Production

Production Editor Douglas B. Graham
Operations Manager Gennaro C. Esposito, Gordon E. Buck (assistant)
Assistant Production Editor Feliciano Madrid
Quality Control Robert L. Young (director), James J. Cox (assistant),
Daniel J. McSweeney, Michael G. Wight (associates)
Art Coordinator Anne B. Landry
Copy Staff Susan B. Galloway (chief), Margery duMond,
Celia Beattie
Picture Department Anne Muñoz-Furlong

Correspondents: Elisabeth Kraemer (Bonn); Margot
Hapgood, Dorothy Bacon, Lesley Coleman (London);
Susan Jonas, Lucy T. Voulgaris (New York); Maria
Vincenza Aloisi, Josephine du Brusle (Paris); Ann
Natanson (Rome). Valuable assistance was also
provided by: Karin B. Pearce (London); Carolyn T.
Chubet, Miriam Hsia, Christina Lieberman (New
York); Mimi Murphy (Rome).

THE CONSULTANTS: James M. Koenig, a professional museum consultant, designs and constructs museum exhibits in his own home workshop. A carpenter
and avid collector of antique woodworking tools,
Koenig is an active member of the Early American
Industries Association and other organizations devoted to the study of early tools. He also designs museum storage systems for the National Park Service.

David X. Manners was a writer of fiction until his
experiences in building his own home turned his
interests toward carpentry and woodworking. Since
that time he has authored some dozen volumes on
how-to subjects, including home workshops and
tools and tool selection. Manners is a former editorial
director of Family Handyman magazine and former
building editor at House Beautiful.

Roswell W. Ard, a civil engineer, is a consulting structural engineer and home inspector who has written
professional papers on wood-frame construction
techniques. He has designed heating, electrical and
motor-control systems and has explored alternate
energy systems, including generators that use solar
energy and wind power.

Harris Mitchell, special consultant for Canada, has
worked in the field of home repair and improvement
for more than two decades. He is editor of the magazine Canadian Homes and author of a syndicated
newspaper column, "You Wanted to Know," as well
as of a number of books on home improvement.

For information about any Time-Life book, please write:
Reader Information
Time-Life Books
541 North Fairbanks Court
Chicago, Illinois 60611

Library of Congress Cataloguing in Publication Data
Time-Life Books.
    The home workshop.
    (Home repair and improvement; 23)
    Includes index.
    1. Workshops. I. Title.
TT152.T55   1980   684'.08   80-13483
ISBN 0-8094-3456-3
ISBN 0-8094-3455-5 (lib. bdg.)

Contents

COLOR PORTFOLIO: Diversity in Shops of Yore ... 32

1 **Where Work Becomes a Pleasure** ... **7**
Downstairs, Upstairs, Even in the Garage ... 8
Built-in Safety: the Surest Kind of Protection ... 10
Guardians against Cold, Damp, Noxious Air ... 12
Better Access and Egress Routes for Materials ... 18
Wanted: a Durable, Cleanable, Slipproof Floor ... 27
Preventing, Detecting and Extinguishing Fire ... 28
Silencing or Confining Noise ... 30

2 **Equipping the Shop for Action** ... **43**
Personalizing a Battery of Portable Tools ... 44
Muscle Men: a Corps of Heavy-duty Power Tools ... 48
Caution—the Watchword for Power-Tool Safety ... 58
The Layout: Putting All the Pieces Together ... 61
Rigging Electric Power to Serve Manifold Needs ... 64
General and Focused Lighting ... 76

3 **Jigs, Benches and Accessories** ... **81**
Building the Best Workbench for Your Workshop ... 82
"Third Hand" Devices to Use with Big Power Tools ... 94
Specialized Work Spaces for Special Pursuits ... 107

4 **A Place where Neatness Counts** ... **115**
Tool Storage: Everything in Its Designated Spot ... 116
Tailored Storage Spaces for All That Miscellany ... 122
Organizing the Workshop's Housekeeping Chores ... 128
Putting Refuse in Its Place ... 132

Acknowledgments and Picture Credits ... **134**

Index/Glossary ... **135**

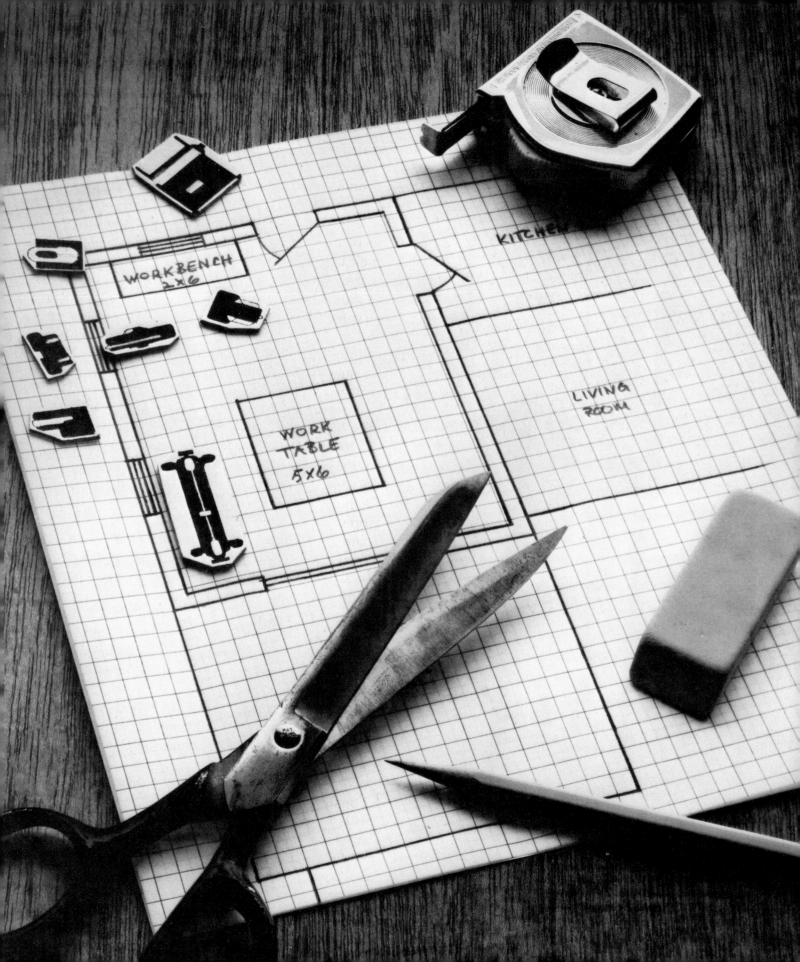

Where Work Becomes a Pleasure

Finding a room that fits. An attached garage being considered for use as a workshop site is drawn to scale on graph paper, complete with doors, windows and permanent work surfaces such as the workbench and worktable. To determine whether the room is big enough for the large power tools planned for it, the homeowner draws scale silhouettes of the tools as they would appear from overhead, then cuts them out and moves them around on the paper to determine the best possible positions.

An amazing number of Americans take care of their own home repairs—so many that it might be considered a national pastime. Seven out of ten homeowners subscribe to the idea of do-it-yourself and own at least a rudimentary collection of tools, and the movement toward self-reliance is growing at the rate of 15 per cent a year. As they add to their knowledge and experience, and acquire more complex tools, most of these home craftsmen yearn for a place in which to practice their newfound skills, a place meticulously organized for making a mess in order to keep the rest of the house running smoothly: in short, a home workshop.

The word *workshop* conjures up an image of a cornucopia of workbenches and power tools, tiers of shelves filled with fascinating hardware and walls festooned with a vast array of hand tools. But most workshops are far more modest. If you want a truly well-stocked workshop with enough elbow room for such large power tools as a drill press and a table saw, you are going to need at least 150 square feet of floor space. In most homes, a space of this size is not easy to come by. For many people a practical home workshop may be nothing more than a converted closet lined with perforated hardboard or stacked with shelves to hold tools, with a fold-down work surface. But the thought and planning that go into its creation can far exceed the shop's modest size.

Whatever the size and the location of your shop, you will want to build into it all the comforts of the rest of the house. Though the shop's purpose may be strictly utilitarian, you will not enjoy working in the winter chill of an unheated cellar or the summer purgatory of an unventilated attic.

You will also want to pay special attention to safety. A workshop is a place fraught with dangers—from the hazards posed by power tools with their high-speed blades and bits, to the threat of fire in everything from combustible liquids to oily rags. To avoid irritating the other members of the household with the whine of power tools, you may need to incorporate soundproofing materials into the walls and ceiling and perhaps even the floor. And you may need to deaden the reverberation of noise to protect your own hearing.

Finally, because tools are the heart and sinew of a workshop, you will want to give considerable thought to their care and storage. How you arrange your tools is of course a matter of personal preference, but certain kinds of tools, particularly cutting tools that must be kept sharp and rust-free, require special kinds of storage in order to remain in good repair. Once such practical matters are taken care of, a home workshop becomes a place that will reward you with satisfactions and savings through all the years you continue to occupy the house.

Downstairs, Upstairs, Even in the Garage

Since few homes come ready-made with an ideal site for a workshop, most homeowners must improvise, using space originally designed for a different purpose. But with a bit of imagination and some thoughtful planning, a surprising number of possibilities emerge.

The site you finally choose will depend on your particular needs and on the amount of time, effort and money you want to invest. Locating a workshop in a spare bedroom, for example, may provide the large work area you need, but if you plan to work with noisy power tools, you will have to do extensive soundproofing. Noise will be less of a factor if you locate the shop in a detached garage, but there you may have to install new electrical wiring and some form of heat.

Noise and the availability of power and light are in fact the two central concerns in evaluating any workshop site. But other factors must also be considered. As you weigh the pros and cons of the various locations, you might begin by asking yourself the following seven questions. Their answers should give you a clearer picture of what sort of environment your shop activities will require. Then use the site descriptions on these two pages to evaluate the specific advantages and disadvantages of your prospective sites.

☐ WHAT KIND OF WORK WILL YOU DO IN THE SHOP? The answer to this question is crucial. Hobby work, such as model building and jewelry making, requires relatively little space and can be done almost anywhere in the house. However, large cabinetry projects require stationary power tools with specific space allotments (pages 48-57), plus room for assembling and painting the projects. And a shop for automotive repairs must be built in a garage.

☐ HOW ACCESSIBLE IS A PROJECTED SITE? It is difficult, if not impossible, to carry heavy, awkward machinery into a workshop through narrow doorways or up long flights of stairs, and equally difficult to transport unwieldly building materials and finished projects in and out of a shop with only one door leading into a long hall. The best access to a workshop is provided by double doors, preferably opening directly to the outside of the house, and a minimum of steps. An outside door not only eliminates the problem of carrying cumbersome objects around corners, but it cuts down on dirt tracked through the house.

☐ WHAT UTILITIES ARE AVAILABLE? All workshops need heat, light and power, and many also need air conditioning to cool the shop in hot weather. Some shops may need a water supply—perhaps for a fire-extinguishing sprinkler system or for cleaning paintbrushes. If you choose a site inside the house, most utilities will probably be available, although you may have to tap several electrical circuits or extend plumbing lines or an existing heating or cooling system. If you select a site separate from the house, you may have to provide new utilities.

☐ CAN YOU CONTROL MOISTURE AND PROVIDE VENTILATION? Excessive dampness is a menace in a workshop: It can rust tools, warp wood and adversely affect new finishes, such as paint and varnish. Locating a shop above ground level reduces the danger of dampness; in a basement, you may have to install a dehumidifier. Improper ventilation can make a shop unbearably hot, stuffy and even dangerous when toxic and flammable fumes are present. The more windows the room has, the better.

☐ HOW MUCH NOISE WILL YOU MAKE? Large power tools are noisy and their vibrations may be carried through the house by ducts and even by wooden structural members. You may have to install soundproofing—especially if you plan to use your shop late at night when other people are asleep.

☐ WHAT WILL YOU DO WITH DIRT AND DUST? Dirt and dust are the inevitable results of workshop activity. Good cleaning systems (page 132) will control most of the mess, but the closer the shop is to living quarters, the harder it will be to keep lighter, airborne particles out of areas where they are unwelcome.

☐ WHAT ARE THE STORAGE POSSIBILITIES? In addition to work space, a workshop needs plenty of room to stow tools, wood, paints, hardware and similar materials. The site you choose should have enough wall or ceiling space to contain all the shelves, cabinets and storage racks your work will require.

Shops that Occupy Entire Rooms

A workshop that takes over a whole room in the house offers one distinct advantage: plenty of floor space for stationary power tools, special work areas and storage of large work materials such as long boards and sheets of plywood.

But before you convert any room into a workshop, consider how the remodeling may affect the resale value of your house. A former recreation room or bedroom that has been converted to a shop may not impress a prospective buyer.

A Workroom in the Basement

For several reasons, a basement is often the most logical location for a workshop. It usually contains the furnace, which means it is already heated, and if it is below ground level, it is generally relatively cool in the summer. Since it is isolated from the rest of the house, dust and dirt are easier to contain, and masonry foundation walls tend to trap sound. Concrete floors provide a sturdy foundation for heavy power tools.

Unfinished basements provide good possibilities for storage: Exposed ceiling joists, for example, are handy supports for convenient overhead lumber racks.

The biggest problem with basement workshops is dampness, caused by water seeping in from outside or by condensation. You can probably overcome the first of these difficulties by waterproofing the inside walls and by building a better drainage system around the outside of the house. Pipes that sweat can be covered with insulation.

Access to basements can also be a problem if the only entrance is through an inside door and down a narrow staircase. In this situation, it may be worthwhile to add a door and steps leading directly to the outside (pages 18-26).

A Spare Room Upstairs

A spare room in the main part of the house is already supplied with heat and electricity and its windows provide natural light and ventilation. But in most cases the spare room will be adjacent to rooms where excessive noise is undesirable, and if the room opens onto a narrow hallway, access may be difficult.

Building double walls or adding sound-proofing insulation to existing walls (page 30) will help reduce the noise level, and if the room is on the ground floor, installing a door to the outside will take care of access. Because dirt may be a problem, a tight-fitting interior door is essential and so is a good vacuum system, to keep sawdust and grime from spreading to other rooms.

Making Use of the Attic

The wide-open empty space of an unfinished attic has many of the attributes of a perfect workshop site. A ridge beam at least 10 feet high contributes useful vertical space and it is especially easy to fit storage under the eaves.

However, an attic shop presents several fairly serious problems. Before you begin to build, check to be sure that the attic floor joists will support a plywood floor and any machinery you are planning to install. The local building inspector can tell you the size and spacing of joists required for your floor span; you may need to add reinforcement.

An attic shop is also less accessible than most other sites: Carrying heavy tools and materials to the third or fourth floor is bound to be inconvenient. And unless the attic has air conditioning or windows, it will be very hot in summer. However, if you install an exhaust fan to cool the shop, you will gain the added benefit of pulling air through the rooms below and cooling them as well.

To reduce the transmission of noise and vibration to the living quarters below, you may have to place rubber mats beneath power tools, or even construct a sound-dampening floor (page 30). Dust filtering down from the attic shop to the rest of the house may also be a problem, but a centralized vacuum system should help. Finally, if you need additional headroom under the eaves, you may have to raise a section of the roof by building a shed dormer, a solution that requires extensive construction.

A Shop that Shares a Room

If you cannot spare an entire room for a shop, with some rearranging you may still be able to create adequate work space in a room already in use. For example, one end of a recreation room can accommodate a shop with enough room for hobbies and other small projects. A garage may be big enough for a small shop area.

The disadvantages are obvious; there will be less privacy and less elbow room. If the shop is inside the house, noise and dirt may inconvenience others who share the room. But with some careful planning of space and some compromises on time schedules, your workshop can usually coexist peacefully in a room that is also used for other activities.

Sharing with a Recreation Room

In a recreation room, or any room in the house with space enough to share with a workshop, the biggest problem will be defining the work area. If possible, designate one part of the room to be used exclusively for shop work. One solution is a permanent partition, separating the shop area from the rest of the room; this will also provide a surface for storage shelves or perforated hardboard (pegboard) tool racks. The partition should be as soundproof as possible, and should have a lockable door.

If a permanent partition is not feasible, consider a movable one such as folding doors or mobile screens. Even movable partitions will muffle noise slightly and slow the spread of dirt and dust. With a movable partition, you can easily expand the workshop into the shared area if you have mounted the workbench and power tools on lockable casters. You then simply push the bench and tools back out of the way when they are not in use.

In a shared shop area, it is especially important to use lockable switches on power tools to prevent unauthorized use, and to store potentially dangerous materials under lock and key.

Sharing the Garage with the Car

Although you may have to add heat and electricity, the garage is a good place to put a workshop because it is isolated—sometimes completely detached—from the rest of the house. This is the obvious place for automotive repair work and other noisy, messy tasks. The wide door provides excellent access to the outside and there is frequently overhead storage room under the rafters of a pitched roof.

In a long, narrow garage, the shop may fit against the end wall. A shop along a side wall needs 3 or 4 feet of clearance; allow room for opening car doors.

Where climate and space allow, you might also consider building a carport for your car and taking over the entire garage for a shop. Or you could gain space on one side of the garage by extending the roof and building a bay underneath it.

Improvised Shops in Unexpected Places

When there is no sizable block of space for a workshop in the house or garage, you might tuck the shop into an overlooked nook or cranny. There may be enough room for a small work area under a basement stairway or in a closet (page 63). Or you could build a hinged worktable to fold down over a washer and dryer and put shelves above for storage.

If the house has a porch, you can enclose it for a shop. In warm climates, you may be able to use an open porch for a workshop, or even a concrete slab sheltered by a simple sun roof. In this case, mount the workbench and heavy tools on wheels so they can be rolled indoors or into a nearby shed for storage. If your yard is large enough and building codes permit it, you can erect a prefabricated utility shed for this purpose.

Built-in Safety: The Surest Kind of Protection

Workshops by their very nature are places in which accidents happen. Some of these accidents involve the careless use of tools: Someone operates a power saw without a blade guard or uses a grinding machine without wearing protective goggles. But a fair number of workshop injuries are caused by environmental conditions. You can prevent accidents by taking safety into account in planning and building your workshop.

Consider, for example, the matter of access, of doors that are wide enough for the passage of bulky objects like sheets of plywood or a completed hi-fi cabinet. If you have space for it, a pair of double doors 72 inches wide is none too large for a workshop, and even a 36-inch door will give you far more maneuvering room than the standard 30- or 32-inch door. Wherever it is possible, these doors should open outward, permitting quick exit in case of fire.

Stairs, like doors, should be designed with easy access in mind. If you must climb or descend in order to reach your workshop, make sure the stairs are not too steep—treads should be at least 10 inches wide and risers no more than 8¼ inches high. For added safety, apply self-sticking nonskid tape or corrugated rubber pads to the treads and paint the nosings (the rounded front edges) bright yellow. If there are more than two steps, attach a strong handrail along one side of the stairway.

Fire, one of the chief hazards of a home workshop (pages 28-29), can be controlled as much by built-in construction features as by accessible fire-fighting equipment. Walls and ceilings, for example, should be fire-retardant gypsum board painted with latex paint, which is less flammable than oil-base paint.

The flooring of the shop (page 27) is another basic safety consideration. It should be durable, skidproof and easy to clean. Both concrete and sheet vinyl are excellent shop flooring materials in terms of wear, for instance, but vinyl is more slippery than concrete when both are covered with sawdust. In addition, the floor should be as free of obstructions as possible. If you must install an electrical raceway to a floor outlet for a freestanding power tool, draw attention to its presence by painting it with black and yellow stripes like those used to alert motorists to highway obstructions.

Color aids are also useful for locating electrical switches and outlets in a hurry, in case you need to turn off the power in an emergency: For this purpose the traditional color is blue. Other safety measures you will want to consider in conjunction with bringing electricity into the shop are a lockable circuit-breaker box to prevent unauthorized use of your power tools, and an abundance of electric outlets so you can use power tools anywhere in the shop without needing a tangle of extension cords. In installing these outlets, make sure they are grounded. Consider using the more expensive ground-fault interrupters in outlets (page 64), as GFIs quickly shut off power in the event of even a minor interruption of current.

Lighting, an integral part of the electrical system, is vital to shop safety. Overhead lighting from fluorescent fixtures is best, providing shadow-free illumination over a wide area. In addition, you will want intense localized light, like that provided by clamp-on desk lights, for some of your workbench or power-tool operations. Wherever light bulbs or fluorescent tubes will be exposed to damage from lumber being swung, they should be shielded with the open metal mesh called hardware cloth. In any area that has a special combustion hazard, as in a spray-painting booth (page 110), be sure to use explosion-proof bulbs.

For safety as well as for your own comfort, the temperature within the workshop should be about 60°. If you have a basement shop, you probably have enough furnace heat, but in a garage you may have to bring in heat, either by tapping an existing system or by installing a self-contained unit (pages 14-15). If you use a portable electric heater, make sure its heating coils are enclosed.

In hot weather you may want to keep the shop tolerable with a window air conditioner, but an exhaust fan will often do the job adequately—and in any event you will need such a fan, to draw off potentially explosive dust and noxious or poisonous fumes.

Almost as insidious as the dangers of too much or too little heat is the invisible hazard of sound (pages 30-31). Long exposure to the whine of power tools can cause fatigue and errors of judgment; it can also damage hearing. Wherever possible, sheathe the shop with materials that muffle sound; dampen the vibrations of power tools by mounting them on rubber pads.

Having designed safety into the shop when you planned it, follow common-sense procedures when you work there. Store potentially dangerous tools in locked cabinets, and flammable liquids in metal cabinets. Use metal trash cans with lids for disposing of debris and empty these containers frequently. Finally, make sure you are not a safety hazard yourself. Wear heavy shoes, preferably with metal toe caps, to shield your feet from an accidentally dropped chisel or piece of lumber. Keep a pair of work gloves in the shop for handling rough lumber, and have a pair of safety goggles or a face shield—or both—on hand, as well as a respirator and good ear plugs.

Since even the most thorough safety precautions can be defeated by a moment's inattention, keep a first-aid kit in the shop where it can easily be found. Paint it a distinct color—green is used in many professional shops—and check its contents occasionally. It should contain, at the minimum, gauze, tape, scissors, bandages, disinfectant, burn ointment, tweezers and an eye-wash solution.

A workshop designed for safety. Although sparsely equipped, this home shop was planned for safety. Easy access is ensured by double doors (right), which admit daylight and open outward for quick exit in case of fire. Walls are covered with fire-retardant Type X wallboard, and are painted with a light shade of fire-resistant latex paint to brighten the shop and improve visibility. On the ceiling, sound-absorbing acoustic tiles dampen noise within the shop. An exhaust fan, installed in the wall at right, pulls fumes and dust out of the room.

Electrical power is distributed through many outlets in different areas of the shop to avoid the need for extension cords, and there is a lockable circuit-breaker subpanel where all the power can be turned off. A metal electrical raceway brings power to the middle of the shop floor. (Do not install such a floor outlet if your shop is subject to flooding.) Overhead, fluorescent light fixtures on adjustable chains can be raised for more head room when it is needed, and all of the fluorescent tubes are shielded with metal

hardware cloth. Above the workbench, a desk lamp provides extra local light for precision work.

Steps from the shop have a handrail, and nonskid strips on the treads; bright color is used to highlight tread nosings, the low ceiling over the stairway, and the electrical raceway on the floor. Near the workbench at right, a metal trash can with a lid is used for oily rags and other flammable trash, while combustible paints and thinners are stored in a metal cabinet. At left, small power tools are kept in a lockable cabinet. Safety goggles, a respirator and a face shield are within easy reach above the workbench.

In case a fire does start, a ceiling smoke detector with an alarm wired to the bedroom provides an early warning. Fire extinguishers, mounted in different locations so that one is at hand near an escape route into the house or through the double doors to the outside, provide the means for fighting the fire. For medical emergencies, a first-aid kit is in plain sight and within easy reach on the wall.

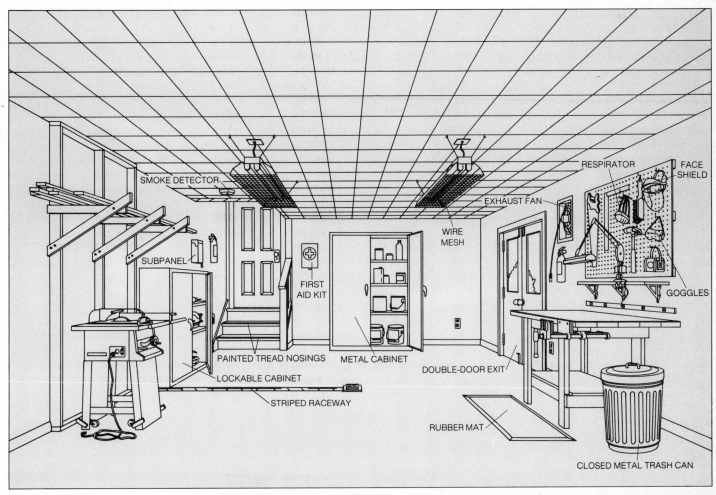

Guardians against Cold, Damp, Noxious Air

Proper temperature, good ventilation and limited humidity are as important in a workshop as in any other room in a house, sometimes more so. These conditions are usually easy to provide. For temperature control, most shops can tap into existing heating and cooling systems, and an ordinary exhaust fan will take care of ventilation. However, excess dampness, which damages tools and lumber by rusting or warping them, is a bigger problem. A number of measures may be taken to solve it, depending on whether the source of the dampness is inside or outside the house.

Ideally, of course, a workshop should be dry to start with. But many basement workshops are plagued by condensation or water seepage. If condensation is the problem, the moisture usually collects on surfaces in a room, particularly on cold windows and cold-water pipes. But water seeping in from outside generally collects in pools on the floor. One test for determining the cause of dampness is to fasten a piece of foil 1 foot square to the inside of a masonry basement wall, sealing all four edges with tape. After two days, check the foil. If moisture has formed on the side of the foil that was facing the wall, the cause is seepage; if moisture has formed on the room side, the cause is condensation.

Excessive humidity is the cause of condensation, and you can roughly measure its level with a homemade sling psychrometer consisting of a wet-bulb and a dry-bulb thermometer taped or tied together (opposite, bottom right). When the psychrometer is whirled through the air, moisture on the wet bulb evaporates, lowering the temperature reading. Humid air absorbs less moisture than dry air, so the smaller the difference between the readings on the two thermometers, the higher the humidity.

Humid air may come from something as obvious as an unvented clothes dryer, which can easily be vented outdoors with a kit from a hardware store. To control condensation dripping from cold-water pipes, cover the pipes with insulation. One handy form, made just for this purpose, covers the pipes like a sleeve. This does not reduce the humidity in the air but it halts the dripping.

The heating system is another possible source of humidity, circulating heated air moistened by the furnace humidifier, downstairs as well as up. A furnace humidifier can be adjusted with its dial control. If moisture condenses on the windows upstairs, the amount of moisture being added to the air should be reduced. You can also place a freestanding dehumidifier in the shop, especially valuable in the summer in a room that is not air-conditioned. These units switch on automatically whenever the air is damp.

In some of these freestanding units the extracted moisture is deposited in a bucket, which must be emptied periodically; in others it flows through a plastic hose into a basement drain or outdoors. In 24 hours, a 14-pint dehumidifier removes up to 14 pints of water from a room with 500 square feet of floor area. Larger and smaller units are also available. For each additional 500 square feet, you will need a dehumidifier with an additional 5- to 6-pint capacity. If condensation from humidity occurs largely in the summer when the air is hot as well as moist, a window air conditioner will alleviate both problems, since cool air carries less moisture than warm.

When the dampness in a basement comes from seepage, first check to see if water is standing near the foundation after a heavy rain; if so, provide a means of diverting it before the next rain. Then check the walls themselves for cracks. Though small cracks do not endanger the structure of a house, they can let water in and should be sealed. Horizontal cracks along a bulging wall and vertical cracks that are wider than ¼ inch and extend more than 4 feet indicate a serious problem that should be investigated by a foundation engineer.

Water that seeps through basement walls in modest amounts can, in many cases, be controlled with a coat of waterproofing paint on the inside. To prepare the wall, clean it thoroughly and use a chemical paint remover to remove any latex or oil-base paint. Then fill any cracks with two coats of waterproof patching mortar or hydraulic cement; the latter will adhere to masonry even when it is wet. If water is seeping through another common trouble spot, the joint between the basement floor and wall, you can seal the joint. First chisel a channel into the joint. Then, if the joint is dry, fill it with two layers of epoxy resin; if it is damp, use hydraulic cement.

In some instances the only way to cure a wet basement is to excavate along the outside of the foundation wall and waterproof it with a thin coat of portland-cement mortar followed by a coat of bituminous sealant. Perforated drain tile is then laid around the perimeter of the foundation at a level lower than the bottom of the footing on a 4-inch bed of gravel; the tile and gravel together channel the water into a dry well or sewer. The enormity of this job—it may require a backhoe—persuades most people to leave the work to a professional.

If a basement lies below the area's water table, sealants, applied either inside or outside, are of little value—water will rise through the floor. The solution is to collect the water in a hole, called a sump, cut into the basement floor; from the hole, a sump pump lifts the water into a pipe that runs through the basement wall into a storm sewer.

To install a sump pump, you must break through the cellar floor with a sledge hammer or rented jackhammer and dig a hole to accommodate the cylindrical metal liner in which the pump sits. A raised wooden cover rests over the hole after the pump is in place, to keep debris out. A separate, unswitched electrical circuit will help assure that the pump will always operate when needed.

Attacking Basement Moisture

Locating the leaks. If pools of water collect near the house foundation, check the condtion of the gutters. Remove debris from them and make sure that every gutter slopes 1 inch for every 16 feet of its length toward a downspout. Downspouts should discharge the water onto a splash block that channels water at least 3 feet away from the walls. Bank soil away from the foundation and plant a ground cover to hold the soil in place. Check basement window frames for leaks and caulk them; clear the window wells of leaves that may block drainage and channel water into the basement.

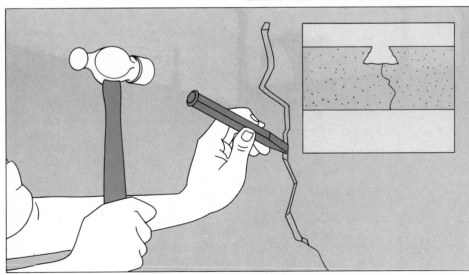

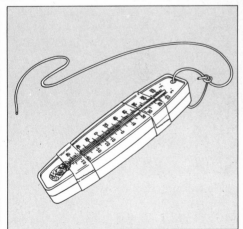

Patching small wall cracks. Using a cold chisel and a ball-peen hammer or small sledge, widen the crack to about ½ inch at the surface, undercutting the edge to form an inverted V about 1 inch wide at the base *(inset)*. Clean away loose masonry with a wire brush and fill the crack with patching mortar or hydraulic cement,

using a pointing trowel to force the mortar down under the lips of the V. Tamp the mortar tightly into the crack with the rounded head of a ball-peen hammer or with a piece of scrap wood. To cure the mortar, sprinkle water on it occasionally for three days and tape a piece of plastic sheeting over it to keep it moist.

Measuring humidity. Tape two bulb thermometers back-to-back and fasten a piece of thin, wet cloth against the bulb of one thermometer by wrapping it with a string. Hold the thermometers in front of a fan or swing them through the air on the end of a string for about a minute. Then add the temperature readings on the two thermometers, multiply the sum by 0.4 and add 15. If the result exceeds 75, the humidity is high enough to be causing damage.

Keeping the Workshop Warm

Heating a workshop means weighing many concerns—economy of operation, availability of space, proximity of existing heat sources. But the most important concern is safety. The lumber, sawdust and flammable materials found in a workshop dictate that the heat source, especially if it involves exposed electric coils or open flame, be isolated from anything combustible.

Since you will rarely want the shop warmer than 60°, a simple plug-in space heater may do the job. But if you need more heat, extending an existing forced-air heating system is the safest option, because the source of the heat is usually in another room, some distance away. Tapping into such an existing heat source is also the least expensive way of acquiring heat, saving you the cost and time of installing an independent heating unit. Most home furnaces produce enough heat to supply at least two additional rooms, and their fans are strong enough to take on the added burden of blowing air through new ductwork.

However, if your workshop is more than 25 feet from the furnace, or if you cannot run a duct to your workshop in a relatively straight line, think twice about taking heat from an existing system: You may lose most of the heat en route from the furnace to the shop. It would also be unwise to tap an existing system if your furnace does not adequately heat your house now.

Among alternative heat sources, the most economical and efficient is probably a wood-burning stove. It does not drain heat from the rest of the house, it can be made to produce heat only when you need it, and it can be fueled in part with scrap wood from the shop. But a wood stove takes up a good bit of room and it can be a fire hazard. It should never be used to heat a shop while you are using chemicals with flammable fumes, or while you are spray-painting. A wood-burning stove also necessitates a scrupulously clean shop: Sawdust settling on the surface of the stove could smolder and burn. Before you decide to install a wood-burning stove, check the local regulations with your building supervisor.

For shops that are too small for a wood-burning stove, an electric base-board heater is in many cases the best solution, though electric heat is expensive. Baseboard heaters fit snugly against the wall, taking up little space, and come in lengths from 28 to 120 inches. Operating on 120 or 240 volts, they use from 500 to 2500 watts of electricity and most models require a separate circuit (*page 64*). The higher the wattage, the greater the heating capacity. To estimate the wattage you need, multiply the number of square feet in your workshop by 10. Some baseboard heaters are equipped with a built-in thermostat; others must be wired to a wall-mounted thermostat.

Taking Heat from a Forced-Air Furnace

1 Cutting a hole in the main duct. With a felt-tipped pen, trace the outline of a 6-inch sheet-metal collar onto the main duct, or plenum, at the top of the furnace. Drill a hole within the circle. Wearing heavy work gloves, enlarge the hole, with a hammer and cold chisel (*left*). Make the opening big enough to admit tin snips; then snip along the outline of the circle.

Fit the collar into the hole and reach inside it to press the collar tabs against the inside of the plenum, fastening the collar in place (*right*). Slide a section of 6-inch round duct into the collar to begin the run. Drill ⅛-inch screw holes through both sides of the joint, secure with sheet-metal screws and seal with duct tape.

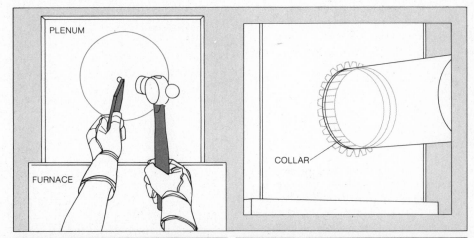

PLENUM

FURNACE

COLLAR

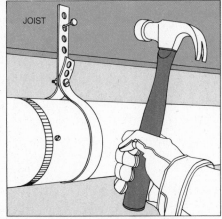

JOIST

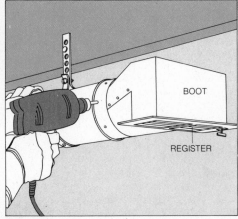

BOOT

REGISTER

2 Supporting the duct. Continue adding sections of duct, suspending the sections at least 1 inch below the ceiling joists with flexible metal hangers placed every 3 feet. Wrap each hanger around the duct, secure it with a bolt and nut, then nail it to the side of the joist. If your workshop has no exposed joists, locate their position using the same method as for locating studs (*page 16*), and fasten the hangers to the ceiling at these positions.

3 Assembling the register. Attach a register to the rectangular opening of a 90° register boot by drilling matching screw holes through the flanges of the register and boot and fastening the two together with sheet-metal screws. (The register should have closing louvers so you can shut off the flow of heat.) Slide the round end of the boot over the end of the last section of duct; drill holes through both and fasten them with sheet-metal screws.

A Wood Stove or Space Heater for Warmth when You Need It

Getting rid of the smoke. An assembly of elbows, Ts and straight sections of stovepipe carries smoke from a wood-burning stove through an insulated trim collar set in a circular opening cut in the wall of the house. Inside, the stovepipe should be at least 18 inches from the ceiling. Insulated pipe runs up the outside of the house and is secured to the wall every 8 feet with a wall band. It ends at a point 3 feet higher than a flat roof, or 2 feet higher than any part of a pitched roof within 10 feet, and it is finally capped (*inset*) to keep wind from blowing the smoke back into the shop.

According to most building codes, a wood-burning stove must stand on a fireproof base, such as brick, slate or marble, at least ⅜ inch thick. It must be at least 36 inches from a combustible wall, and no closer than 18 inches to a masonry wall or a stud wall protected by a heat shield of ¼-inch asbestos millboard covered with sheet metal. The heat shield is mounted on the wall with 1-inch porcelain spacers to provide air space between the shield and the wall.

Wiring an electric baseboard heater. Shut off power at the service panel, remove the heater's wiring-box cover, and run plastic-sheathed electrical cable from the main electrical panel or from a subpanel (*page 67*) into the wiring box. Secure the cable with a cable clamp at the knockout hole. Connect the black cable wire to the black heater wire and join the white cable wire to the white heater wire, using wire caps. Connect the bare cable wire to the grounding screw in the wiring box (*left inset*). Anchor a furring strip to the masonry wall, first using a masonry bit to drill through the strip and into the wall. Tap screw anchors into the drilled holes in the wall, then use sheet-metal screws to attach the strip to the wall. With screws through predrilled holes on the heater back, mount the heater on the strip. Replace the heater cover.

If the unit does not have a built-in thermostat, connect it to a wall-mounted thermostat (*right inset*). Run color-coded wire already connected to the heater through metal raceway to a convenient location on the workshop wall. Fasten the raceway to the wall with flathead screws through knockout holes located on the back of the raceway. Screw the thermostat backplate to the wall and connect the color-coded wire to the appropriately colored backplate terminals. Finally, snap on the thermostat cover.

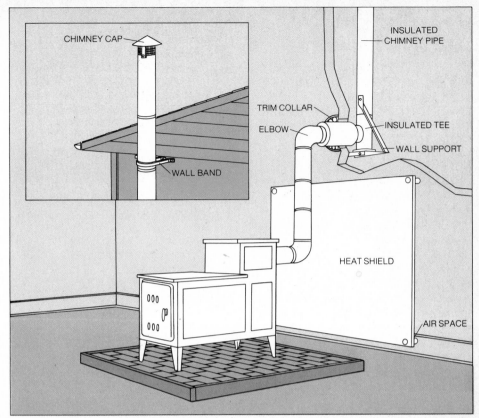

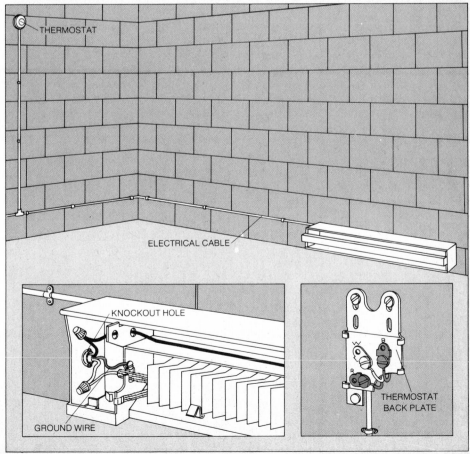

Installing an Exhaust Fan

Opening windows and doors may provide enough fresh air in summer to get rid of unpleasant workshop fumes and airborne dust, but in cold weather these accumulate in the shop and also may migrate through the house. Unless you are working with a paint sprayer, which requires an especially powerful fan and a special mounting *(page 110),* a standard kitchen exhaust fan provides adequate ventilation. It should be vented directly outdoors, through an opening cut in the outside wall or through a hole in a piece of plywood set in a window.

For home workshops up to 1,700 cubic feet in size, a fan that moves 425 cubic feet of air per minute is adequate, and is available at many appliance and electrical-supply stores. Larger fans may have to be specially ordered. To calculate the fan size you do need, divide the number of cubic feet in your workshop by 4, the number of minutes in which the fan should completely change the air. Match the result with the fan's CFM rating, the cubic feet of air per minute that the fan will move.

The physical dimensions of the fan should also influence your choice. If you are cutting an opening for it in a stud wall, you will want the fan to fit between two studs, so you will not have to cut through a stud. Some fans have mounting holes 16 inches apart, for attaching directly to a pair of studs; others require a frame for the fan housing *(opposite, top),* which is then set into a stud wall.

For safety, a fan should have an enclosed motor to eliminate the danger of sparks that could ignite flammable or explosive fumes such as those from contact cement, gasoline, paint thinner or paint remover. The fan should be equipped with a damper or shutters that open and close automatically to keep out cold air, and should have a noise rating, called the sone level, no higher than 10. Before cutting into a wall to install a fan, be sure the selected area of the wall is free of internal wire or plumbing.

A Fan Built into a Stud Wall

1 **Cutting the inside opening.** Drill a starting hole for the cut about midway between two studs; drill through both inside and outside walls. (To locate stud positions, use a magnetic stud finder or drill an angled hole and insert a wire that you can measure when it touches a stud.) For a standard 12-inch-square exhaust fan, which requires a 13-inch-square opening, draw parallel lines from stud to stud 7¼ inches above and below the drilled hole, using a level. Drill holes at each corner through inside and outside walls. Widen the drilled hole and, with a keyhole saw or saber saw, cut through the inside wall to each stud. Cut along the edges of the studs, then across the two horizontal lines. Remove the wallboard or plaster and lath and the insulation.

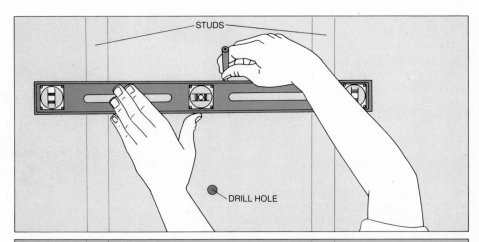

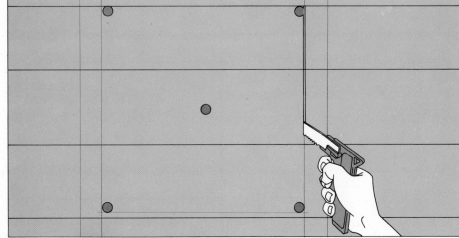

2 **Cutting the outside opening.** Using the drilled holes as points of reference, mark and cut an identical hole through the exterior siding and sheathing from the outside. Measure the depth of the wall from the exterior surface of the sheathing to the surface of the interior wall. Rip a piece of 1-inch lumber to this exact width, long enough to make a square frame with interior dimensions of 13 inches on a side—1 inch larger than the dimensions of the fan.

3 **Inserting the frame.** Slip the frame into the opening, lining up the edge of the frame with the surface of the interior wall. Nail the frame to both of the studs. On the exterior, mark the positions of screw holes for the fan mounting on the frame edges and drill pilot holes. Spread weatherproof caulking along the edges of the frame, then set the fan in the frame and screw it in place *(inset)*. Caulk again around the edges of the fan. Inside, cover the joint between the wall and the fan frame with molding mitered to fit, and paint the frame to match the interior wall.

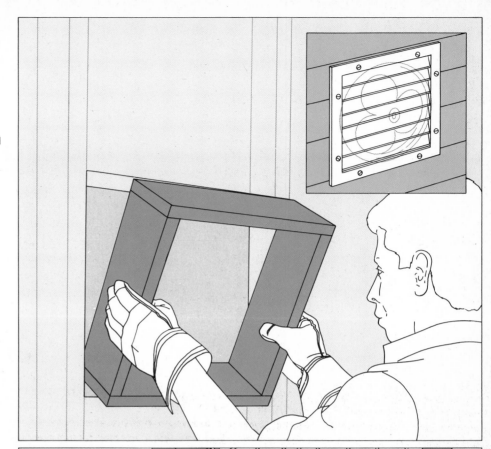

4 **Wiring the fan.** From an outlet box that has a switch nearby, run a length of two-conductor armored cable through a knockout opening in the fan junction box. Connect the motor wires as shown on page 75, Step 2. Then, with the power shut off, run two-conductor-with-ground cable from the switch box, through metal conduit, to a nearby electrical box, connecting the wires as you would if you were tapping power at a junction box, as shown on page 68.

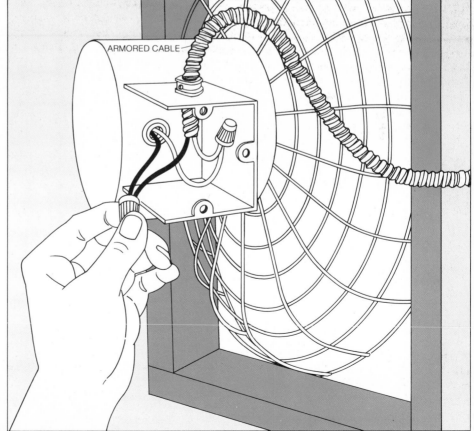

ARMORED CABLE

Better Access and Egress Routes for Materials

The fragile interior of your house can seem like an obstacle course when you need to maneuver bulky materials or projects through it on the way to and from your workshop. For safety and convenience, you need an opening into the shop that is reasonably direct and can admit a 4-by-8 panel of ¾-inch plywood.

A simple slot in an outside wall may do *(opposite, top),* but far better is a doorway big enough to admit two people carrying a large bookcase or a bed frame *(opposite, bottom).* The location of your workshop, as well as the construction of your house, will determine the difficulty of installing either.

With some resourcefulness and foresight, you may be able to provide temporary access to a shop by simply rearranging furniture, fixtures and appliances. In many instances, however, the obstacle will be an immovable part of the house—a projecting wall, a narrow doorway, perhaps a winding staircase. Even if you can manage to thread materials through the house to the shop, you will find it very inconvenient to do so regularly. Nor will you appreciate cleaning up the sawdust that you are likely to track along the way. The solution is to build a new, direct access route, either a pass-through or a new outside entrance.

The easiest kind of pass-through to build in a frame house is a vertical doorway to the outside only 6 to 8 inches wide. This enables you to slip 4-by-8 panels and awkwardly shaped pieces of lumber directly into your workshop, if it is on the first floor, or into the nearest first-floor room if your shop is in the basement. In a wood-frame wall, such a vertical pass-through can be fitted between two existing studs in the wall with very little carpentry and no risk of doing damage to the structure.

A pass-through provides access for panels and long boards, but to move out a finished project such as a bookcase 8 feet tall, or simply to be able to walk directly in and out of the workshop, you will need a new entrance from outside. If your shop is below grade, you can cut through the wall *(page 24)* and install an exterior prehung door *(page 25),* available in 32- or 36-inch widths from a lumberyard. When ordering such a prehung door, specify the desired jamb width and indicate that you will need a door that swings into the basement.

To install a door to a typical below-grade basement workshop, you must also build an areaway consisting of a floor slab and a three-sided retaining wall outside the foundation wall, with steps that rise to ground level. To carry rainwater away, the slab must either house a drain connected with an existing drainage system around the house foundation, or be covered by a weatherproof steel cellar door and set on a concrete cap that protects the retaining walls from rain.

If your foundation does not already have a perimeter drainage system, the cellar door will probably be less expensive than installing a drainpipe. And even if you do have the drainage system, a cellar door will reduce your dependence on the drain and will keep snow and leaves out of the areaway.

In choosing the location for a basement entrance, choose a place on the foundation wall where plumbing pipes and electrical cables will not interfere with construction and, insofar as possible, where the grade is lowest and slopes away from the foundation wall.

To order a manufactured cellar door, you will need to measure the height of the grade above the basement floor at the proposed door location, either from a window or from holes drilled through the wall. The most common cellar-door size is 6 feet long and 4 feet 7 inches wide; the frame is 1 foot 7½ inches deep at the high end next to the house. Once you have laid out the areaway outside the wall, you may want a professional with heavy equipment to excavate from the ground level to the house footings.

To pour the slab, footing and concrete cap, you will need about three fourths of a cubic yard of concrete. Order it from a building-materials supplier in a ready-mix truck and lay 1-by-8 planks across your yard to cart it to the site in wheelbarrow loads. To build the retaining wall, use 8-by-8-by-16- or 12-by-12-by-16-inch blocks, depending on building-code requirements. Your building code may also require you to tie both the new footing and the areaway walls every 2 feet to the old footing and wall with metal reinforcing bars, called rebar, inserted in holes drilled in the existing footing and wall.

To make the areaway waterproof, trowel a mixture of 1 part portland cement to 2½ parts sand on the exterior sides of the walls. Spread the mixture from the top of the wall down to the footing, banking it into a curve at the joint between the first course of blocks and the footing. Let it dry for 24 hours, roughen it with a wire brush and let it harden for an additional 24 hours.

For steps, install steel stringers sold by the manufacturers of steel cellar doors, and fit the stringer slots with 2-by-10 wood treads. Such steps are far easier to install than concrete ones.

Pass-throughs and Areaways

A pass-through in a frame wall. A narrow vertical pass-through framed between adjacent wall studs admits 4-by-8 panels of plywood or wallboard into a first-floor workshop. The door of the pass-through is ¾-inch plywood; it swings inward on two ¾-inch offset hinges. Spring-action catches, screwed to the stud on one side of the pass-through and to the door, keep the door shut; weather stripping blocks drafts. A hasp and lock secure the door on the inside.

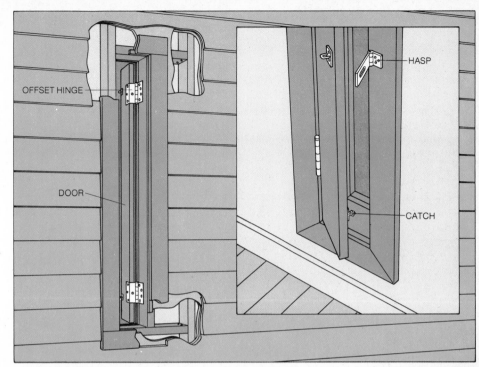

OFFSET HINGE

DOOR

HASP

CATCH

A cellar door. A sloping steel door set atop a three-sided concrete-block retaining wall forms a weatherproof passage to a basement workshop. The retaining wall is sealed against water at the top by a beveled concrete cap and on the outer sides by two coats of portland-cement-and-sand. The foundation of the wall is a turned-down slab—a slab with footings all along its edges. Stairs for the passageway consist of steel stringers nailed to the sides of the retaining wall and fitted with 2-by-10 wood treads. To keep out cold air, the basement wall itself contains a door, a prehung unit that has been installed in a frame of 2-by-8s.

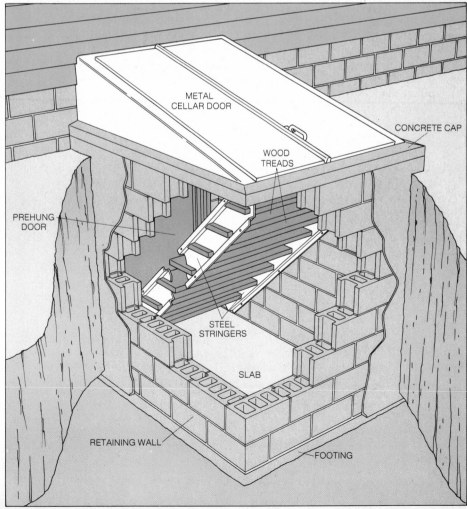

METAL CELLAR DOOR

CONCRETE CAP

WOOD TREADS

PREHUNG DOOR

STEEL STRINGERS

SLAB

RETAINING WALL

FOOTING

A Stud-Wall Slot for Plywood

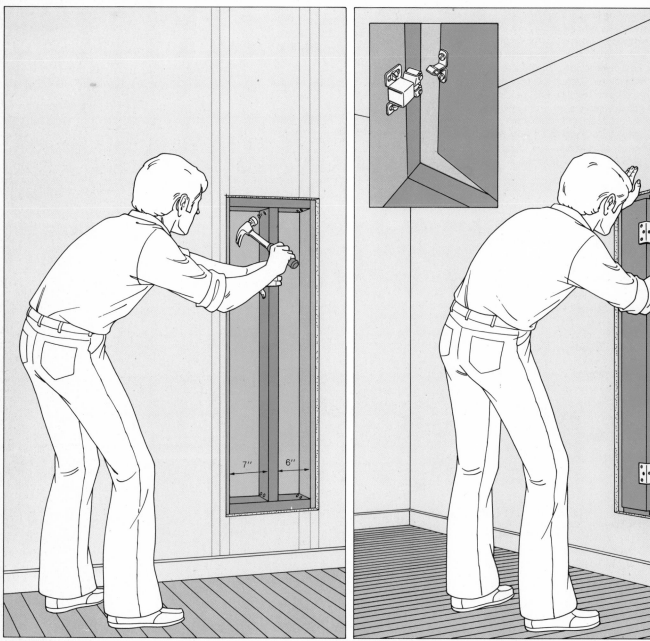

1 Framing the opening. Cut an opening in the inside of the wall (*page 16*), starting 4 to 8 inches above the baseboard. Extend the opening 50 inches up the wall along the edges of two adjacent studs. Cut two 2-by-4s, each about 14½ inches long, to fit horizontally between the studs; toenail them to both studs across the top and bottom of the opening. Then cut a 2-by-4 to fit vertically between the horizontal pieces, 7 inches from one stud, 6 inches from the other.

From inside the house, drill through the exterior sheathing and siding of the narrower half of the slot to mark the exterior opening. Then cut that opening from outside (*page 16*).

2 Hinging the door. Using two offset hinges to avoid driving screws into a plywood edge, fasten a ¾-inch-thick plywood door, cut to fit the narrower opening, to the center 2-by-4. Locate one hinge 3 inches from the top of the door, the other hinge 4 inches from the bottom. Mount two spring-action catches (*inset*) near the edge of the door and on the stud. Apply weather stripping around the outside of the door to save heat. On the inside, screw a hasp and staple so the door can be padlocked. Inside and out, frame the opening with molding, using filler strips of wood to lift the molding flush with the walls. Patch the recess in the wider part of the slot with wallboard before the interior molding is installed.

Building a Basement Areaway

1 Squaring the building lines. To lay out building lines at right angles with the house, use the 3-4-5 triangle method. To do this, mark the inside corners of the areaway on the bottom of the siding, using the dimensions specified by the cellar-door manufacturer. Tack a long 1-by-4 to the basement wall below the siding. The ends of this board should be several inches beyond the marks on the siding. Under each siding mark, drive a corner nail into the top edge of the 1-by-4. Then drive another pair of nails into the same edge, each nail 3 feet in from a corner nail.

Hook measuring tapes to one corner nail and to a nail 3 feet inward. Have a helper cross these tapes so the 4-foot line on the corner-nail tape meets the 5-foot line on the diagonal tape. Drive a stake at this point; the outside tape forms a right angle with the house. Use a carpenter's level atop a straight board to set the top of the stake level with the top edge of the 1-by-4. Drive a nail into the top of the stake. Establish the opposite edge line in the same way.

Use string to extend the edge lines beyond the nails in the stakes and to two more stakes that mark the ends of the areaway. Measure the diagonals of the resulting rectangle; adjust the stakes to make the diagonals equal.

RIGHT ANGLE

3'

4'

5'

2 Setting up batter boards. To establish reference points that you can use to reconstruct the building lines later, after excavation, build a pair of right-angled batter boards. Make each pair from two 1-by-6 boards nailed to three 2-by-4 stakes driven into the ground 5 feet beyond the outside corners of the areaway, thus forming the right angle. Use a string and a line level to set the batter boards at exactly the same height as the marker board. Extend the building lines with string to nails in the batter boards.

Use nails in the batter boards to mark the locations of the footing trench and slab (inset). For safety, have a professional excavate the area to a point 2 feet outside the actual building lines, and to the depth of the top of the existing house footings. Reconstruct the building lines by stretching strings between the nails on the batter boards and on the marker board. Then use a plumb bob, dropping it from the stretched strings to the bottom of the excavation, to position stakes there that will transfer the building lines for the footing trench and the slab.

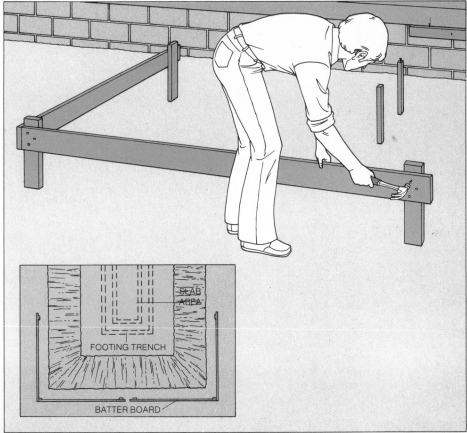

SLAB AREA

FOOTING TRENCH

BATTER BOARD

3 **Leveling the footing trench and slab.** Between the building lines, dig the U-shaped footing trench 16 inches wide and 8 inches deep. Then, in the slab area inside the U, slice out 4 inches of soil, angling the soil sides slightly so they will not crumble when the concrete is poured. Level the bottom of the footing trench by driving 1-by-2 stakes in a staggered pattern from the corners of the trench and marking each stake at the height of the top of the house footing, using a 4-foot level. Make a second mark 4 inches down from the first on each stake beside the slab area to determine the height for the bottom of the slab; and make a mark 8 inches down on all the stakes to indicate the bottom of the footing. Deepen the excavation where necessary, but do not fill where it is too deep.

Lay 4-mil polyethylene plastic over the slab-and-trench area, and cover it with wire mesh made of 10-gauge wire with 6-inch squares *(inset)*. Pour concrete for both the slab and the trench at one time, up to the highest marks on the stakes. Cover the hardened concrete with sheets of plastic and let it cure for seven days. During that time, lift the plastic off and mist the concrete from time to time with water.

SLAB AREA

FOOTING TRENCH

WIRE MESH

PLASTIC FILM

4 **Building the areaway wall.** Reestablish the building lines for the three-sided concrete-block wall by replacing the ground-level strings *(Step 2)*. Transfer these lines to the hardened footing by dropping a plumb bob from the strings to the footing and marking the footing, thus locating the inside and outside corners of the areaway walls. Snap chalk lines between the marks to outline the walls. To determine how many blocks you will need to build each side of the wall, lay blocks along the outline end-to-end in a dry run, without mortar. Then, at the corners and ends of the walls, lay stepped sets of blocks called leads; mortar the blocks together and make each lead three courses high.

Fill in between the leads with more blocks, using a taut string as a guide to keep the walls straight, and check often with a level to make sure the wall is both plumb and level. In every third course, place wire-mesh reinforcement in the mortar bed. Build the wall to slightly above grade and to within 3 inches of the areaway height recommended by the door manufacturer.

Installing a Fabricated Cellar Door

1 **Building forms for a concrete cap.** With masonry nails, fasten 1-by-6 form boards to the outsides of the areaway walls, setting the top edges of the boards 3 inches above the tops of the blocks. Drive the nails into the ends and center of each wall. For added reinforcement, drive two 1-by-4 stakes on each side and nail through the stakes and boards into the blocks.

Fasten another line of 1-by-6 form boards along the inside of the top course, but set their top edges 4 inches above the tops of the blocks. To brace these boards, cut three 1-by-4s to fit between the bottoms of the form boards and the slab; then nail one brace up the center of each wall. Face-nail a 10-inch 1-by-4 over each brace and form board. To brace the boards from the sides, nail a 1-by-4 cross brace between the side walls and another between the end wall and the first cross brace (*inset*). Fill each core in the top course of blocks halfway with crushed newspaper before pouring the concrete cap.

2 **Beveling the cap.** As you fill the form with concrete, bevel the concrete from the inside to the outside, to allow rain to drain off the cap. Measure the length and width of the cellar-door frame and mark the house wall and the outside form boards where the outside edges of the frame will fall. Pour the concrete into the forms and trowel it flat between the inside form and the marks; slope the concrete from the marks to the lower outside form.

3 Fitting the doorframe. With a helper, set
the cellar-door frame on the concrete cap, tight
against the house wall. If the top back edge
extends up over siding, outline the back of the
frame with chalk on the siding, disregarding
the header flange. Remove the frame and cut out
the siding along the outline. Slip the frame into
place by inserting the header flange underneath
the siding, then rest the base of the frame on
the flat part of the concrete cap. Drill into the cap
through the mounting holes in the base and
secure the frame to the concrete with lag bolts
and lead anchors.

If the top back edge of the frame butts against
masonry (inset), simply set the back of the frame
against the wall and fasten the header flange
to the wall with lead anchors and lag bolts. Then
cut a ¼-inch-deep slot in a horizontal mortar
joint just above the header flange, insert a piece
of metal flashing and bend it over the flange.
Caulk the mortar joint where the flashing is inserted into the wall.

Place the doors on the frame according to the
manufacturer's instructions. Caulk around the exterior of the frame with a butyl-base caulk.

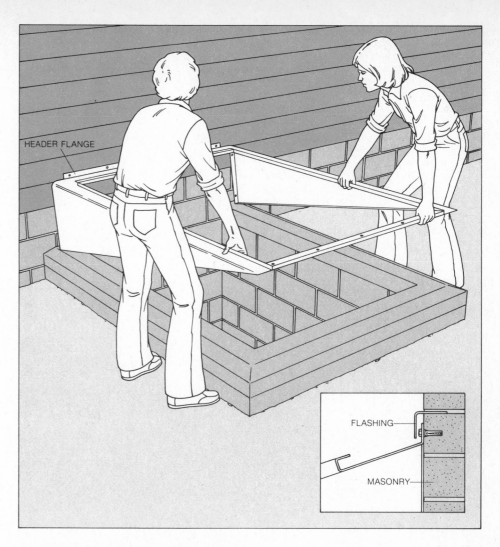

Installing a Basement Door

1 Opening the basement wall. Working in the
new areaway outside the basement wall, mark the
width of the door opening to be cut on the
concrete block immediately below the siding. Usually the width will be the width of the frame of
a prehung door plus 3¾ inches. Put the marks
on vertical mortar joints if possible. To outline
the opening, drop a plumb bob from the marks to
the floor and snap a chalk line on the wall.
Score from top to bottom along these lines using a
circular saw with a carbide-tipped blade; wear
goggles, a respirator and earmuffs and work the
saw blade slowly into the block. Check the
blade frequently and take a break whenever it
gets hot. Similarly score the wall on the inside.

With a cold chisel and small sledge hammer,
break out the block between the scored lines,
from the sill plate at the top, down to the footing. Mortar the footing in the opening and lay a
level course of 4-by-4-by-16 solid-concrete
blocks as a base for the prehung door's threshold.

2 **Installing the rough frame.** To create nailing surfaces at the sides of the rough doorframe, nail scraps of wood in the open cores of cut blocks along the sides of the opening (inset). To these nailers, nail the 2-by-8 sides of the rough frame, extending from the threshold base to the sill plate. Measure the height of the prehung doorframe, add ¼ inch for shims, and mark this height on the sidepieces of the rough frame. For the top of the rough frame, toenail a 2-by-8 between the two sides above the marked lines. Repair any chipped blocks with mortar. Insulate the space between the top of the rough frame and the sill plate with fiberglass insulation and cover it on both sides with ¾-inch plywood.

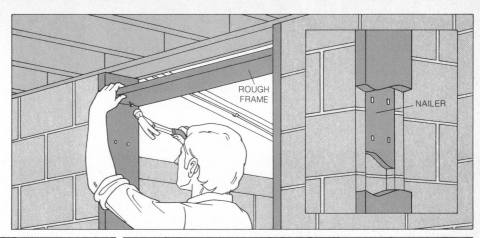

3 **Setting the doorframe in place.** With a helper, set the prehung door in the opening, swinging toward the inside, with the inside edge of its frame flush with the inside edge of the rough frame. Shim the bottom of a side jamb if necessary to level the unit. To center the unit, shim both sides between the jambs and the rough frame; place pairs of shims near the top, at the middle and near the bottom.

Plumb the doorjambs with a level, adjusting the shims to move the jambs at the top or bottom as necessary. Remove the jamb braces installed by the manufacturer. Open the door and drive 16-penny masonry nails through the top and bottom of the jamb on the hinged side of the door, through the shims and partway into the rough frame, but not into the concrete block.

4 **Adjusting the jamb on the latch side.** If the top corner of the door protrudes into the house, loosen the shims on the latch side, hold a block of wood against this jamb near the bottom, and tap it gently with a hammer until the door is flush with the jamb at both top and bottom. Reverse the procedure if the door protrudes at the bottom. Tighten the shims at the top and bottom and drive 16-penny nails partway into the rough frame, nailing at each set of shims.

For final adjustments, loosen or tighten the center shims and nail them in place; insert pairs of shims between the head jamb and the top of the rough frame, nail them in place and trim them flush with the jamb. Set all nails, then cover the rough frame and the shims with moldings on both sides of the doorframe.

5 Installing a threshold. Set an aluminum threshold, matching the width of the door, across the bottom of the opening on the base of concrete blocks. Close the door to make sure it will fit over the threshold; align the bevel of the threshold with the outside face of the door. Mark through the threshold screw holes onto the concrete blocks. Remove the threshold and use a masonry bit to drill holes 1½ inches deep in the concrete blocks. Insert plastic screw anchors in the holes, set the threshold across the opening and screw it in place. Slide rubber weatherproofing into grooves in the threshold.

Assembling the Outside Stairway

Installing stringers and treads. To install steel stringers, measure from the areaway floor 8¼ inches up one of the side walls. Mark a horizontal line on the wall through that point, using chalk and a level. With a helper, hold one stringer against the wall, so its lower anchor hole is lined up with the level line on the wall, and the angled top is flat against the outer wall. Mark the positions of the stringer's boltholes on the wall, and anchor the stringer in place with 1¼-inch masonry nails.

Place the other stringer against the facing wall, but before you nail it in place, check its alignment with the anchored stringer. Insert a 2-by-10 board into a facing pair of slots near the middle of the stairway and place a level on the board. Adjust the alignment to level the tread, then nail the second stringer to the wall, and insert 2-by-10 treads of pressure-treated lumber in all the slots. Toenail the treads into the side walls with eightpenny masonry nails (*inset*).

Wanted: A Durable, Cleanable, Slipproof Floor

A workshop floor need not be pretty, but it must be strong—it is the one floor in the house that you should not have to worry about damaging. It must withstand the considerable weight of a workbench and stationary power tools, and it also must be tough enough to stand up to any chemical solvent, grease or heavy lumber that you drop on it. Nevertheless, like the floor in your other workshop, the kitchen, it should be safe and comfortable, since you will spend countless hours standing on it.

Happily, the concrete floors of many basements and garages, where workshops are usually located, satisfy most of these requirements without any modification. A concrete slab, the most durable and slip-resistant of all floor materials, is as stable as the ground it rests upon. Yet because it almost always is in direct contact with the ground, it will feel cold underfoot and, far worse, may even be damp. A wet concrete floor is not merely uncomfortable—it is unacceptably dangerous in a home shop, where electrically powered tools pose a shock hazard. Such a floor must be dry (page 12), whether you intend to leave it bare or finish it.

Even a dry concrete floor, no matter how old, may require treatments. Some slabs undergo a chronic deterioration called dusting: The concrete is constantly crumbling into a powder at the surface because it was improperly mixed or cured during construction. You can arrest this deterioration by coating the concrete with a penetrating fluosilicate concrete hardener, which is available at hardware stores.

Strong as it is, concrete may crack and buckle, usually when the ground below settles slightly. If a crack is less than an inch wide, patch it with latex concrete filler. To fix wider cracks over a large area, you may need to break up the concrete in the damaged area with a sledge hammer, remove the old concrete and replace that area of the slab.

After you remove the damaged concrete, dig 4 inches below the bottom of the slab and fill the hole with ¾-inch gravel to the level of the bottom of the slab. Then lay a piece of reinforcing wire mesh, made of 10-gauge wires spaced 6 inches apart in both directions, over the gravel and coat the edges of the hole with an epoxy bonding agent recommended for concrete. Finally, fill the hole with fresh concrete, level it with a straightedged board and cure the concrete for three days by sprinkling water on it and keeping it covered with plastic.

Painting a concrete floor is an inexpensive way to relieve the slab of its gray drabness. The type of coating that is easiest to apply is latex concrete paint, which is specially designed to resist the alkali that most slabs contain. For a more durable coating, slower-drying oil-base concrete paints penetrate the concrete and are more resistant to scuffing. Most durable of all, but far more expensive than latex or oil-base paints, are epoxy and epoxy-polyurethane paints, which sometimes come in two parts—resin and hardener—that you must mix together.

Before applying any of these coatings, remove any grease or oil with a spray degreaser, available at automotive-supply stores. If the slab has never been painted, and the paint manufacturer recommends that you neutralize the alkali in the raw concrete, scrub the concrete with a solution of muriatic acid. To mix the solution, pour 1 part acid into 5 parts water, wearing rubber gloves, overshoes, a respirator and goggles; never pour water into the acid. With the area as well ventilated as possible, scrub the solution into the concrete with a long-handled floor brush. When the solution stops bubbling, flush it with clear water and either push the water into a drain or mop it up. Allow the floor to dry before painting it.

Even painted concrete is cold and hard on your feet, and will be harder still on any wooden tools or projects that you accidentally drop. If you expect to do most of your work standing in one spot, in front of a workbench, for instance, the simplest solution is to cushion the floor there with a rubber mat. If you expect to have several work areas, you may want to cover the entire floor with a more comfortable surfacing material, such as vinyl-asbestos floor tile—which is also much easier to clean.

Before the tiles are laid, the slab must be thoroughly cleaned and smoothed of any irregularities. Bumps or depressions left in a concrete floor will ghost through the tiles soon after they are laid. To fill depressions, use latex concrete filler and level the filler with a straightedge. To smooth off bumps, use an electric concrete grinder, which you can rent from a tool-rental store.

Do not coat the concrete with a concrete sealer—the mastic for the tiles will not adhere well to it. But the alkali of the concrete should be neutralized, and if the slab has previously been painted with an oil-base paint, this must be professionally removed, though latex paint may be left. To test for oil-base paint, carefully wet a small area of the paint with a solution of 2 teaspoons of lye dissolved in a cup of water. If the paint deteriorates within 10 minutes, it is oil-base.

Workshop floors that are not in basements or garages are usually made of wood, which is rarely cold, wet or hard, but is more vulnerable to damage than concrete. To protect a wood floor, you can cover it with vinyl-asbestos tiles, but it is often easier and cheaper to use vinyl-asbestos sheeting, the modern equivalent of linoleum. Vinyl sheeting comes in rolls ranging in width from 6 to 15 feet; you can install it simply by laying the sheets on the workshop floor and tacking them around the perimeter of the room.

Most wood floors are strong enough to bear the weight of common shop tools, but if you have professional shop machines—some of which weigh 600 pounds—you may have to reinforce the floor joists by nailing a matching joist to each existing one. For a workshop in an attic, where floor joists are typically undersized, this shoring up is often needed even for average-weight stationary tools.

Preventing, Detecting and Extinguishing Fire

In any home workshop, the proximity of flammable materials to potential ignition sources makes fire protection a matter of top priority. Wood, sawdust, paint, thinners and solvents inevitably accumulate, and many work areas also contain heat- and spark-producing tools. Frequently a nearby appliance, such as a furnace or hot-water heater, has a pilot light or automatic ignition device, and this constitutes another potential hazard.

Coping with the threat of fire in a workshop involves three basic strategies: following safety rules for working with and storing materials; equipping the shop area with fire-detection and fire-fighting tools; and providing barriers that will keep a fire from spreading.

Prevention is the first line of defense, and here thoughtful use and storage of flammable liquids are essential. Liquids that vaporize at room temperature, such as gasoline, can explode in the presence of a cigarette or even a tiny spark in a light switch; such liquids should always be stored and used outdoors. Slightly less volatile liquids, such as paint, paint removers and some solvents, should be stored in tightly closed metal containers. Use these liquids only in an area that is well ventilated (pages 16-17 and 110-112) if you must use them indoors.

Good housekeeping is another fire-prevention tactic in the workshop, as it is anywhere. If oil-soaked rags—such as those used to apply wood stain or linseed oil—are wadded up and dropped in a waste bin, they can ignite spontaneously; they heat up as oil molecules oxidize until the flash point is reached and they burst into flames. To prevent this, wash such rags and hang them in the open so any heat generated can dissipate. If you do not plan to reuse them, place the rags in a closed metal container, such as a metal garbage can with a lid, until you can dispose of them.

Workshop oil spills are often blotted up with sawdust, but the resulting mess is very flammable and should be cleaned up at once. For other sawdust accumulations, you can install a central vacuuming system (pages 132-133).

The concentrated use of electrical tools in a workshop makes adequate circuitry and proper wiring essential. Overloaded circuits and short circuits are common causes of shop fires; information on a safe electrical system for a workshop is on pages 64-79.

The second line of defense against fire is to detect it in its earliest stages. Every workshop should have a strategically located, operative smoke detector. Although models wired to a central alarm are available, and are probably preferable for a shop isolated from the rest of the house, the most commonly used detectors are the battery-operated models. They are simplicity itself to install, consisting only of a backplate or mounting bracket onto which the unit is snapped. Most units contain a test button, which you should push once a month to make sure the alarm is in working order. Lacking such a button, you can blow cigarette or incense smoke toward the unit to check the alarm's effectiveness.

There are two basic types of smoke detectors, operating on different principles. In the ionization type, smoke interrupts the flow of current through a field of ionized atoms lying between two terminals; in the photoelectric type, the entering smoke deflects a beam of light between two photoelectric cells. Ionization detectors, which are extremely sensitive, sometimes sound an alarm when no fire threat is present, reacting even to the minimal smoke of a dull power-saw blade working its way through a knot. Photoelectric detectors are triggered only by smokier fires.

Both detectors, however, respond to particulate matter in the air, and so they can be triggered by such things as fine sawdust. In a workshop, they should not be placed near a table saw or a sander, and their vents should be vacuumed periodically to prevent dust build-ups.

Another piece of equipment essential for any home workshop is a multipurpose fire extinguisher that holds at least 5 pounds of fire-quenching chemicals. It should be hung on a bracket near the doorway, at a height convenient for adults and children; all members of the household should be taught how to use it. The only maintenance it requires is checking of the pressure gauge once a month to make sure the needle is in the "safe" zone—usually designated by a wedge-shaped area between the labels RECHARGE and OVERCHARGED. If the needle is not within the safe zone, take the extinguisher to a service shop to have it adjusted, or replace it with a new one.

If you have basic plumbing skills, you may want to install an automatic sprinkler system in the shop. When triggered, a sprinkler system sprays a fine mist that smothers a fire by cutting off the oxygen supply, so it is effective even against grease and electrical fires. If it is connected to an alarm, the system usually can be shut off in time to prevent serious water damage to shop equipment.

Even though you may be doing your best to prevent a shop fire from starting or to stop such a fire quickly, you should take additional steps to protect the rest of your home in the event of a shop fire. By installing horizontal 2-by-4 blocks—called fire stops—between studs in shop walls still to be finished, you can interrupt the chimney-like effect these tall, vertical spaces would otherwise have. Covering the shop walls and ceiling with fire-resistant Type X gypsum wallboard greatly slows the spread of fire, as does a fire-rated or solid-core door at the shop entrance. Any door will impede the progress of fire most effectively if it fits snugly and is weather-stripped.

Allies in Fighting Fire

Anatomy of a fire extinguisher. A reliable tool for fighting small fires is a multipurpose fire extinguisher. Its special dry-chemical mix, expelled under pressure, is effective against all three major classes of fires: burning wood or other combustibles (Class A), oil- or grease-fed flames (Class B), and electrical blazes (Class C). Any unit that can handle all three types is marked ABC.

To operate an extinguisher, first release the seal by pulling the ring pin out of its slot. Then, standing at least 8 feet away from the fire and near a door, point the nozzle at the fire and squeeze the release handle. Sweep the spray back and forth over the center of the fire until the canister is empty (usually about 10 seconds). Call local fire authorities immediately, even if the fire appears to be completely extinguished.

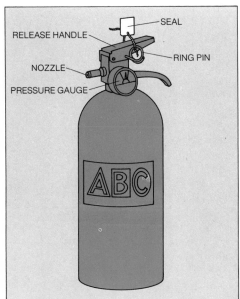

A sentry that signals smoke. To install a battery-operated smoke detector, first check that the battery is wired to the alarm and is in place in its pocket—in the model shown, on the back of the unit. For most detectors, you then screw a special mounting bracket to the wall or ceiling and twist or slide the unit onto the bracket. With some smoke detectors, however, the battery is inside the unit and the backplate of the unit is the mounting device, so that you must remove the cover to attach the backplate to the ceiling or wall and to periodically replace the battery.

Place a ceiling-mounted detector as close to the center of the ceiling as possible and at least 1 foot from a wall; place a wall-mounted detector high on the wall but at least 6 inches below the ceiling. Air circulates less freely where walls and ceilings meet, and smoke might not reach the alarm until a fire has grown large.

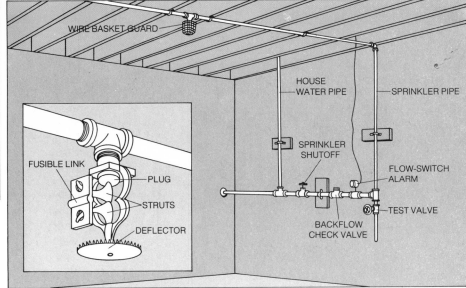

Anatomy of a sprinkler system. A heat-sensitive sprinkler head (*inset*) is the heart of an automatic sprinkler system. When heat in the room reaches a threshold temperature, usually 165°, a fusible link in the head melts, allowing water in the pipe to push out a plug. With the plug removed, water flows out and hits the deflector, which transforms the stream into a fine mist.

One sprinkler head will blanket about 100 to 150 square feet, so one or two are generally enough to protect most workshops. Be careful not to place the head near a heat source, where high temperatures might set it off accidentally. A sprinkler head can also malfunction if it is bumped, so, in a workshop, you should protect it with a basket-shaped metal guard.

In addition to the network of pipes and sprinkler heads, the system should have a separate shutoff valve, a backflow check valve to keep water in the sprinkler system from entering the house supply, a test valve, and—most important—a flow-switch alarm that sounds an alarm elsewhere when the sprinkler system is activated. If possible, put the shutoff valve outside the shop or at least near the door, so that you can turn it off without entering the shop.

Silencing or Confining the Noise of the Workshop

A workshop is a noisy place. The high whine of a table saw ripping through plywood, the roar of a bench grinder as it sharpens a mower blade, the hearty thump of an air compressor operating a spray gun, even just steady hammering or the buzz of a portable drill—for the worker all these sounds can become annoying and even dangerous when they increase fatigue. If the shop is not detached from the house, the cacophony that issues from the work area is sure to irritate other occupants of the house.

To reduce the passage of shop noise to other areas, you must deal with the two ways that sound travels: through the air, and through solid materials such as wood and wallboard. To block the first path from the inside out, you have only to seal openings between the shop and its surroundings. You can install rubber weather stripping around any doors—provided the heating system does not depend on air circulation beneath the doors—and seal joints between wallboard panels and along floor and ceiling lines with acoustic caulking.

If heating ducts run from the workshop to other parts of the house, you can line them as far as you can reach with a special insulation coated with neoprene rubber to prevent insulation fibers from getting into the air.

More troublesome is the passage of sound through solid surfaces—the shop floor, walls and ceiling. For example, when noise hits wallboard nailed directly to studs, it travels through the wallboard, through the studs and through the wallboard on the other side with little diminution. Techniques for reducing such sound travel involve one or both of two basic strategies: creating as wide and dense a barrier as possible and isolating barrier parts from each other so the sound cannot be conducted through.

You can fit insulation batts between studs or install special flexible metal strips, called resilient channels, between wallboard and studs. For an even more effective sound barrier between rooms, you can erect special walls built with staggered studs or doubled sets of studs (opposite, top).

The floor of a workshop does not contribute to noise problems unless the shop is above other parts of the house. In most such cases, it is simpler to soundproof the ceiling of the room below than to rip up and modify the floor of the shop. However, if you are putting your shop in an unfinished attic, building a sound-proof floor there (opposite, bottom) is the better solution.

Acoustic ceiling tile will help quiet a shop by greatly reducing reverberation, though it is quite ineffective in blocking noise transmission between rooms.

There are also ways of reducing noise inside a shop, and of protecting yourself from the noise that remains. Pads placed under machines or the legs of the tool stands will minimize noise-causing vibration. Any thick, resilient material—rubber, cork, or layers of felt—will do the job, but molded neoprene antivibration pads, called isolation mounts, are available at many rubber-goods stores.

The most effective, cheapest and easiest way of guarding against the harmful effects of noise is to wear ear protectors. Many hardware and sporting goods stores that carry gun supplies also sell sound-dampening earmuffs—which look like stereo earphones—or special earplugs for blocking loud noises. (Earplugs designed to be worn while swimming or sleeping are not very effective against the levels of noise encountered in a shop.) Though the earmuffs do a better job, the less expensive plugs are more comfortable, particularly if the job requires you to wear goggles.

Blocking Noise at the Source

Pads to minimize vibration. Mounting tools on pieces of neoprene antivibration padding reduces the vibration and noise from the tool. Parallel grooves on the top of each ⅜-inch-thick pad are set at right angles to grooves on the bottom, to interrupt the transference of vibration; if you use more than one layer of padding, stack the pieces so the grooves do not interlock.

Enclose each mounting bolt with a section of garden hose and add rubber washers at each end (inset) to isolate the bolts from the table and the pad. Mounting holes must be large enough to accept this assembly. You can also place sections of padding under each foot of a tool stand.

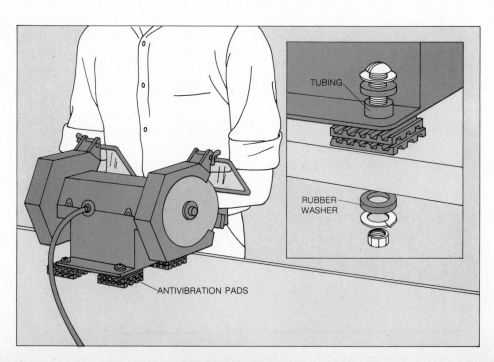

TUBING

RUBBER WASHER

ANTIVIBRATION PADS

Preventing Transmission of Sound Room-to-Room

A well-soundproofed shop. Several techniques for soundproofing a shop are shown at right. The travel of noise through the ceiling to the room above is reduced by batts of fiberglass insulation stapled between ceiling joists. Resilient metal channels (*left inset*) run perpendicular to ceiling joists and separate the ceiling wallboard from joists to further reduce the passage of sound. The narrow flanges of the channels are screwed to the joists, and the wallboard is screwed to the wider flanges.

To soundproof a finished ceiling, nail 2-inch-deep Z-furring strips (*left inset*) to the ceiling and install a second layer of wallboard over the strips, inserting 1-inch-thick sheets of insulation as you go. Acoustic tiles can be glued to any ceiling to dampen reverberations within the shop.

Existing walls can be soundproofed with the techniques used for ceilings, or a new wall can be built. The soundproof wall here has 2-by-6 top and bottom plates, with 2-by-4 studs alternately staggered to opposite edges of the plates. Because each stud touches wallboard on only one side of the wall, less sound is transmitted. An alternative is to erect a second wall with 2-by-4 studs spaced 1 inch away from an existing wall, filling the space between with insulation.

Airborne noise is blocked by a solid-core door, edged with neoprene-rubber seals (*right inset*), at the shop entrance. The wall duct is lined with rubber-coated insulation that absorbs sound. Acoustic caulking at floor and ceiling lines halts the passage of sound at these points.

Building a soundproof floor. To soundproof as you finish an unfinished attic floor, first install batts of 3-inch fiberglass insulation between the open floor joists. Nail ½-inch plywood over the joists as a subfloor and top the plywood with ½-inch resilient fiberboard. Then glue—do not nail—2-by-3 furring strips to the fiberboard, installing them parallel with the joists below and centered between the joists. This isolates the top level of the floor from the joists and keeps noise from traveling to the room below. Nail a layer of ½-inch plywood over the furring strips, and finish with sheet vinyl or other floor covering.

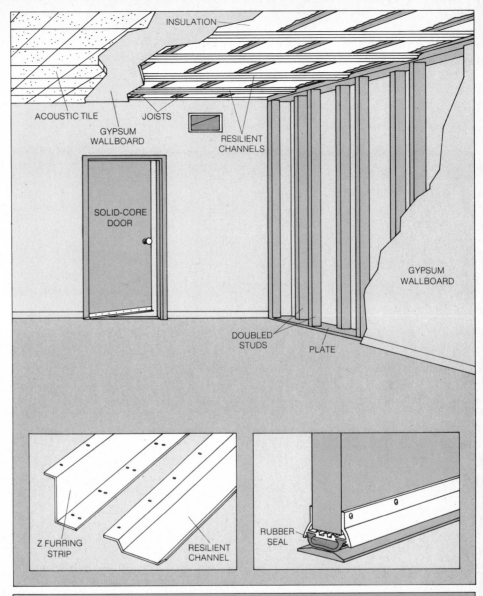

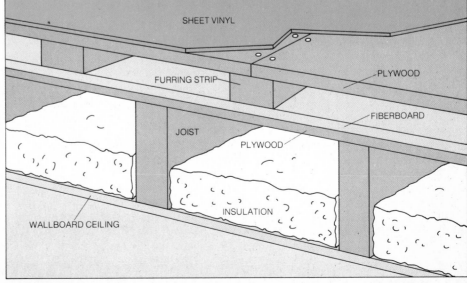

Diversity in Shops of Yore

In times past, when towns were small and essentially self-sufficient, the local woodworking shop had to be manned by a craftsman of myriad skills. His workshop was, perforce, a place equipped for making or repairing virtually anything from a parlor chair to a wagon wheel, a button or a gunstock, and if he could do the associated metalwork, so much the better. The Dominy family, whose remarkable shops and tools are shown on the following pages, is a classic example of this kind of wondrous versatility.

Skilled cabinetmakers, wheelwrights, clockmakers, carpenters, metalsmiths and handymen, three generations of Dominy menfolk—from the mid-18th Century to the mid-19th—maintained both a woodworking and a metalworking shop in rural East Hampton, New York. In these compact and well-conceived spaces, built on the family homestead, the Dominys were equipped to cast, turn, hammer, saw, thread, drill, carve or burnish almost everything a neighbor could want from wood or metal.

The tools upon which the Dominys depended numbered well over a thousand. All of them were powered by human muscle directly or, as with the wheel lathe (pages 36-37), by a mechanism that was itself driven by hand or foot.

The notion of multipurpose or combination tools had scarcely begun to influence tool design, so most of the Dominys' tools served a single purpose. Consequently, 44 taps were needed for making screw holes in metal, 23 gauges for measuring turned work, and 50-odd clock- and watchmaker's files to shape and clean the metal parts of timepieces.

With few native toolmakers to turn to before the Industrial Revolution, the Dominys got many tools the way most American wood- and metalworkers did: by purchasing European goods. A common economy was to buy the tool heads—the steel gouge or file or chisel—from abroad, then fashion the wood handle at home. Sometimes, however, the Dominys made a tool entirely: The demands of some task might inspire the creation of a special plane, for example. Or they might convert a broken iron or steel piece into something new—like the 17th Century sword or dagger blade that became a turning chisel (page 36).

The workshops were as efficient and orderly as the times allowed. The value of daylight led Nathaniel Dominy IV, who built the woodworking shop around 1750, to provide a workbench at each of three windows; the Dominys simply moved during the day to work wherever the light was best. The multiplicity of tools provoked a multitude of open wall and ceiling storage racks, fitted into every available space.

Sawdust, wood shavings, a clutter of wood and metal scraps were the order of the day, though the Dominys reportedly made a weekly ritual of cleanup. Then the floors were swept, the odds and ends put away, and the massive workbenches burnished with wood chips to keep them smooth and splinter-free.

The traditions established by three generations of Dominys were not to pass to a fourth. Like handcraftsmen everywhere, great-grandson Nathaniel Dominy VII (1827-1910) could not compete with cheaper, machine-made goods. Though he kept the shop intact, he settled for working as a jeweler and handyman. Several decades after his death, the Dominy house was torn down and the shop buildings moved to another site.

Miraculously, the tools survived a decade of dispersal among a museum, an antique shop and various attics around East Hampton. In 1957 they were collected, along with some Dominy-made case clocks, furniture and other pieces, and moved to the Henry Francis du Pont Winterthur Museum in Delaware. There, with the aid of photographs, floor plans and elevations made 17 years earlier by the Historic American Buildings Survey, they were installed in reconstructions of the original workshops.

The exhibits provide a unique glimpse of a way of life that may no longer be practicable. But the qualities that made these shops work for the Dominys—versatility, self-sufficiency, convenience and having the right tools for each job—are as relevant to today's amateur craftsman as they were to the professionals of old.

A rack of bits and braces. Taking up a minimum amount of space, some three dozen woodworking bits and other special-purpose hole cutters are tucked between a pair of rough studs. The top-row tools have versatile four-sided tapered wooden blocks that were inserted into the similarly four-sided socket of the wooden brace hanging on the wall at right above them. The other braces, of later vintage, take more familiar steel-shanked bits. Below the rack are some of the Dominys' bench planes.

Workbenches: the Fundamental Tools

Three massive workbenches, each positioned to catch its daily share of sunlight, lined the Dominys' woodworking shop. The largest, set along the east, or morning, wall, at left in the photograph, had as its main surface a solid slab of polished red oak 12 feet long, 17½ inches wide and 5½ inches thick. A thinner, supplementary board, laid along the bench at the back, added another 11 inches of width. Two smaller joiner's benches were each about 6 feet long.

All three benches had double screw vises and each also had some means of supporting the free end of a board while the other end was in the vise. The benches are low by modern standards, with work surfaces scarcely 28 inches high. But the height served well in getting the most out of hand tools: As the craftsman bore down from above, he could apply the full strength of his hands or arms.

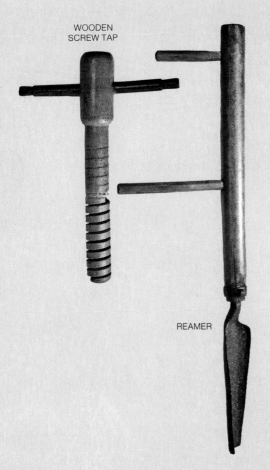

WOODEN
SCREW TAP

REAMER

A joiner's jumbleshop. Many of the Dominy tools are archaic. The wood clamp hanging to the left of the rear door could set a curve in four chair slats at a time. Propped up nearby is the long, angled sole of a cooper's jointer plane, which beveled the edges of barrel staves. Suspended in the foreground are, from left to right, a wood-handled cant hook for moving oversized logs, a 7-foot crosscut saw, and just behind them a pair of two-man frame saws for slicing heavy stock. The mahogany tea table was built in 1796 to be used by the Dominy family.

SASH FILLISTER PLANE

DRAWKNIFE

MALLET

BOW SAW OR FRAME SAW

The Great Wheel Lathe: A Primer for Apprentices

The wheel lathe, introduced in the latter half of the 16th Century, had become a wonderfully efficient engine for turning and shaping circular wood parts by the time the Dominys built theirs around 1770. Compared with the pole lathe, a truly ancient foot-treadle device that the Dominys also employed, the wheel lathe provided smoother, continuous rotation at higher speeds, making possible subtle shapings even on very hard woods.

The stock was held between upright arms, or puppets, which fitted into a track along the lathe bed and could be adjusted left and right to accommodate stock of varying sizes. Alternatively, the puppets could be replaced with a special arbor-and-cross attachment that held and turned a circular slab of wood for hollowing, or dishing, its surface. The tea table on pages 34-35 was given its tray shape in this manner.

The wheel lathe had one disadvantage: It required power from a second person—usually a son or apprentice. But the helper had little to do while turning the crank except watch the master craftsman as he gouged and chiseled the whirling wood, so cranking the wheel provided an excellent chance to learn the business.

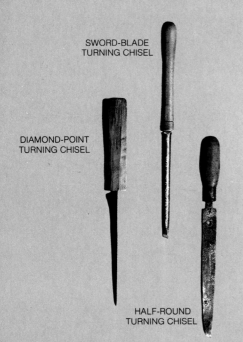

SWORD-BLADE
TURNING CHISEL

DIAMOND-POINT
TURNING CHISEL

HALF-ROUND
TURNING CHISEL

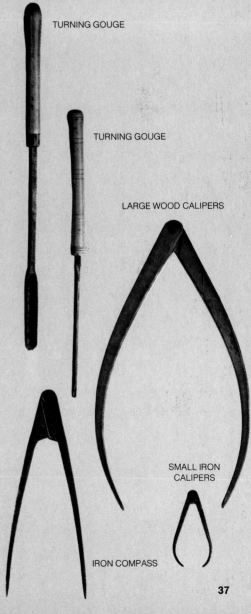

Turns for the better. A length of white pine takes shape as a table leg on the Dominys' wheel lathe. The craftsman addressed the work from the far side of the lathe, with the handle of his cutting tool steadied on an adjustable tool rest. The apprentice turning the crank faced the master. Since the various cutting tasks required a wide range of turning speeds, interchangeable pulley wheels were used to gear up or down. Tools shown here that were used with the lathe include gouges for making the first rough cuts and chisels for refining them. Calipers and compasses measured progress.

TURNING GOUGE

TURNING GOUGE

LARGE WOOD CALIPERS

SMALL IRON CALIPERS

IRON COMPASS

The Clock Shop: Elegant Precision in Little Space

In a building scarcely more than 10 by 14 feet in size, three generations of Dominys shaped metal clockworks—wheels, pendulums, weights, escapements, dials and hands—and made replacement parts for everything from pocket watches to guns and plows.

Besides the shop proper *(right)*, the clock shop included an annex with a large brick forge and an attic that housed the forge's bellows. Since virtually everything the Dominys produced had to be made from scratch, the forge was of necessity the starting place for most commissions. There metals were heated to a temperature suitable for shaping with a hammer and anvil or were melted for casting in handmade wooden molds *(near right, top)*. Parts were then taken into the shop, the castings checked against templates, and each piece put through a series of refining steps.

Because the Dominys' metalworking was mostly devoted to clock- and watch-making, most of the tools in the clock shop were small, like the bone- and steel-headed hammers opposite, which were used to rivet the tiny gear wheels of a watch onto their shafts. But a good-sized bench vise, like that at the rear of the room, had its place too. It might hold a movement plate while it was being filed or grip a tiny polishing lathe so both the craftsman's hands were left free.

The Dominys also favored a number of labor-saving engines: hand- or foot-treadle devices such as the bench lathe in the foreground, a screw-thread cutter and the wheel cutter on page 40.

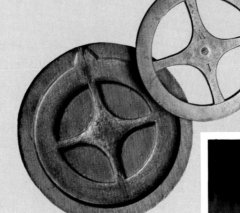

WOOD CLOCK-WHEEL MOLD
AND BRASS TEMPLATE

HOUR-HAND
TEMPLATES

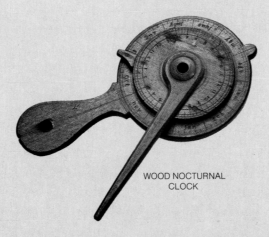

WOOD NOCTURNAL
CLOCK

Orderly retreat. This clock shop features a work stool that fits beneath a hip-high bench, abundant light and little clutter—all essential to the painstaking work of a clockmaker. The tall clock that stands at the back was made in 1799 for David Gardiner of Flushing, New York, and was delivered with instructions: "1st Take out those things that are deposited in the bottom of the Case—then take it out of ye Box & Rear it where you intend it shall stand."

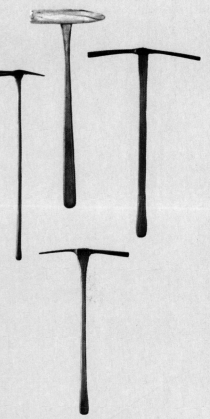

STEEL- AND BONE-HEADED HAMMERS

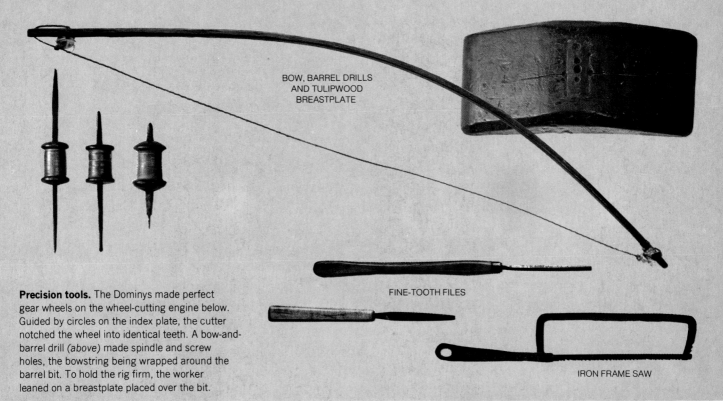

BOW, BARREL DRILLS
AND TULIPWOOD
BREASTPLATE

FINE-TOOTH FILES

IRON FRAME SAW

Precision tools. The Dominys made perfect gear wheels on the wheel-cutting engine below. Guided by circles on the index plate, the cutter notched the wheel into identical teeth. A bow-and-barrel drill (*above*) made spindle and screw holes, the bowstring being wrapped around the barrel bit. To hold the rig firm, the worker leaned on a breastplate placed over the bit.

A Sextet of Basic Tools: The Six Simple Machines

"Give me a place to stand and I will move the earth," said the Greek scientist Archimedes, extolling the properties of the lever. Though Archimedes somewhat overstated the case, his remark does indicate how greatly a simple tool can augment the power of the human body. The lever and five other devices known to the ancient Greeks—the wedge, the inclined plane, the screw, the wheel and axle and the pulley—are held to be the six basic tools from which humans assembled the myriad other tools that have shaped our world.

Traditionally the six are called the "simple machines," though in fact not all of them have moving parts. What they do share is a single mechanical principle that explains how a great weight can be moved with a small expenditure of force. Stated succinctly, in the language of algebra, this principle says that driving force, multiplied by the distance moved at the driving end, equals working force multiplied by the distance moved at the working end.

The lever is the simplest illustration of this principle. Essentially a straight rod, the lever exerts a powerful working force when it is moved on a pivoting point, or fulcrum. The long handle of a crowbar being used to pry up the lid of a crate pivots on the edge of the crate to lift the lid—and the nails that secured it. Pliers, scissors and metal snips consist of two levers that pivot on a single fulcrum.

On pliers and metal snips, where the fulcrum is close to the jaws, or working end, the long handles transfer great force to the short jaws. The wire-cutting edges of a pair of locking-grip pliers can sever a ¼-inch steel rod. On the other hand, the long jaws of a pair of paper shears gain in working distance what they lose in working force: The shears cut several inches in one stroke.

The blades of shears illustrate yet another simple machine: the wedge. The tapered shape of the wedge allows it to pierce and separate materials efficiently. Stone Age people used a crude wedge, in the form of a sharp rock, to scrape the hair from animal hides and to cut meat into manageable pieces.

More sophisticated examples of the wedge include the blade of a hatchet, the edge of a chisel and the tip of a nail: All are wedges that split wood fibers.

The inclined plane, sometimes considered a variant of the wedge, is used exclusively to split weight from gravity's pull—to lift. Ramps provide an obvious example of how the inclined plane uses increased distance to decrease the force required to raise a load. Everyone agrees that climbing an angled ramp is much easier than scaling a vertical wall.

The screw, another simple machine, is actually an inclined plane spiraling around a post. In its original form, the screw was a mechanical device used to raise loads. One of the most famous screws of antiquity was Archimedes' water screw, an irrigation machine consisting of a screw that revolved inside an open-ended cylinder to lift water from one level to another. In one of its modern forms, a screw lifts a cork from a bottle and, in the form of a spiraling drill bit, reams wood out of a hole.

Rotary action is also essential to the wheel and axle. Recognized as a valuable achievement 5,000 years ago, by Sumerian kings who included wheeled vehicles among the treasures to be buried with them, the principle of the wheel and axle has had innumerable applications. A wrench removing a lag bolt is in effect a spoke in a wheel, and the bolt is the axle.

A specialized use of the wheel produces the final simple machine, the pulley—a device for lifting. The basic pulley consists of a rope passed over a wheel with a groove in its rim, and allows the worker to remain stationary while moving a load to a distant point.

The block and tackle—a more sophisticated example of the pulley—has two wheels, one stationary, the other attached to the load being lifted. Both wheels have several grooves around their rims, enabling rope to be passed around them several times. Manually operated elevators, once in common use, worked by means of a block-and-tackle mechanism, enabling one attendant to raise a cageful of freight or people with an easy downward pull.

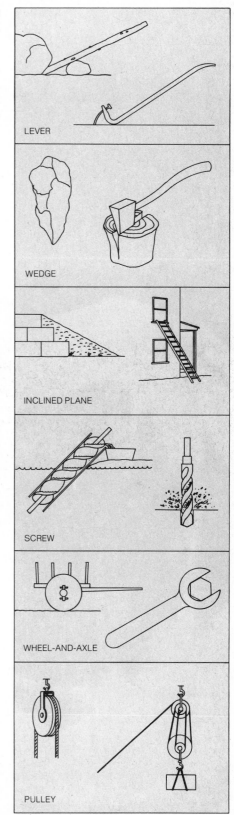

LEVER

WEDGE

INCLINED PLANE

SCREW

WHEEL-AND-AXLE

PULLEY

2 Equipping the Shop for Action

Power and versatility. The plastic-sheathed three-conductor cable at far left awaits installation in a heavy-duty electric circuit for carrying power to this drill press and a shop's worth of other tools. Once hooked up, the versatile drill press converts electricity into motion and, besides drilling, performs a variety of tasks that range from sanding to cutting square holes for mortises.

Not everyone creating a home workshop is as fortunate as a certain hardware-store owner in Denver, Colorado. This particular gentleman built himself a 44-by-28-foot shop, then erected his home on top of it. Unconstrained by limitations of space or budget, he equipped his shop with hundreds of the finest hand tools and an array of power tools for every contingency—a lathe, a table saw, various sanders and shapers, even a large industrial metal-cutting saw.

Most people approach the making of a workshop in a much more conventional manner: The house comes first, and the shop and its contents are fitted into whatever space and budget are left over. Frequently this calls for careful planning, and some compromises. Like a football coach selecting members of his team, the homeowner choosing the working elements of a shop is surrounded by many candidates for his attention, each offering special attributes and skills. Equipping a shop, like choosing a team, is often a matter of putting together an ensemble that will work well together.

Space, of course, dictates the size and composition of the workshop ensemble. If you can afford to devote a whole basement to your shop, or an entire garage, you can think in terms of such space-consuming power tools as a table saw, with accessory tables for holding long boards as they pass through the saw. But even if your space is limited or your shop must share space with other family activities, you can still equip it with power tools; you will simply have to be more selective and more ingenious. It is perfectly possible to put power tools into a shop confined to a single wall or to the inside of a closet, if you choose tools that need less working room, take up less storage space and can perhaps be folded down or rolled out of the way when not in use.

Though power tools and the electricity needed to run them are likely to be the primary concerns in the equipping of a modern workshop, in fact the first tools acquired for any shop are apt to be its hand tools. A collection of these, selected for quality, long life and good design, are the bedrock of any tool kit—as they have been ever since humans first used sharp-edged stones to put points on sticks. The hand tools available today are a testament to how far we have come. In addition to the basic saws, hammers, screwdrivers and pliers, a craftsman can buy, for example, chisels made of Sheffield steel with interchangeable rosewood handles, German or Italian riffle files curved at the end in at least a dozen different versions of a shallow S, and Japanese handsaws that cut on the pull stroke and leave a kerf as narrow as that of a knife. Truly, the roster of tools available to equip a modern workshop is enough to start even a neophyte on the way to becoming a skilled craftsman.

Personalizing a Battery of Portable Tools

Almost any home workshop begins with a collection of hand tools assembled haphazardly over months and even years, without plan and long before any conscious thought of equipping a workshop has taken hold. So when the idea does surface, the first order of business is to take stock of what is on hand and what additional tools are needed.

In selecting tools, you will want to consider, for example, the kinds of projects you contemplate. But the main consideration, and the key to selecting hand tools, is quality. When you are equipping a workshop, look for reputable brand names and for tools that have been given medium-to-high ratings in consumer tests. Such tools will not be low-priced, but well-made tools provide decades of service and sometimes last for a life-time. Also, it is possible to find bargains.

To cut costs, watch for sales, but be sure the sale price includes a normal guarantee. Buy tools in sets—screwdrivers, chisels and wrenches are generally less expensive when purchased this way, although the initial investment will be higher than for a smaller number of individual items. Stores that cater to professionals with top-of-the-line tools at less-than-retail prices are often interested in selling to nonprofessionals as well. And finally, there are garage sales and country auctions, where you may be able to find rock-bottom prices, but do examine the merchandise with care.

In equipping your workshop, you will not buy everything at once, of course. Begin with the essentials, then at intervals add other tools. It helps to make a purchase plan and stick to it. That way, you avoid impulse purchases and the acquisition of gimmicky tools that may be in fashion at the moment but in the long run will prove of limited value.

On this and the facing page, various types of hand tools are grouped according to function, and general guidelines are given for judging their quality and usefulness. The chart that follows is intended as a guide to selecting tools for specific kinds of work, enabling you to decide which tools match your requirements and which will be used infrequently. The list is not all-inclusive: Many highly specialized tools have been omitted. Nor does it include "found" tools—cotton swabs, toothbrushes, tweezers and the like—which are endlessly useful for all sorts of workshop chores.

Chisels

Four wood chisels with blades ranging in width from ¼ to 1 inch suffice for most basic jobs. Look for metal-capped, high-impact plastic handles and a washer between the blade and the handle to act as a shock absorber. Another mark of quality is price: The more a chisel costs, the better the grade of steel in the blade.

For advanced projects, many home craftsmen add two types of specialty chisels: paring chisels, for delicate work, and mortise chisels, for joinery. For metalwork, the standard tool is a cold chisel with a flat ½-inch blade. For masonry work, a brickset is used to split bricks.

Clamps

Clamps come in various shapes, sizes and materials for a variety of jobs. C clamps, usually cast iron or aluminum, are the most useful. A screw clamp, made up of two wooden jaws and two steel spindles, is more versatile than a C clamp and less likely to mar work, but costs more.

A bar clamp may be bought in two parts that fit on the ends of a ¾-inch galvanized pipe to span a long distance. A web clamp, similar in principle to an automobile seat belt, secures odd-shaped pieces by exerting even pressure along a tough woven strap. Corner clamps hold miter joints for gluing and nailing.

Cutting Tools

At least five saws form the common complement of a home workshop. The ripsaw and crosscut saw are used for freehand cuts with and across the grain; the backsaw is used in a miter box; the coping and keyhole saws are used for cutting curves. All should have polished blades to reduce friction as they pass through wood. To further reduce friction, the larger blades of rip- and crosscut saws should be taper-ground, that is, machined so that the blade is thicker near the teeth than at the top.

Examine the teeth of all saws for sharpness and uniformity. Check the feel of the handle and the type and number of fasteners that attach the handle to the blade. Large saws should have three such fasteners, removable so the handle can be replaced if necessary.

Drilling Tools (Manual)

Although largely replaced by electric models, hand drills are still used in hard-to-reach places and for delicate work. The common egg-beater-action drill is accurate for holes up to ¼ inch in diameter; better models have metal rather than plastic gears. A push drill with a ratchet mechanism bores small holes in delicate work and pilot holes for screws. For larger holes the centuries-old brace and bit is still ideal, but be sure the brace has a reversible ratchet for work in tight areas.

Files and Rasps

The basic file is half-round in shape, 10 inches long, with rows of coarse blade-like ridges on the rounded side and crisscrossed, or "double-cut," ridges on the flat side; it is adaptable enough for trimming either metal or wood. Second in usefulness is the 10-inch half-round rasp, with raised, pointed teeth, for use only on wood. Other files and rasps, more specialized, include flat, round and triangular types for trimming odd-shaped wood or metal. Two helpful accessories are a handle of wood or plastic that can be switched from file to file as needed and a stiff wire brush, called a file card, that cleans shavings from the file teeth.

Similar in function to files are forming tools, thin sheets of rough, perforated steel locked within plastic handles. Though they do not supplant files, forming tools make quick work of such tasks as trimming the edges of wallboard, vinyl tile, plywood and similar materials.

Hammers

Hammers are more specialized than is often thought. A curved-claw hammer pulls nails smoothly, but for prying apart nailed construction a straight-claw hammer is more useful. The tempered head of a ball-peen hammer is meant for striking cold chisels and other metal tools, while a two-headed mallet, with replaceable rubber and plastic faces, is used on chisels and for shaping sheet metal.

The finest claw and ball-peen hammer heads are made of drop-forged steel, not cast steel, and are seamless and highly polished. The choice of handles is largely a matter of taste, but buy a weight that suits the job; 7, 12, 16 and 24 ounces are the most common.

Measurers and Markers

Tools for accurate measuring and marking come in various shapes, sizes and materials. Of prime importance are rulers, especially a flexible steel tape. Ideally this tape should be marked in incremental feet and inches as well as cumulative inches, and at 16-inch intervals it should be highlighted to help locate stud positions. Some tapes come with useful tables printed on the reverse side; all need a sturdy case that can accept replacement tapes. The tapes themselves should have a plastic coating, which prolongs the life of the markings.

A 6-foot folding extension ruler made of hard wood is also useful; look for one with a brass inset that slides out for measuring the inside dimensions of such things as door openings. In all measuring and marking tools, examine the workmanship. Levels should have either metal bodies or metal edges, plus vials that are replaceable. Check combination squares for rigid steel bodies and look for two small but useful built-in accessories, a bubble level and a marking awl.

Miscellaneous

Tools to round out a collection can be of many different types, from basic to highly specialized. Buy miscellaneous items, such as putty knives and nail sets, with the same care you would use in buying hammers. Use mail-order houses to locate specialty tools. Some of these tools are highly ornamental, such as brass fin-

ger planes for miniature work, while others are special in that they make a specific task possible or easier, like a dovetail saw for precision cutting. Local contractors or hardware stores can probably give you the names and addresses of some specialty-tool companies.

Planes

The block plane, for trimming end grain, and the jack plane, for shaving along the grain, are the two essential planing tools. Both should have high-quality steel blades and precisely machined adjusting mechanisms that hold their positions and allow exact control over the amount of wood to be shaved.

Specialty planes that may be added to the workshop later include a longer plane for truing the edges of long boards; rabbet and plow planes for cutting recesses; and a spokeshave—a drawknife for paring curves.

Pliers

Often thought of as multipurpose tools, pliers actually have specialized purposes and should be used only on jobs for which they were designed. A pair of 8-inch slip-joint pliers is for bending and gripping. Diagonal-cutting pliers cut wire and small nails. A pair of locking-grip pliers can be adjusted to clamp onto an object, acting as a wrench. Long-nose pliers are able to reach into recessed areas and are especially handy for making terminal loops on electrical wires. In general, look for pliers that are made of chrome-plated steel with strong joints and plastic-coated handles.

Portable Power Tools

Small portable power tools have become practically indispensable in the home workshop. An electric hand drill can bore, sand, polish, grind, even drive screws. Circular saws, routers and orbital sanders far outpace their hand-tool counterparts. Moreover, some manufacturers now make stands and tables for portable tools, enabling them to be used much like the costlier, stationary ones.

When purchasing small power tools, buy items of at least medium quality. Check for plastic double-insulated bodies, heavy-duty electrical cords, perma-

nently lubricated bearings, and safety features such as triggers that are hard to press accidently and brakes that stop motors as soon as the triggers are released. Some models have variable-speed and reversible controls. Compare models to get as many of these features as you can.

Screwdrivers

Every tool collection needs at least four common sizes of flat-tipped screwdrivers for single-slot screws and two sizes of Phillips screwdrivers for cross-slot screws. In Canada you will also need square-tipped Robertson screwdrivers. The tips and shafts of these types should be made of chrome-vanadium steel. The handle may be either wood or plastic, but a plastic handle with a rubber cover makes the best shock insulator for screwdrivers used in electrical work.

In addition to these basic types, a spiral ratchet screwdriver, which converts forward motion on the handle into twisting motion on the shank, can speed jobs requiring the setting of a great many screws. It comes in several sizes, the most useful being 14 inches long, and has as many as four interchangeable bits.

Wrenches

The most useful wrench is the 10-inch adjustable wrench with smooth jaws that open to grip nuts and boltheads up to 1 inch wide. It should be made of drop-forged steel with a corrosion-resistant chrome finish. Other types are open-end wrenches with fixed jaw widths, which slip around nuts and boltheads from the side, and box wrenches, which fit over nuts and bolts and are especially suited to hexagonal nuts and boltheads. Combination wrenches combine the two types, but separate sets of open-end and box wrenches can be more convenient, especially when two wrenches of the same size are needed at one time.

Socket wrenches, driven by handles with ratchet mechanisms, speed the task of tightening bolts and of working in tight spots. A good basic model has a ⅜-inch-wide drive post and sockets with six interior corners; adapters to the drive post of this type let the handle be used with sockets that need ¼- or ½-inch posts. Buy metric-standard wrenches if you will work on foreign bicycles or cars.

The Right Tool to Make the Task Easier

Tools	Basic Household Maintenance	Plumbing	Electrical Repair	Masonry	Carpentry	Metalworking	Woodworking
CHISELS							
Brickset chisel				★			
Cold chisel	☆	☆		★		★	
Paring chisels							★
Wood chisels	☆		☆		★		★
CLAMPS							
Bar clamp					★		★
C clamp	★				★		★
Screw clamp							★
Web clamp	☆						★
CUTTING TOOLS							
Backsaw and miter box		☆			★		★
Coping saw	☆				★		★
Crosscut saw and ripsaw	★				★		★
Dovetail saw					☆		★
Hacksaw	★	★			☆	★	
Keyhole saw		★	★		☆		
Pipe cutter		★	★				
Tin snips	☆		☆			★	
Utility knife	★		★		☆		
Wire stripper			★				
DRILLING TOOLS (MANUAL)							
Brace and bit					☆		☆
Hand drill	☆				☆		★
Push drill	☆						★
FILES							
Flat file	☆					★	
Forming tools					☆		☆
Rasp					★		★
Round and half-round files	★					★	☆
Triangular file					★	★	
HAMMERS							
Ball-peen hammer	★	☆		★		★	
Bricklayer's hammer		★		★			
Claw hammer	★	★	☆	★	★		★
Soft-faced mallet				☆		★	★
Tack hammer	☆						
MEASURING AND MARKING TOOLS							
Awl					★		★
Center punch						☆	
Chalk line				★	★		
Combination square	★				★		★
Flexible tape	★	★	★	★	★		★
Folding rule	☆				★		★
Level	★	★		★	★		☆
Marking gauge					☆		☆
Steel square	☆			★	★		★
MISCELLANEOUS							
Bench vise		★			★	★	★

★—Essential ☆—Desirable

Tools	Basic Household Maintenance	Plumbing	Electrical Repair	Masonry	Carpentry	Metalworking	Woodworking
File card						★	☆
Nail set	☆				★		★
Plunger	★	★					
Pointing trowel				★			
Propane torch		★				★	
Pry bar	★			☆	★	★	
Putty knife	★				☆	★	
Staple gun	★		☆		☆		
Star drill				★			
Voltage tester			★				
Whetstone	☆				★		★
PLANES							
Block plane	★				★		★
Jack plane	☆				★		☆
Jointer plane							☆
Rabbet plane							☆
Spokeshave							☆
PLIERS							
Channel-joint pliers		★					
Diagonal-cutting pliers	☆		★				
Electrician's pliers			★				
Locking-grip pliers	★	★			★	★	
Long-nosed pliers	☆	★	★				
Slip-joint pliers	★	★			★	☆	☆
PORTABLE POWER TOOLS							
Belt sander					☆		☆
Circular saw	☆				★		☆
Electric drill	★	★	★	★	★	★	★
Orbital sander	☆				☆		★
Router					☆		★
Saber saw	☆		☆		★	☆	☆
SCREWDRIVERS							
Flat-tipped screwdrivers	★	★			★		★
Offset screwdriver			☆				☆
Phillips-head screwdrivers	★	★	★				☆
Spiral ratchet screwdriver	☆				★		☆
WRENCHES							
Adjustable wrench	★	★			★		☆
Basin wrench		★					
Box and open wrenches	☆				☆		
Pipe wrench		★					
Socket wrench	☆	★				★	
Spud wrench		★					

Determining your tool needs. In the left-hand column of this chart, tools are listed in groups according to their functions. Each of the next seven columns is headed by a work category. To find out which tools are required for a given type of work, read down any one of these seven columns. To determine how useful a particular tool can be, locate it under its function category in the first column, then read across the chart. The tools that are essential to a specific type of work are marked by a solid star; tools that are helpful in advanced, special or infrequent tasks are indicated by an open star. Of course, these designations are not rigid; for example, the spiral ratchet screwdriver that is indispensable to a person who works with piano hinges may be considered a specialty tool by someone who makes a hobby of model building.

Muscle Men: A Corps of Heavy-duty Power Tools

The equipment that best defines the capabilities of a home workshop is its complement of stationary power tools. Along with a solidly built workbench, these machines will make the shop a realm of true craftsmanship.

Stationary tools ensure machine precision and production efficiency. They also carry hefty price tags. No home shop needs to have every power tool, and most will include just one or two. In selecting the tools, take into account the kinds of work you do, the amount of it you can anticipate, the floor space of your shop and the cost of each tool.

About 80 per cent of your power-tool work probably will involve the cutting of wood—with the remainder taken up by drilling, joining, smoothing and finishing tasks. In that case, a stationary saw may be all you need.

Whether you select a table saw or a radial-arm saw is largely a question of personal preference. A good table saw is massive, durable, simple in design and simple to use. It is the preferred tool for cutting large panels of wood—an important concern if much of your work involves plywood. A radial-arm saw is more versatile; it can be used for sanding and planing as well as for cutting. It is also easier to use for repeating a single procedure many times, and its blade is above the table and wholly visible, which, adherents claim, makes it safer.

Though many professionals contend that the multipurpose drill press is a logical second purchase, that decision again hinges on the kind of work you plan to do. Many furniture builders would rather have a band saw, for instance. It is the perfect tool for compound cutting or for removing wood from two or more sides of a block, and it can cut through stacked pieces of wood to produce several identical parts. Hobbyists may prefer a jig saw, whose fine blade can cut intricate shapes in lightweight materials.

Other power tools are in a sense satellite tools. The job of the bench grinder is to keep other tools sharp, a specialized function that nevertheless makes it useful in even a general-purpose shop. The jointer-planer, which planes, miters or rabbets the edge of a board, is generally teamed with a power saw that provides boards with the requisite precision-cut edges. When used as a plane, the jointer-planer produces the glass-smooth surfaces that are particularly desirable in cabinetmaking.

Before buying any of these machines, consider how much work you can reasonably expect to get from each one. A shop that contains many machines gives you the luxury of using each tool only for the function it performs best, and saves you set-up time—changing accessories or fashioning jigs. But if your need for a specialized tool is limited, you can often adapt another tool to do double duty. A drill press fitted with molding blades can serve as a shaper, for example; a radial-arm saw equipped with sanding accessories will make an adequate substitute for a disk sander.

Space limitations in your workshop will also affect your choice of power tools; each tool, in addition to taking up floor space, requires operating space around it. In a well-equipped, well-planned cabinetmaking shop, the table saw, jointer-planer, drill press, lathe and band saw need a minimum of 120 square feet. If you lack that space, you might better invest in a compact multipurpose shop tool that combines the functions of several specialized machines. A multipurpose tool occupies as little as 12 square feet and can be stored against the wall when not in use. It will be expensive, but its cost may well be less than the cumulative price of the individual tools it replaces.

Price is indeed the final factor in selecting power tools. If your budget is tight, choose the most versatile tools, such as the radial-arm saw and the drill press, and add accessories as needed. One money-saving option is to buy tools minus the motor; a single motor can be shifted to drive several power tools. Another economy measure is to purchase secondhand tools; insist, however, that you be allowed to put a tool through its paces before you buy it.

Before buying bargain tools, compare them with competitive brands. Open the tool's housing and take a good look at its inner workings. Size it up in terms of weight and rigidity. Even to an untrained eye, a difference in quality will usually be visible between bargain tools and more costly ones.

Finally, learn to read specification sheets provided by the manufacturers. With this information, you can be sure you are comparing apples with apples as you evaluate similar tools for their motor capacities and performance capabilities.

The Basic Cutting Tool: A Table Saw

Sizing up a table saw. The table saw, also called a bench saw, provides a flat, stationary work surface on which building materials—usually wood, but occasionally light metals—can be accurately guided over a rotating circular saw blade that projects through a slot in the tabletop. The table saw mechanizes a wide range of cutting techniques, including ripping, crosscutting, miter cutting and sawing compound angles. The machine's motor-driven arbor—the axle on which the saw blade revolves—can be raised or lowered to vary the blade's cutting depth, and tilted so that the blade will cut at

angles. To guide the work past the blade, the table has a rip fence and a miter gauge.

A typical home table saw comes with a 10-inch blade capable of cutting 3¼ inches deep. Other commonly found blade diameters range from 8 to 12 inches. For cutting wide panels, look for a table that extends to make rip cuts up to 24 inches wide, the capacity needed in most home workshops. To support the work conveniently, the table should have 10 or 12 inches of surface from its front edge to the front of the blade when the blade is set for a 1-inch cutting depth.

A ¾- to 1-horsepower motor is common in home tools, but the speed ratio may vary; a motor speed of 5,500 revolutions per minute is desirable for the high-speed blades needed for cutting dadoes and moldings (*below*).

The table saw's safety features are important considerations. Shop for a saw that has a plastic or metal blade guard to shield the cutting edge, a splitting device to separate the cut wood and keep it from binding on the blade, and antikickback fingers to catch the work and keep it from flying back if the wood should bind.

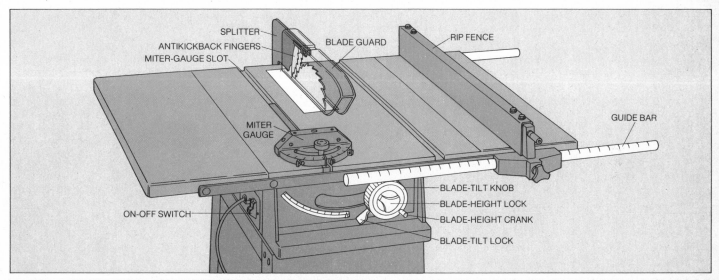

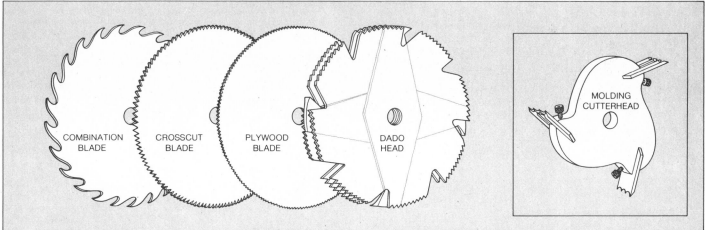

Table-saw blades and accessories. To get the most use from a table saw, outfit it with a full complement of blades and special cutting heads. The blade sold with most saws is a combination blade designed to work efficiently on both crosscuts and rip cuts. For cleaner edges and a narrower kerf on these cuts, a hollow-ground combination blade has teeth set directly in line with the body of the blade, which is ground thinner than its cutting edge.

More specialized is the crosscut blade, which has twice as many teeth as the combination blade and is less likely to cause splintering when cutting across wood grain. A plywood blade is specially tempered to stand up to the glue and the layers of variable graining in plywood; the blade's many small teeth minimize splintering.

For cutting dadoes, the table saw takes a dado head, which consists of two circular blades as-

sembled around a variable number of inner blades called chippers. The chippers cut away wood between the two main blades. On quality dado heads the main blades are hollow-ground.

For cutting more intricate profiles, a molding cutterhead is used as a mount for three identically contoured blades that are fastened into it with screws (*inset*). Blades for the cutterhead are available in many different profiles.

Space requirements of a table saw. To rip a long board into narrower sections, you line up one edge of the stock against the ripping fence and then push the entire length of the board over the blade. There must be adequate space both in front and in back of the table to accommodate the full length of the board, and also room for a movable back stand (*pages 98-99*) to support the cut sections as they come through the saw.

Since long pieces of lumber are also crosscut, the table saw requires space on both sides as well, although it is usually possible to give the saw a quarter turn, especially if it is mounted on heavy-duty locking casters. Given these requirements, the ideal place for a table saw is at the center of the workshop.

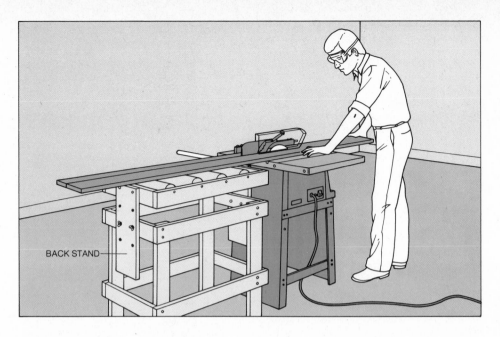

BACK STAND

A Versatile Alternative: The Radial-arm Saw

Selecting a radial-arm saw. This saw operates on a principle directly opposite to that of its counterpart, the table saw: For all but the rip cut, the blade moves while the wood remains stationary, and the cut is made from above rather than beneath the work. Since the blade rides along a track, tilts 100° right or left in its yoke and swivels 360° beneath a support arm that is adjustable both laterally and vertically, the saw has much of the mobility and flexibility of a portable power saw. And since the blade also can be locked in any of its paths, the radial-arm saw offers great precision.

A typical radial-arm saw for the home workshop has a blade 10 inches in diameter. It cuts to a maximum depth of 3 inches, crosscuts boards 13 inches wide and handles rip cuts up to 24½ inches wide. Look for a saw with a heavy cast-iron arm and a motor rating of at least 2 horsepower. Consider also the tool's braking capacity. Automatic braking is a real convenience, but lacking that, the blade should at least have a manual brake, since a coasting blade can be dangerous. Other desirable features are floating blade guards and adjustable antikick-back fingers for protection during rip cuts.

Elaborate radial-arm-saw models offer options such as multiple arbors and variable speed control. More important is the availability of special accessories that broaden the saw's capabilities beyond making simple straight cuts. Properly equipped, a radial-arm saw can cut rabbets or dadoes and can also perform routing, shaping, sanding and drilling chores.

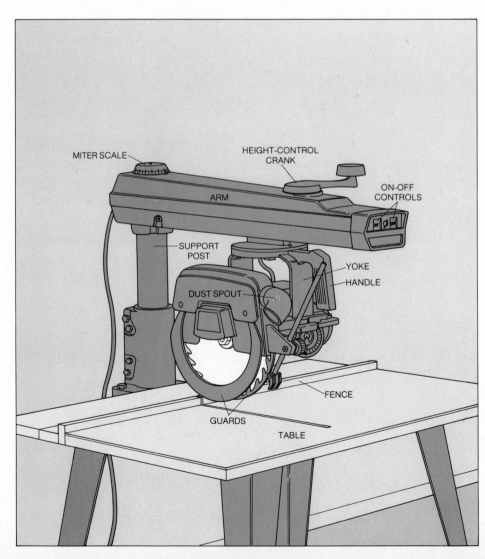

MITER SCALE

HEIGHT-CONTROL CRANK

ON-OFF CONTROLS

ARM

SUPPORT POST

YOKE

HANDLE

DUST SPOUT

FENCE

GUARDS

TABLE

Radial-arm-saw accessories. By removing the standard circular blade and tilting the saw's motor in its yoke, you can fit the radial-arm saw with accessories that cut complex profiles into wood and speed up finishing chores. Very useful is the shaping accessory, shown with its special blade guard in place *(top, near right)*, and with the guard removed *(inset)*; note the two-part fence on each side of the cutterhead that guides wood evenly past the contoured blades. The saw's motor speed of 3,450 revolutions per minute is adequate for shaping wood.

For certain planing tasks, such as cutting wide bevels on the surface of a raised panel, the radial-arm saw is fitted with a circular planing attachment *(top, far right)* that revolves at speeds sufficiently high to produce very smooth work. A saber-saw attachment *(bottom, near right)* transforms this revolving action into the up-and-down motion of the jig-saw blade, for cutting along intricately curving lines. A drum sanding attachment that lowers into a notch in the table *(bottom, far right)* lets you use the saw's spinning action to smooth wood edges held against the drum at table level. The drum can also be raised and angled to operate in other positions, or replaced with a sanding disk.

A special chuck converts the radial-arm saw for use with a variety of drill and router bits. The saw can also be used with the same selection of blades as the table saw, including dado blades.

Space for a radial-arm saw. Like a table saw, the radial-arm saw requires sufficient space on both sides to accommodate long pieces of lumber—ideally 10 to 12 feet. Unlike a table saw, however, the radial-arm saw works efficiently backed against a workshop wall. In rip cutting, the blade is set sideways; in crosscutting, the lumber is lined up against the fence at the back of the table and the saw is pulled forward along its arm to make the cut, then pushed back behind the fence to complete the action. The machine itself occupies roughly 6 square feet and requires a few feet of maneuvering space in front for its operator. Worktables on either side of the saw are useful for supporting long boards.

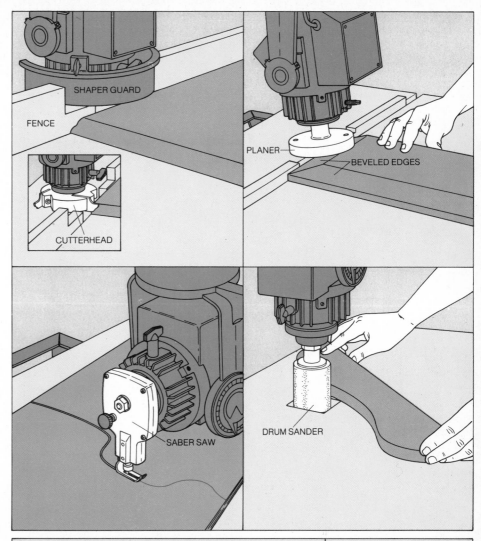

SHAPER GUARD

FENCE

CUTTERHEAD

PLANER

BEVELED EDGES

SABER SAW

DRUM SANDER

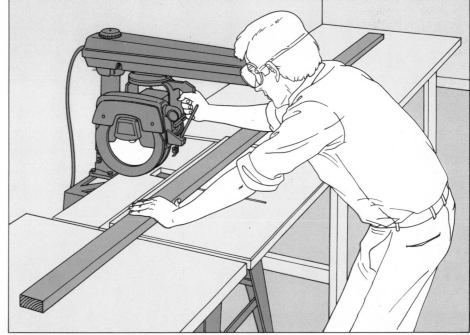

Adding a Saw to Cut Curves

A deep-cutting band saw. Prized for its ability to cut curved lines and for its unmatched depth of cut, a band saw has a continuous blade driven in one direction around two wheels, one above the other, encased in a metal housing. Only the section of blade above the worktable is exposed. For woodworking, the saw blade moves at very high speeds, 2,000 to 3,000 feet per minute; for cutting metal, the machine can be outfitted with special blades and run at lower speeds.

The size of a band saw is determined by its throat, the distance from the blade to the vertical arm at the tool's back. Band-saw capacity is rated by maximum depth of cut. An average home tool has a throat of 10 to 12 inches and will cut through wood 6 inches thick. Most home band saws have ½-horsepower motors and use blades from ⅛ to ½ inch wide. The more powerful the motor, the wider the blade it can drive.

Band-saw tables are generally small but they should tilt 45° for angular cuts. An adjustable ripping fence and miter gauge are common accessories, but not all tables are slotted to accept them. Blade-tension indicators make it easy to set the proper tension for each blade width.

The space requirements of a band saw are much like those of a radial-arm saw. Maneuvering space is needed in front and on both sides, depending on the length of the boards to be cut.

A tight-turning jig saw. Sometimes called a scroll saw, this tool has a slender blade, $\frac{1}{16}$ to ¼ inch wide, mounted under tension between two chucks, one above, one below its worktable. The blade operates with a rapid up-and-down motion. This is a lightweight saw designed for cutting intricate shapes in thin materials. Within its more limited capacity and at slower cutting speeds, the jig saw performs much the same tasks as a band saw. Since almost all jig saws operate at variable speeds, they can be used to cut a wide range of materials.

Jig saws for the home shop have maximum cutting depths just under 2 inches and, as with a band saw, the width of the throat is a primary consideration. Good home models measure 24 inches from blade to vertical support; others have throats ranging from 15 to 20 inches. Jig-saw motors are generally rated at ⅓ horsepower.

Some jig saws are designed to convert to saber-saw action: A heavy-gauge blade fits into the lower chuck, and the arm that holds the top chuck swings out of the way. Other features to look for are built-in lights, spring-loaded guards that hold the work against the table, and blowers that keep the cutting area clear of sawdust.

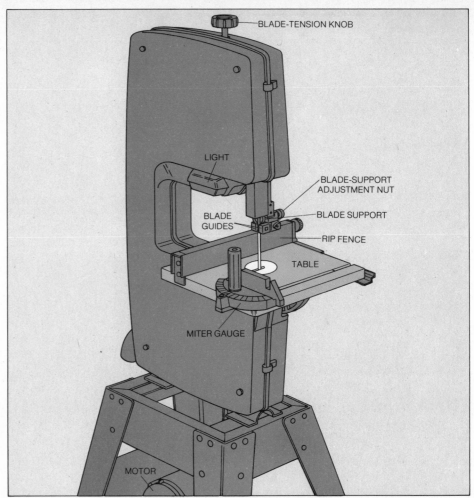

BLADE-TENSION KNOB

LIGHT

BLADE-SUPPORT ADJUSTMENT NUT

BLADE GUIDES

BLADE SUPPORT

RIP FENCE

TABLE

MITER GAUGE

MOTOR

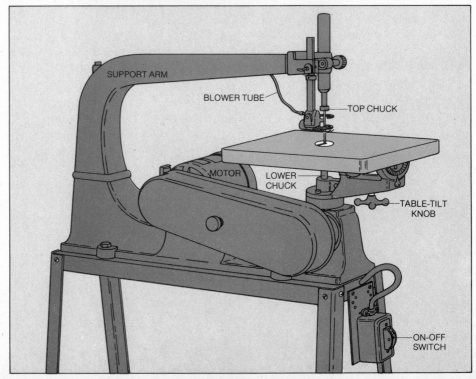

SUPPORT ARM

BLOWER TUBE

TOP CHUCK

MOTOR

LOWER CHUCK

TABLE-TILT KNOB

ON-OFF SWITCH

The Convertible Drill Press

Sizing up a drill press. Originally designed just to drill precise holes, today a drill press cuts perfect circular openings as much as 6 inches in diameter. With accessories, it can also fashion perfectly square mortises, cut plugs, and function as a router, planer, shaper or sander.

The capacity of a drill press is determined by the distance from the column behind the work table to the center of the spindle that turns the drill. A typical tool measures 7 inches from column to spindle. Only the column length differentiates floor-model drill presses from bench models, but the longer the column the greater the thickness of work the tool can accommodate, since the worktable slides on the column to increase the vertical distance between the tabletop and the chuck that grips the drill bit.

The spindle of a drill press is covered by a metal sleeve known as its quill. Both spindle and quill rest inside the drill-press head when not in use (and thus are not seen in this drawing). The quill is lowered, by means of a feed lever, to drill holes of varying depths, the maximum depth depending on the distance the quill travels; for home tools, quill travel ranges from 2½ to 4½ inches. An adjustable depth-stop limits the quill's extension and well-made tools have a spring action that returns the quill to the starting point.

The worktable is usually small, but it should be equipped with flanges and slots for use in clamping the work. Motor sizes vary from ⅓ to ½ horsepower, but the real key to a drill's versatility is the range of its spindle speeds.

Drill-press accessories. The most elaborate of the drill-press accessories is the mortising attachment *(near right)*, with a yoke that clamps on the drill-press quill. The yoke holds a square, hollow chisel that will cut the corners of a mortise, but an auger-like bit inside the hollow square actually does the bulk of the cutting.

The common twist bit *(far right)* is sold in many sizes and will cut through metal and plastic as well as through wood. The brad-point bit has a center point to guide the drill and sharp lips at the outside that enable it to drill extremely smooth holes. A spade bit makes quick work of holes up to 1½ inches in diameter. For even larger openings, the hole saw is sold in both fixed and adjustable diameters. The cutting edge of the fly cutter extends out on its horizontal arm to produce holes up to 6 inches in diameter.

A plug cutter produces wood plugs for concealing boltholes or screw holes, and cuts the short dowels for glued joints. The drill press also mounts router bits to cut shaped edges and slots.

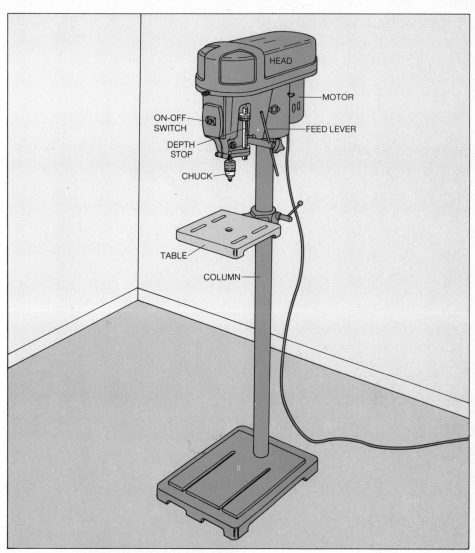

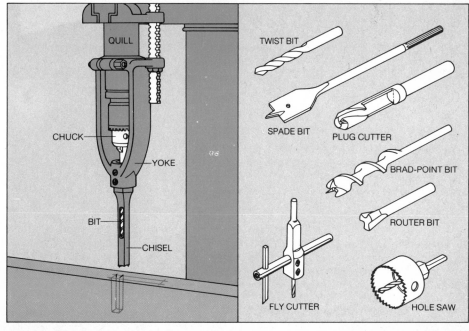

A Jointer to Smooth Edges

Choosing a jointer-planer. The jointer-planer, commonly called a jointer, is used to smooth and square the edges of boards and panels before they are fitted together. You will probably want to use a power saw to cut the wood close to size, anticipating how much stock the jointer will remove. The jointer can cut rabbets and tenons for joints and shape the bevels, tapers and recesses of furniture parts.

Jointers well suited to the home workshop have blades that are 4 inches wide and capable of cuts ⅛ to ⅜ inch deep. Most models have spring-loaded blade guards that push aside as the work passes over the blades (*inset*). The front table adjusts to raise or lower the wood relative to the blade and thus controls the depth of cut.

A large table supports the work more conveniently than a smaller one; look for one at least 27 inches long. Look also for a long rabbeting ledge. The fence should tilt in both directions and have automatic stops at 45° and 90°. The motor should be rated at ⅓ to ½ horsepower. A jointer requires space in both front and back for running through long pieces of lumber.

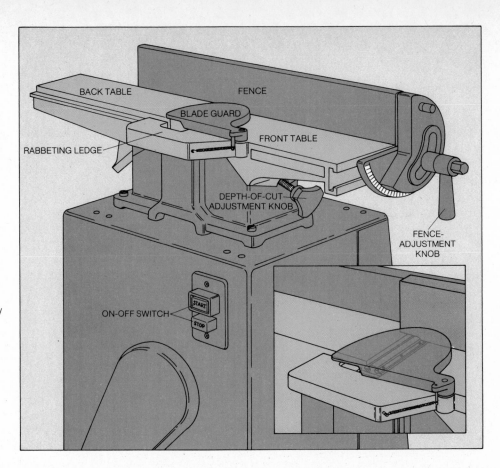

A Shaper to Carve Moldings

Selecting a shaper. This specialized tool cuts moldings with complicated contours and decorates wood surfaces with intricate shapes. The shaper's vertical spindle is fitted with heavy, three-lipped blades that bite into the wood from the side. The spindle can be adjusted to position the blades at varying heights. For most jobs the forward, or in-feed, half of the shaper's double fence is positioned to determine the depth of a cut; the out-feed fence simply supports the work as it passes beyond the blades. This fence can also be removed for freehand work.

The smoothness of a shaper's cut is determined by the speed of its spindle. Home models commonly run at 9,000 to 10,000 revolutions per minute. The motor should be at least ½ horsepower; 1 horsepower is not excessive. Spindle diameter is commonly ½ inch, and the height adjustment of the spindle is usually ⅞ inch.

Features to look for are ball-bearing construction, a reversible motor, independently adjustable fences, spring-loaded jigs for holding the work, and a ring-shaped blade guard for use in freehand work. A shaper requires at least 6 feet of working space in front and at both sides.

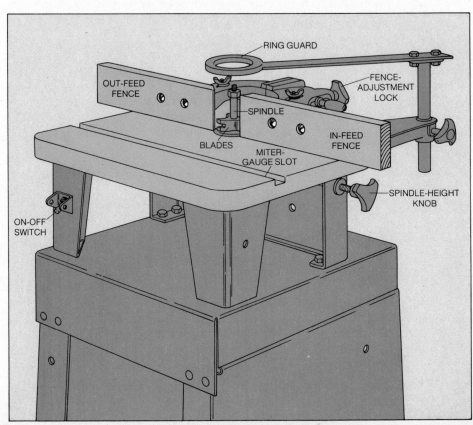

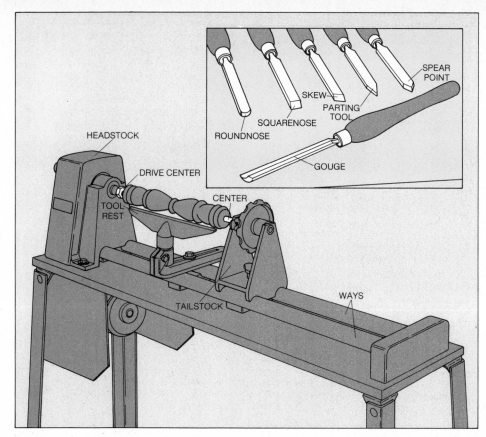

A Lathe for Spinning Curves

Choosing a lathe. Unlike most shaping tools, which turn a blade, the lathe turns the wood, and the wood is scraped and sheared by hand-held chisels steadied against an adjustable tool rest. For spindle turnings, such as chair legs or balustrades, the wood is clamped between two centers—a drive center in the headstock and a holding center in the movable tailstock, which adjusts to accommodate the spindle's length. Work can also be mounted on the drive center alone—to turn hand-carved bowls, for example.

A lathe's capacity is described in terms of maximum spindle length and maximum diameter of stock that can be turned above the guides, or "ways," of the lathe bed. A typical home-workshop lathe opens to 36 inches between centers and accepts 10- to 14-inch-diameter stock. It is powered by a ⅓- to ½-horsepower motor and provides a fairly wide range of rotation speeds. In high-precision, vibration-free lathes, the ways are heavy cast iron. Home lathes are more commonly constructed of pipe; insist on one with twin-rail ways.

To make effective use of a lathe, you will need a full range of chisel shapes and sizes. Six basic chisel shapes are shown in the inset.

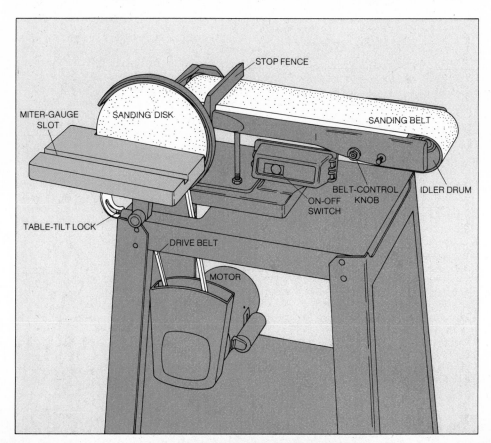

A Sander to Finish the Work

Stationary belt and disk sanders. Though belt sanders and disk sanders can be bought separately, the best sanding tool incorporates both functions. Disk widths range from 8 to 12 inches; common belt sizes are 4-by-36 and 6-by-48 inches. The greater the abrasive surface, the faster the work goes. A 1-horsepower motor is desirable, though many sanders function acceptably on ½ to ¾ horsepower.

The belt sander runs a continuous abrasive belt around two drums—one driven by the motor, the other idling. Positioned horizontally, the belt is used for sanding surfaces and lengthwise edges; for such operations the stock rests on the belt, one of its edges braced against the stop fence. The belt can also be positioned vertically for smoothing an end grain.

The disk sander is a rotating plate of steel or aluminum faced with abrasive sanding papers. A disk removes stock very quickly but always leaves sanding marks. It is most useful for smoothing end grains, miter cuts and curved edges. The table in front of the disk is always used to support the work. It should be adjustable, tilting to facilitate the sanding of angled cuts, and it should be slotted for a miter gauge.

The Tools' Tool: A Grinder

Selecting a bench grinder. This relatively inexpensive tool is mostly used to maintain other shop tools by keeping their cutting edges sharp. But it is also helpful for such jobs as grinding off rivets or smoothing welded joints. The model most practical for home-workshop use has a very basic ¼- to ½-horsepower motor and two aluminum-oxide grinding wheels. The motor should be fully encased, and the wheels fitted with covers and clear-plastic eye shields that expose just a small part of each wheel.

Home-workshop bench grinders generally have wheel diameters ranging from 4 to 8 inches, and wheel widths varying from ½ to 1 inch. A tool equipped with one medium-coarse wheel and one medium-fine wheel is versatile enough to handle most workshop tasks. Adjustable tool rests are essential features; they ensure the correct tool position for sharpening an edge. Built-in water trays and flexible gooseneck lamps are other convenient features to look for.

To minimize vibration, bench grinders need solid support. Though sometimes sold with their own heavy-duty pedestals, grinders are more often bolted to a workbench. A bench grinder requires only sufficient space in front of it to accommodate the length of tool handles.

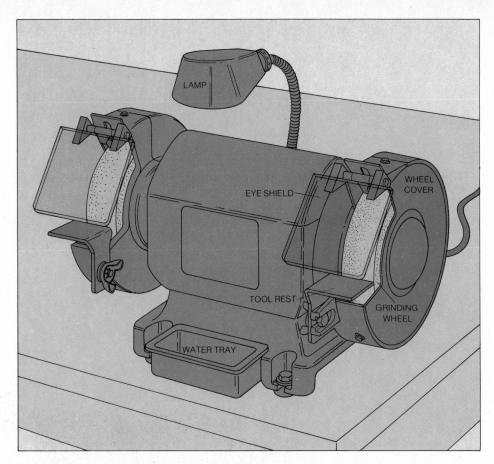

A Workshop in a Single Tool

Evaluating a multipurpose tool. In a small workshop, a well-engineered multipurpose power tool offers an alternative to a roomful of specialized machines. The Shopsmith power tool shown at right occupies only 12 square feet and utilizes a 2-horsepower, variable-speed motor, auxiliary spindles and an adjustable tubular-steel frame to incorporate the capacities of five separate tools. It functions as a 10-inch table saw, a 12-inch disk sander, a 16½-inch drill press, a 34-inch lathe and a horizontal boring machine. With appropriate accessories, this machine can be further adapted for use as a band saw, jig saw, jointer and belt sander.

The key to this tool's versatility is a movable power plant, housed in a headstock that slides along heavy steel ways and can be locked at any point. The ways are also movable: Normally locked horizontally, they can be tilted upright to position the motor's drive shaft for vertical work. For precision in cutting, drilling and shaping, the worktable, miter gauge, rip fence, extension table and tool rest are all adjustable. Homemade back stands and auxiliary work surfaces (*pages 96-99*) are especially practical with such a tool.

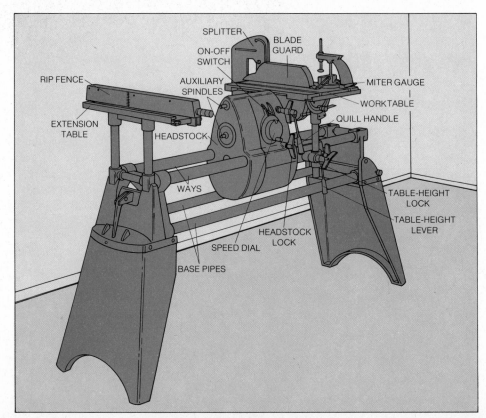

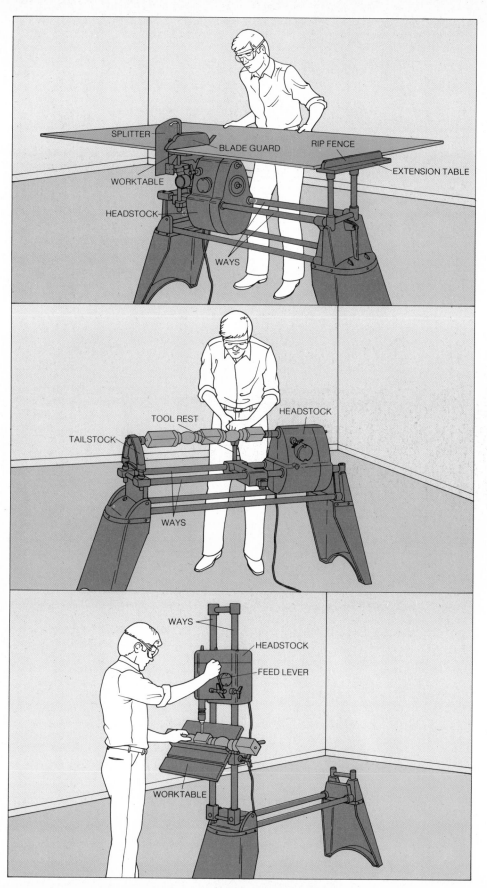

SPLITTER
BLADE GUARD
RIP FENCE
WORKTABLE
EXTENSION TABLE
HEADSTOCK
WAYS

TOOL REST
HEADSTOCK
TAILSTOCK
WAYS

WAYS
HEADSTOCK
FEED LEVER
WORKTABLE

Metamorphoses of a multipurpose tool. Three very different jobs—sawing, turning and drilling precise holes—require three distinct setups on the multipurpose tool. Changing the tool's function involves shifting the position of the head-stock and spindle, installing the proper bit, blade or disk, and assembling the appropriate work-support jigs. With practice, you can make these setups quickly.

For sawing a wide panel (*top, left*), the head-stock is shifted along the ways to position the cir-cular blade; the miter gauge is removed; and both worktable and extension table are set in place to support the wood. The rip fence guides the edge of the panel as the cut is being made, and the splitter behind the blade guard makes the procedure safer.

When the tool is to be used as a lathe (*center, left*), the headstock is again adjusted laterally—this time to accommodate the length of the wood being turned. Lathe centers are attached to the drive shaft and to a tailstock attachment that locks in place at one end of the frame. Work-table and extension table are removed, and the same carriage that supported the worktable now holds a tool rest that steadies the chisel.

For a vertical drill press (*bottom, left*), the tubular-steel ways are tilted upright and locked in position. Both headstock and worktable are raised or lowered along these columns to accom-modate the size of the piece being drilled; the worktable also tilts to support the work at any angle. As with a conventional drill press, the op-erator uses a feed lever to lower the quill.

Caution—The Watchword for Power-Tool Safety

A common—and generally well-founded —wisdom among workshop professionals is that a novice tool-user is less likely to have accidents than an experienced one: The potential dangers of a tool will intimidate the novice into using it correctly. Injuries are more likely to occur as he becomes more skilled, takes short cuts, and grows careless.

Given the amount of wood in the home, most accidents in home workshops are cuts sustained in working with wood, and the worst offenders are power tools. But hand tools can cause injuries too. You can avoid accidents by adopting certain standard precautions.

You should begin by choosing the right tool for the job. Do not substitute a screwdriver for a prying tool or a hatchet for a hammer. Not only do you risk hurting yourself but you will probably ruin the tool. The screwdriver shaft may bend out of true and the hatchet head may chip, throwing hazardous flecks of metal. Equally important, keep tools in good repair. Check handles and hammer heads to be sure they are seated firmly and are

not cracked; keep cutting tools sharp. A dull chisel is difficult to control and may slip. It will also require more time to do the job, taxing your patience and making you more accident-prone.

While a sharp tool is safer than a dull one, you should cultivate a healthy respect for cutting tools. Never put your hand in front of a chisel blade you are using. In particular, do not hold the work in one hand and the chisel in the other; clamp the work on a bench. Always store sharp tools with the cutting edges shielded.

As with hand tools, you should keep power tools properly adjusted and lubricated. Before adjusting them, however, make sure all the moving parts have come to a complete stop; never reach over a spinning saw blade or a revolving grinding wheel. If the adjustment is a major one, unplug the machine.

Get into the habit of using safety aids. Leave guards, shields and antikickback devices in place unless the work makes it impossible to use them; in that case, exercise extreme caution. Use notched

push sticks and hold-down blocks as extensions of your hands whenever the work brings your hands to within 3 inches of a moving blade or sanding belt.

Power tools can also be dangerous because they involve electricity. To avoid shocks, make sure all the tools are properly grounded and check all electrical connections frequently for exposed or loose wires. Never operate a power tool while standing on a wet surface; keep the power cord away from moving blades, belts, wheels and spinning shafts.

It is especially important with power tools that you dress for the job. Wear a face shield and goggles when you use a table saw, lathe or grinding wheel; add a dust mask when you use a belt or orbital sander. Use earplugs to save your hearing and your nerves. Avoid loose clothing and work gloves that could catch in fast-moving parts: Button or roll up your shirt sleeves, tuck in your shirt, tie back long hair and remove your necktie.

Finally, stop when you are tired. Fatigue probably causes a majority of the accidents in a home workshop.

Common Causes of Accidents

The table saw: kickback. The kickback of a table saw can throw a piece of lumber at you or cause your hand to slip into the spinning blade. It occurs during rip cuts when the cut edges of wood pinch together behind the blade. A blade can also bind if it is dull or dirty, if it is set more than ⅛ inch above the surface of the work, if blade and rip fence are not aligned, or if the wood is warped or cupped. If a blade binds or slows, turn off the power immediately.

To prevent kickback, most table saws are equipped with a splitter and antikickback fingers as part of the blade guard. These should be used for any cut made through the wood (*page 49*). But you can also guard against kickback by steering the wood carefully as you feed it through the saw. Hook two fingers of your right hand over the rip fence to hold the wood against the fence and the table as you push the wood through with your left hand. Check the alignment of the rip fence and blade at frequent intervals by holding a carpenter's square against the fence and the front edge of the saw table; the two should form a perfect right angle. If they do not, use the microset knob at the end of the fence to realign the fence.

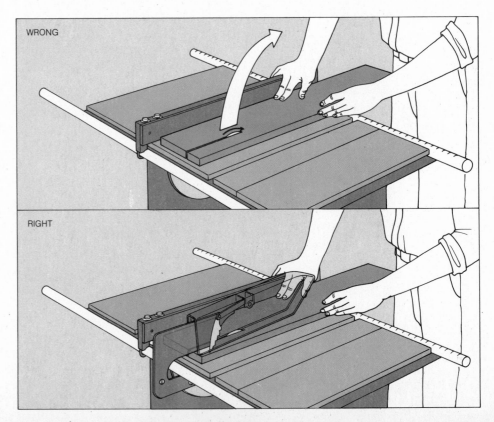

WRONG

RIGHT

The drill press: twirling the work. The spinning bit of a drill press, when lowered into a piece of wood, tends to set the wood atwirl too, twisting it out of your hands. Never operate a drill press without bracing the work against the vertical column at the back of the machine, or anchoring it with clamps at the edges of the table. Be especially careful not to let clothing or hair get caught by the spinning bit.

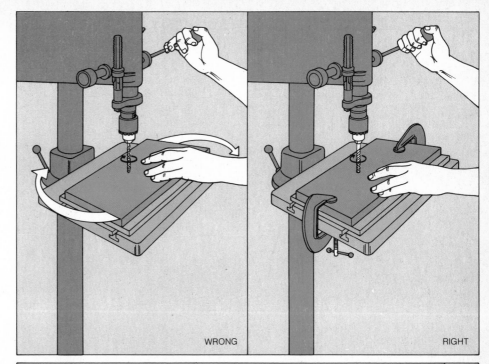

WRONG RIGHT

The lathe: flipping the chisel. When you shape wood on a lathe, the position of the chisel changes constantly as it cuts into the wood, lengthening the distance between the tool rest and the chisel edge. Eventually this distance may become so great that the chisel dips downward, hitting wood below the midpoint of the work. This can cause the chisel to catch in the spinning wood and flip upward, out of your hands. To prevent this, reset the tool rest closer to the work often enough so the rest is never more than ¼ inch away from the work.

A chisel may also be kicked by a lathe during the early, rough stages of work before a smoothly contoured surface is established. You can avoid this by starting the work at low speed and by keeping your chisels and gouges sharp.

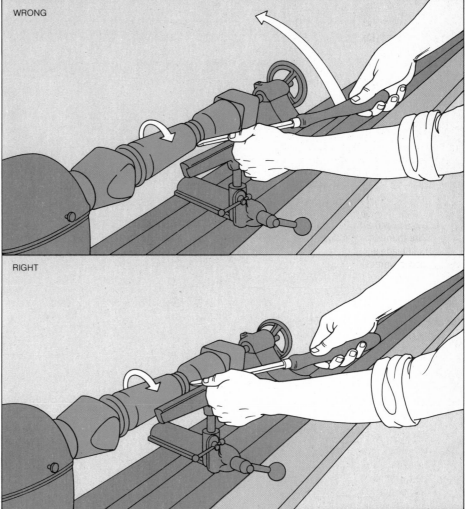

WRONG

RIGHT

The belt sander: catapulting the work. A belt sander has enough speed to rip a board out of your hands and launch it across the room, leaving no protection between your fingers and the spinning sandpaper. To avoid this, always feed the wood *against* the direction of the belt's rotation and protect your pushing hand from the belt by using a push stick.

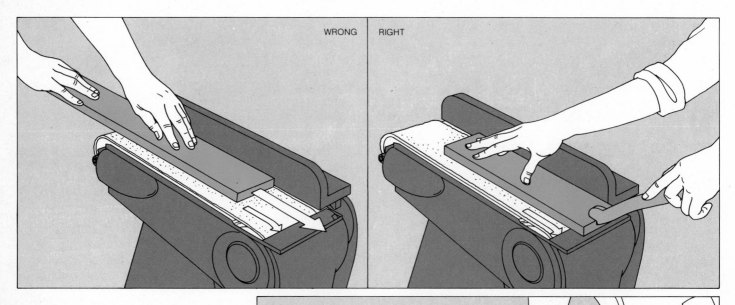

WRONG   RIGHT

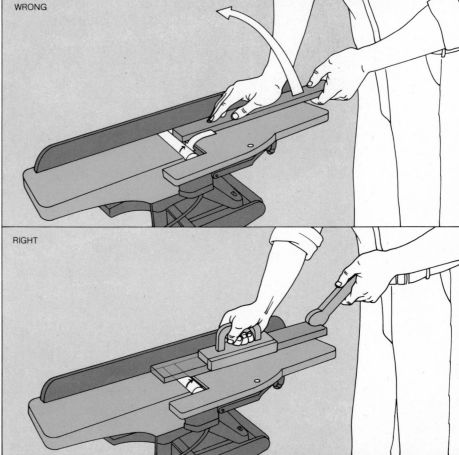

WRONG

RIGHT

The jointer: yanking the wood. In planing, the knives of a jointer-planer can grab the end of a piece of wood and pull it—and possibly your hand—into the machine. Avoid this by planing wood no thinner than ½ inch and no less than 12 inches long; the thickness and length of the wood will enable you to keep it firmly under control. Safety aids such as a hold-down block (*bottom*) will also help to keep the wood flat against the work surface, and a push stick will keep it moving forward at an even rate. Always use the spring guard over the blades (*page 54— omitted here for the sake of clarity*) to protect your hands. To avoid kickback, set the jointer for small bites when planing hardwoods.

Putting the Pieces Together

Almost as crucial as planning a shop for safety is planning it for efficiency. No matter what its shape and size, or how special its purpose, a shop should be arranged to conserve space and motion. Tools should be grouped according to function, with storage for their accessories and spare parts nearby. Electricity should be available where it is needed, for both light and power, and cleanup facilities should be readily accessible.

You can, of course, eventually arrive at a more or less suitable shop simply by pushing and shoving cabinets and tools around. But if you invest a little time and thought in a preliminary layout, and plan your shop on paper, you can not only sort out your priorities, but save yourself from such costly mistakes as buying a power tool too large for your shop.

Begin your layout on standard graph paper with a floor plan of the existing space. Drawing to scale, note the locations of windows, doors, stairs, supporting columns and other permanent architectural features. If the shop is in the basement, include anything that intrudes on the shop space—a furnace, a water heater, a freezer, a washer and dryer. If the shop is in the garage, indicate the space you will need to reserve for the car.

Consider next what partitions or enclosures may be added to the shop. You may, for example, need to create a separate sanding area, isolating its dust from a workbench devoted to electronics. If you are adding a spray booth, indicate where it will be placed (page 110).

Once the basics are on your plan, make cutouts, drawn to scale, of the workbenches, cabinets and power tools you intend to install, and move them around until you find a satisfactory arrangement. In plotting the location of power tools, remember to allow for sufficient work space around the tool (page 48) and for the possible addition of auxiliary work surfaces (page 94). Remember, too, that power tools should be arranged in the sequence in which they will be used. In woodworking, for instance, the natural progression is from cutting and shaping (a saw, jointer and lathe), to assembly (a drill press), to finishing (a sander).

As you move your components around, think about power and light. With proper planning, you may be able to reduce the number of new fixtures required. Try to place a workbench or a lathe near a window, to benefit from natural light, and wherever possible, place power tools near existing outlets. You will need overhead shadow-free light for a table saw, sander or jointer, but a drill press, band saw or jig saw can go into a less well-lit corner since it is possible to equip any of them with a gooseneck lamp.

Finally, be prepared to consider trade-offs on space. You may, for instance, decide to buy a radial-arm saw, which fits against a wall, rather than a table saw, which requires 10 feet of space all around. Or you may decide to build a fold-down workbench (page 89).

You can also save space by mounting bulky tools on roll-away stands that can be pushed into a corner or under a workbench when not in use. Or you can elect to do without stationary power tools altogether, opting for the smaller tabletop versions or portable hand-held power tools instead. Such spacesaving tricks have an added benefit: They allow you to keep the design of your workshop flexible, so that it will adapt to your changing interests and needs.

Plotting a Traffic Pattern

A stepsaving circle. In this capacious, well-equipped shop, tools and work surfaces are arranged in a circle to follow the natural flow of a typical woodworking project. Storage is located near the saw, jointer and lathe, which are commonly used at the start of a job. If more space is needed for pushing long pieces of lumber through the saw or jointer, either tool can be lined up with the shop's double doors. A jig saw and a band saw for shaping are lined up along the wall with a drill press, which is used in assembly.

Nearby stands a worktable for assembly; the table is set out from the wall to leave space for running long boards through the belt sander during finishing operations. The shop's main workbench stands between two windows, to make optimum use of natural light.

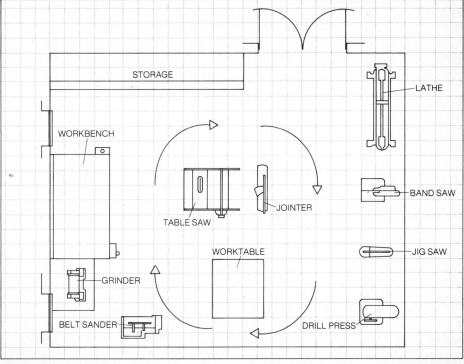

Two Shop Layouts for Smaller Rooms

Two full shops for small spaces. Work flows in a U—from storage to cutting and shaping, through assembly to finishing—in these two woodworking shops designed for a smaller space than that occupied by the circular shop on the preceding page. In one shop (*left*), a radial-arm saw replaces the table saw because it can be put against the wall, freeing the center of the shop for finishing operations. In the other (*right*), a central peninsula contains the workbench, saw and jointer. One advantage of this arrangement is that both sides of the workbench can be used. When necessary, in this particular shop the double doors can be opened to provide more space for using the saw and jointer.

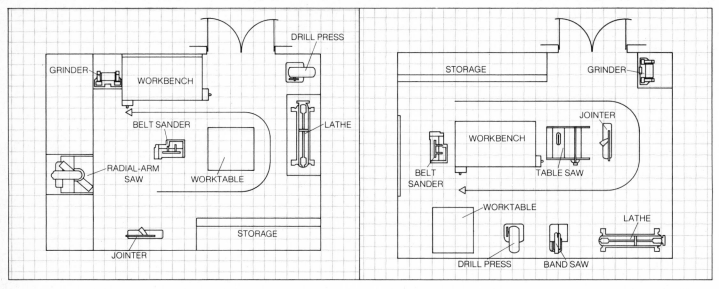

Three Shops Designed for Tight Quarters

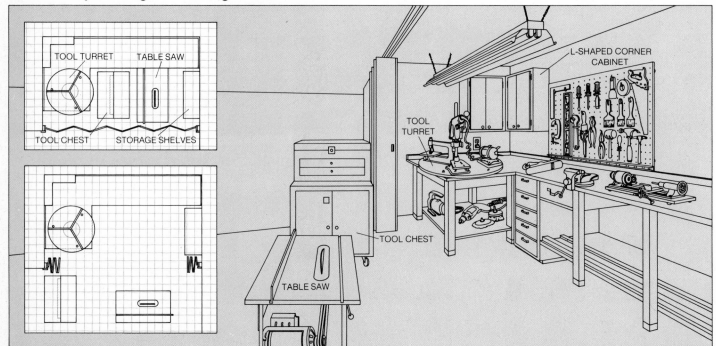

The expandable shop. This shop, fitted into an alcove behind folding doors (*top inset*), solves the problem of a shop that must share space with a recreation room, den or garage. Large components, such as the tool chest and the table saw, have been mounted on locking casters and can be rolled out into the adjacent space when the folding doors are open (*bottom inset*).

With the saw and the chest rolled outside, the L-shaped workbench offers a work surface large enough for a small lathe and a revolving tool turret—actually a heavy-duty Lazy Susan that can be locked in any one of three positions (*page 113*) to allow convenient use of small power tools—a jig saw, a drill stand and a grinder. Shelves below the bench and pegboard on the wall provide tool-storage space.

The one-wall shop. This shop, set at the end of a garage (*inset*), has only one wall for storage and work space. A workbench that covers most of the wall expands to an L-shaped surface when the hinged flap on its left side is raised. Overhead racks suspended from the ceiling provide storage space for lumber. Fluorescent-light fixtures attached to the bottom of the rack and to a storage cabinet provide light for the bench. The car can be moved out of the way in order to open up more work space.

Although this shop does not have enough room for a table saw, a jig saw, or a shaper, a special power table (*right*) converts their hand-held equivalents—circular saw, saber saw and router—into stationary tools that can virtually duplicate their tasks. Available by mail order, the table is made of 16-gauge metal and stands 30 inches high. Its top has interchangeable templates and brackets for clamping tools, upside down, to the table's underside; there is also a rip fence that slides on the tabletop.

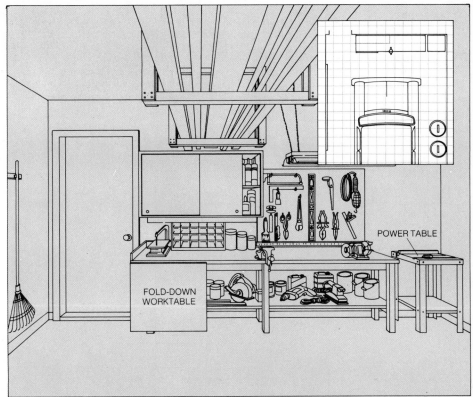

POWER TABLE

FOLD-DOWN
WORKTABLE

The closet shop. A shop in a closet can offer more than just a convenient place to organize and store tools. You can attach a small fold-down work surface to the inside of the closet door, provided the door is solid, not hollow-core. Make the work surface of ¾-inch plywood and support it with heavy-duty folding brackets. You can position it at a height convenient for standing or sitting, whichever you prefer.

To extend the work surface, build a stationary shelf at the same height inside the closet, supporting it, and any other shelves you install, with 2-by-4s nailed to the studs in the closet walls. The work-surface shelf must be recessed 3 inches from the front of the closet to accommodate the folded table when the door is closed. A clamp-on work lamp provides light.

A tool caddy (*page 104*) on the floor holds the most commonly used hand tools for jobs done elsewhere; other tools are stored in a wheeled chest that can be rolled out of the closet as needed. If locking casters are used, the top of this chest can also serve as auxiliary work surface.

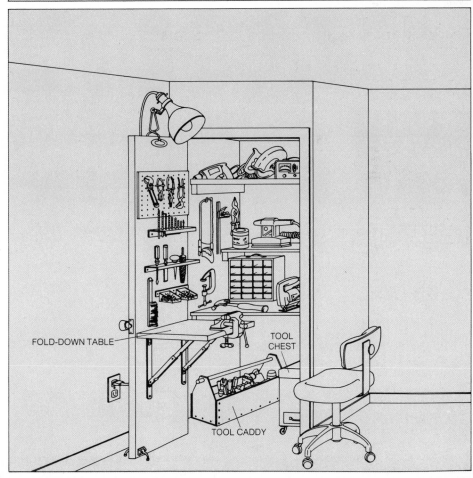

FOLD-DOWN TABLE

TOOL
CHEST

TOOL CADDY

Rigging Electric Power to Serve Manifold Needs

A home workshop requires heavy-duty wiring and special fixtures to satisfy the needs of large power tools, provide enough outlets to keep tool cords out of harm's way and supply sufficient light for both craftsmanship and safety.

Channeling of electrical power to convenient shop locations is accomplished in one of three ways. If there is already an electric circuit in the area, it may be that all you need to do is tap into it for new outlets and perhaps replace an ordinary incandescent-bulb socket with a more efficient fluorescent fixture. Alternatively, if there is no circuit on site, perhaps one or more existing circuits in other locations can be tapped to serve the shop. Or, finally, you can install the desired number of circuits, originating at the main service panel.

To determine whether an existing circuit has enough spare capacity to be tapped for the workshop, shut off the circuit at the main service panel by turning off its breaker or by removing its fuse. Check all around the house to find the electric devices and outlets left without power, and add up the wattage of the greatest number of devices likely to be turned on at any one time. Divide this combined wattage by 120 to obtain the amperage needed, and subtract this am-

perage from the ampere rating that is stamped on the circuit breaker or fuse. If the result is 10 or more amperes, the circuit has enough spare capacity to run almost any portable power tool; if the result is less than 10 and greater than 2, the circuit can be used only for additional lighting.

However, if your shop will contain stationary power tools or an electric space heater, you should install new circuits to handle the additional load. These can be started at the main service panel or, if the main panel is not located close to the workshop, you can install a smaller, auxiliary service panel, called a subpanel, and run a heavy-duty cable to it from the main panel. Unless you are skilled at working inside a main panel, leave this part of the job to an electrician; he will also be able to tell you whether or not your main panel has enough capacity to handle the added circuits.

In selecting a subpanel, check its box for certain characteristics. The box should have two separate bus bars, or terminals—one for ground wires and one for neutral wires. The neutral bus bar must be completely insulated electrically from the metal of the box; that is, it should lack the bonding screw that touches both the bus bar and the box in a main panel.

Conversely, the ground-wire bus bar should be electrically connected to the subpanel box. In addition, the subpanel should have space for at least four circuit breakers and fittings for a lock.

No matter how you channel power to the workshop, you can reduce the chance of shock by installing ground-fault interrupters (GFIs). These devices, which are capable of detecting minute amounts of current leaking out of the circuit, cut off the circuit in 1/40 of a second, before such a leak can cause harm. A GFI can be purchased either as a circuit breaker that will protect an entire circuit or as a receptacle that will protect only itself and the portion of the circuit wired through it.

Whether or not you install GFIs, it is essential that you match the circuit's wire size to the capacity of its circuit breaker or fuse. For 15-ampere lighting circuits—or, in Canada, all 120-volt circuits—use No. 14 copper wire; for 20-ampere portable power-tool circuits, use No. 12 wire; use No. 12 wire also for 20-ampere heavy-duty 240-volt circuits.

Before you start wiring, plan the job on paper and use the plan as a shopping list for parts. You may also be required to show the plan to your electrical inspector in order to get a permit for the work.

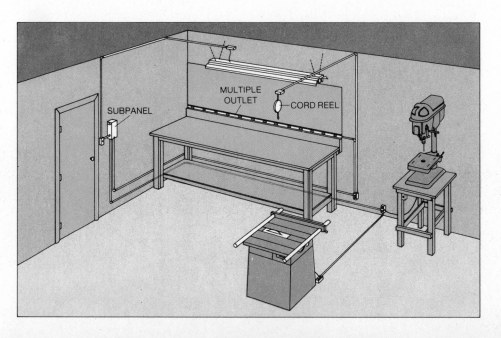

An all-purpose wiring layout. The shop wiring illustrated provides several conveniences. A subpanel near the door feeds one circuit through a switch to a fluorescent light above the workbench. Another circuit from the subpanel provides power to a string of outlets along the back of the bench for portable power tools, to an overhead outlet on a cord reel, and to a standard wall outlet. A third circuit powers outlets located near stationary shop tools, including a floor outlet for the table saw.

All circuit cables are encased by steel conduit. While the circuit breaker for the fluorescent light normally would be left on at all times, those for the bench outlets and the stationary power tools can be shut off and the subpanel locked to keep children from using tools without supervision.

Pathways for Electric Wires

Crossing the house. To extend an electric cable to the workshop from a power source in another part of the house, use the framing members of an unfinished basement, crawl space or attic as pathways. Secure the cable to the framing members with cable staples every 4 feet and within a foot of each end. To run cable across joists, staple it to 1-by-2s that you have fastened to the joists; in a basement, you may be able to use a girder or the edge of a sill plate as a route for the cable (*below*).

Within a wall. Run cable inside a wall by drilling through the framing member called the top plate (if you are working in the attic) and into the space between studs. Then drill through the corresponding framing member, called the sole plate, from the basement below. Insert an electrician's fish tape (a reel of flexible steel with a hook at one end) through the top hole until it catches the end of a second fish tape, which has been inserted from below by a helper. Draw the tapes through one hole until a hooked end protrudes, and attach the cable to that hook with electrical tape (*inset*). Then draw the fish tape and cable through the wall.

Some walls have horizontal braces, called firestops, nailed between studs about 4 feet above the floor. If a fish tape strikes such an obstruction, cut a small opening in the wall at the level of the firestop and chisel a groove for the cable into one edge of the firestop. Fish the cable past the firestop and staple it into the groove, then nail a protective metal plate over the groove. Patch the hole with spackle or wallboard.

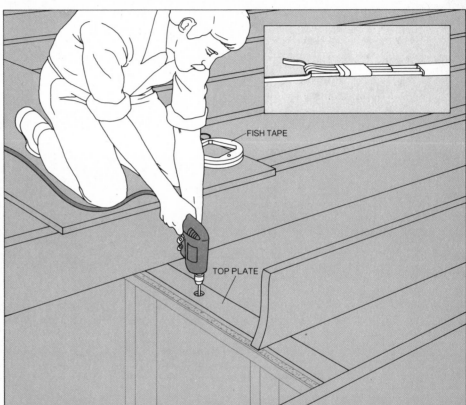

FISH TAPE

TOP PLATE

Through concrete block. Run wire horizontally through a concrete-block wall by drilling with a masonry bit and enlarging the hole as necessary with a star drill and a hand sledge. Caution: Wear goggles while making holes in masonry. Make the hole 3 inches in from the side of the block to reach a hollow space inside.

To run cable along the outside of a concrete-block wall, secure the cable to the block with cable straps held by screws and plastic screw anchors. If exposed cable runs where it may be subject to damage, protect it by threading it through metal cable conduit.

Installing a Subpanel

1 **Clamping in the new cable.** Run No. 8, three-conductor-with-ground cable from the main panel to the subpanel location, leaving 5 feet of extra cable at the main-panel end and 2 extra feet at the subpanel end. If the cable will run into the subpanel from its back through a hole in the wall, first thread a cable clamp over the cable and slide the clamp to the wall, leaving a 2-foot end. Then tighten the clamp to the cable and strip the cable sheathing back to the clamp. If the cable will enter the subpanel from the side, first mount the subpanel (*Step 2*) and bring the cable into it, then clamp the cable and strip its sheathing, as described above.

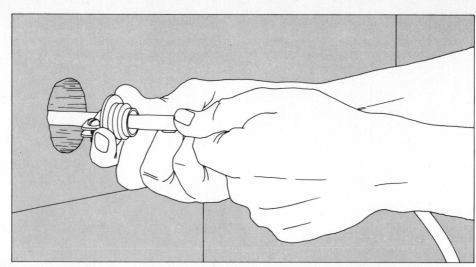

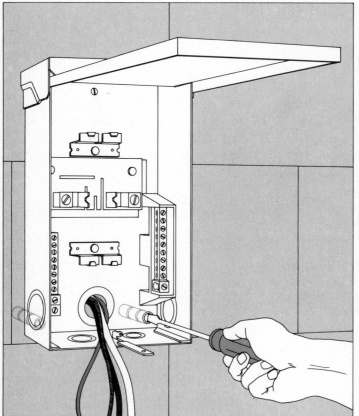

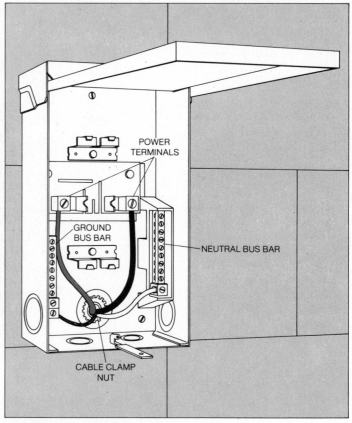

2 **Mounting the subpanel.** Hold the subpanel against the wall. If the cable is to enter from the rear, thread it temporarily through the hole in the wall so the subpanel can fit flush against the wall. Have a helper mark the position of the subpanel mounting holes. Then remove the subpanel from the wall and drill holes at the marks. Insert lead or plastic screw anchors into the holes and mount the subpanel, driving screws into the screw anchors.

If the wall is likely to be damp, as basement walls sometimes are, mount the subpanel on a piece of ¾-inch plywood anchored to the wall.

3 **Connecting the power wires.** Tighten the retaining nut of the cable clamp against the subpanel, and separate the four cable wires. Connect the bare ground wire to a large terminal on the ground bus bar; then connect the white neutral wire to the large terminal on the insulated neutral bus bar, the black power-carrying wire to one power terminal and the red power-carrying wire to the other power terminal.

4 **Installing a circuit breaker.** Snap a circuit breaker designed for your subpanel onto a holder provided for it. In this model, a standard 120-volt breaker, suitable for a lighting circuit, first slips onto a bracket and then is pressed onto a blade connected to one 120-volt power terminal. A 240-volt breaker engages two brackets and two blades, side by side; with each blade connected to a separate 120-volt terminal, the combined capacity of the breaker is 240 volts.

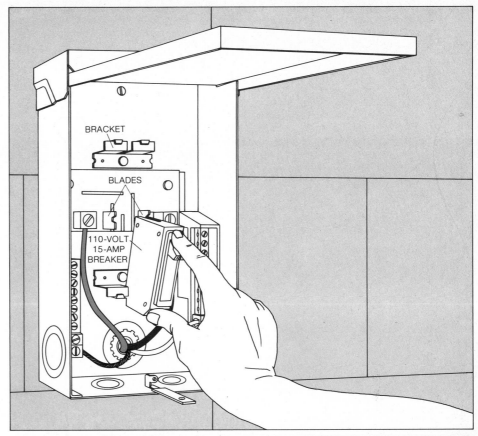

BRACKET

BLADES

110-VOLT
15-AMP
BREAKER

5 **Wiring a GFI breaker.** Snap a 120- or 240-volt GFI breaker (ground-fault interrupter—see page 64) in place as in Step 4. Uncoil its white neutral wire and lead it to the insulated neutral bus bar of the subpanel. Cut the wire to fit and strip off ½ inch of insulation. Fasten the wire to any free terminal on the neutral bus bar.

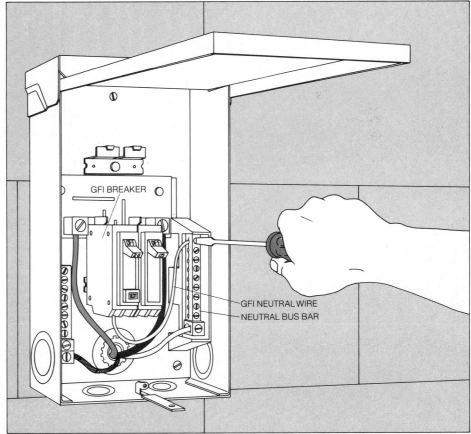

GFI BREAKER

GFI NEUTRAL WIRE
NEUTRAL BUS BAR

Extending Existing Circuits

1 **Locating a cable for tapping.** Select a junction box that you suspect is wired to a circuit with extra capacity. Turn on all switches in this circuit, then turn off all the power at the main panel, either by snapping off all the circuit breakers or by removing all the fuses. To be sure the power is off, open the junction box and test all combinations of wires and the metal parts of the box with a neon-bulb voltage tester. If the bulb stays dark, switch on the breaker you think controls the wires in the box, and repeat the tests. If the tester bulb lights, you know you have found a cable on that circuit.

To be sure the cable is not a part of the circuit controlled by a switch, have a helper operate switches on the circuit while you test to see if the flow of current in the cable is interrupted. If it is not, you have found a wire suitable for tapping. Turn off the power again.

In some cases, several circuits share a single junction box. If they do, take careful note of the wiring pattern in the box; disconnected wires must always be reconnected in their original pattern. Do not tap into aluminum wiring.

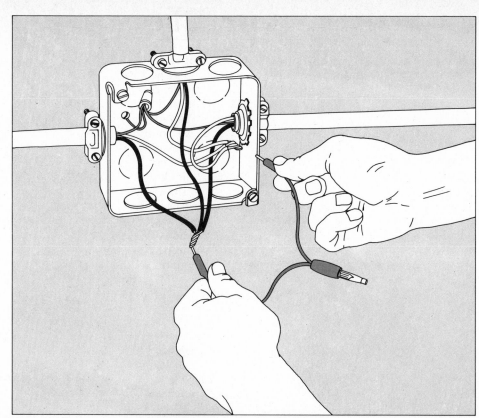

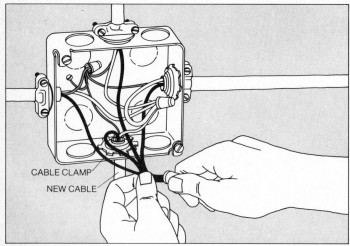

CABLE CLAMP
NEW CABLE

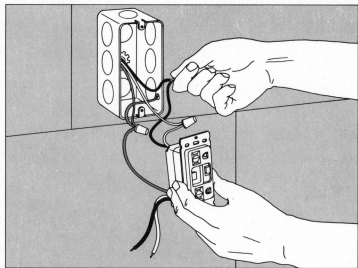

2 **Adding a new cable.** Strip 6 inches of sheathing from the end of a new run of two-conductor-with-ground cable, then strip ¾ inch of insulation from the end of each wire in the cable. Fasten the cable into the junction box with a cable clamp and nut. Using wire caps, connect the cable's bare copper wire to the other bare copper ground wires in the box, and to the green ground jumper wire. Then connect the cable's white neutral wire to the white wires, and finally, the black wire to the black wires.

If the junction box contains more than one circuit, make certain you know which cables belong to each circuit. Do not connect new black and white wires to cables on two different circuits.

3 **Wiring a GFI receptacle.** To install a surface-style GFI outlet at the workshop end of the new cable, fasten a 3½-inch-deep surface box to the wall; if the cable enters the box from the back, first strip and fasten the new cable to the box as for a subpanel. Connect the cable bare copper wire to the GFI receptacle green wire and a green jumper wire from the box; the cable white wire to the receptacle white wire marked LINE; the cable black wire to the receptacle black wire marked LINE. The remaining black and white receptacle wires, marked LOAD, can run to additional outlets, as needed; cover unused LOAD wires with small wire caps.

The Options in Shop Circuits

Once you have brought electrical power to the shop, it must be distributed. Wires must lead to outlets, and the wires must be protected from hard knocks. Tools powered by separate motors may need power cords and switches.

Various types of outlets are available to fit almost any workshop situation. A common duplex receptacle in a surface-mounted box can drive a tool placed along a wall. A floor outlet fed by flat conduit can power a freestanding tool in the middle of the room. Multi-outlet strips are convenient above a workbench, where several small power tools may be used on one job. Finally, an extension-cord reel hung from the ceiling lets tools go freely about the room.

To protect the wires that feed these outlets, there are various options. Armored cable, with its spiraling metal cover, offers security and installation ease at some expense of appearance. Thin-walled metal conduit, called EMT, costs more but gives good protection and good looks. Conduit is also made from plastic tubes, joined with cemented plastic fittings. The neatest but costliest option is painted rectangular metal raceway.

If you are installing new circuits from a subpanel or main panel, you have a choice of voltages: 120 or 240. A 240-volt circuit is essential for some tools, such as an arc welder or certain models of radial-arm saws, and for many air-conditioning units; a 240-volt circuit can also be used to provide power to a string of 120-volt outlets, providing twice as much power as a 120-volt circuit in the same size wire.

Note: In Canada, do not ground outlet boxes as shown in the drawings. Instead, fasten the bare ground wire of each cable or the green wire of a flexible cord directly to the box with a screw. For a receptacle, extend one of the bare wires to the green grounding screw.

Different voltages from the same cable. In this schematic drawing of a 240-volt cable, the electrical patterns of the alternating current passing through three wires explain how the cable can carry 240 volts and in addition simultaneously carry two different 120-volt circuits. The voltage in the black wire alternates from positive 120 volts to negative 120 volts and back again in relation to the white wire. Meanwhile, the voltage in the red wire alternates from negative 120 volts to positive 120 volts and back. Thus, when the voltage in the red wire is positive 120 volts, the voltage in the black wire is negative 120 volts, a difference of 240 volts. An electrical device that is connected to the black wire and the white wire will therefore receive only 120 volts, as would a device connected to the red wire and the white wire. However, a device that is connected to the black wire and the red wire will receive 240 volts.

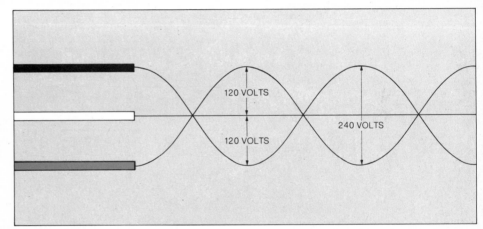

Using Conduit to Carry a 120-Volt Circuit

1 Laying out the conduit path. Select a position for the first outlet or junction box along a run of conduit. Choose a knockout opening in the subpanel at an appropriate location for the circuit you are running, and use a straightedge to mark vertical and horizontal paths for the conduit from the subpanel to the box and beyond. Remove the knockout with a hammer and punch. Insert a conduit connector in the hole and secure the connector with its retaining nut (inset).

2 Cutting sections of conduit. For each straight run along the pathway, starting at the subpanel, slip a fitting of the required shape onto the far end of a length of conduit, hold or prop the conduit against the pathway and mark where it joins the previous fitting. (At the subpanel, this fitting will be the conduit connector installed in Step 1.) At the point marked, cut the conduit with a hacksaw and ream the inside rim with a round file to remove burrs, which can cut into cable. Mark and cut other sections until you have all the conduit you need for the entire run.

3 Running cable through the conduit. Starting in the middle of the run and working toward both ends, push two-conductor-with-ground cable through the disassembled sections of conduit and their fittings until the cable emerges from the two ends of the run; then pull it taut. Reassemble the conduit pieces and tighten the setscrews of the fittings. Fasten the conduit to the wall with straps, held with screws in screw anchors, every 4 feet and within a foot of each end.

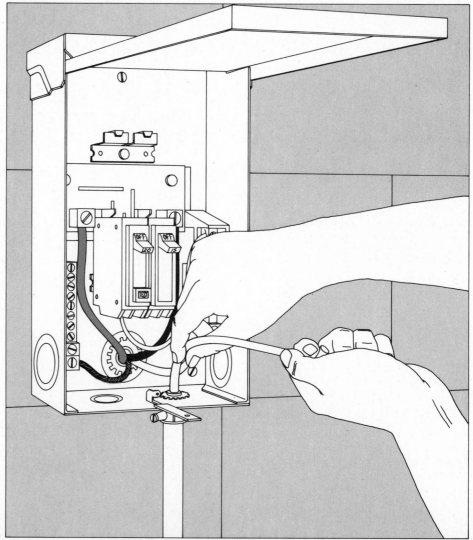

4 **Wiring the circuit to the subpanel.** To wire the circuit cable to a 120-volt GFI breaker, connect the bare wire of the cable to the grounding bus bar, then connect the white neutral wire to the terminal on the breaker marked with a white dot and labeled LOAD NEUTRAL, the black wire to the terminal labeled LOAD. Prepare the wires for connecting by stripping them to a depth indicated by a guide on the side of the breaker. Then insert the wire into the appropriate terminal opening and tighten the terminal setscrew.

To wire a standard 120-volt breaker (not a GFI), attach the ground wire of the cable to the grounding bus, the neutral wire of the cable to the neutral bus and the black wire to the terminal of the circuit breaker.

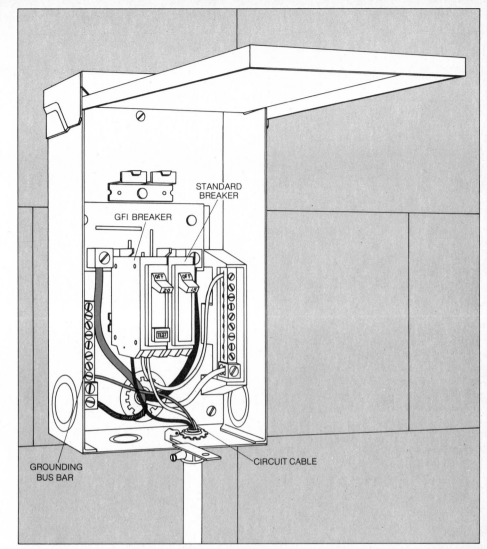

STANDARD BREAKER

GFI BREAKER

GROUNDING BUS BAR

CIRCUIT CABLE

5 **Wiring the circuit to an outlet.** At the outlet-box end of a run of conduit, strip 6 inches of sheathing from the end of the cable and, using wire caps, connect the bare wire of the cable to a pair of green jumper wires. Attach one jumper wire to a screw terminal on the wall of the box and the other to the green grounding terminal of the receptacle. Connect the white wire of the cable to a silver terminal of the receptacle and the black wire to a brass terminal.

To extend the wiring from one outlet to another, connect the appropriate wires of the next length of cable to the green jumper wires and to the remaining silver and brass terminals of the receptacle. If the cable feeding the second outlet comes from a junction box, wait until all the cables from the junction box are in place before making any wire connections, then join the wires as described on page 68.

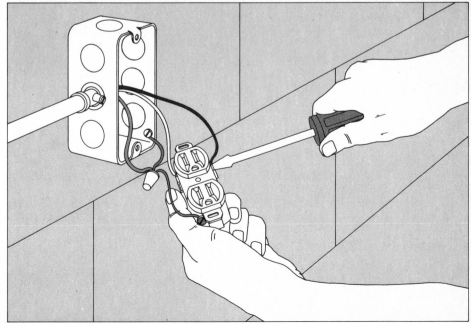

Special Outlets to Bring Power Closer to the Job

A multi-outlet strip. Screw the base of a multi-outlet strip onto the wall along the small junction box made for that strip. Place the junction box at the end where the power will enter, and run conduit and cable to it. Using a wire cap, connect the bare cable wire to the green wire of the outlet strip; then, at the other end of the outlet strip, connect the green wire to a grounding clip that clamps into the outlet-strip base.

Using wire caps or flat pressure connectors made for your outlet strip, join the white cable wire to the white outlet wire and join the black cable wire to the black outlet wire. At the opposite end of the outlet strip, fold over the free ends of the black and the white wires twice, and wrap each end separately with electrical tape. Finally, snap the outlet strip onto the base.

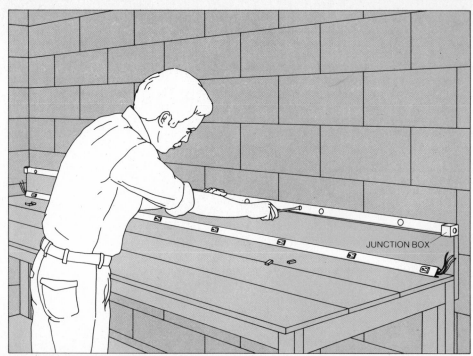

JUNCTION BOX

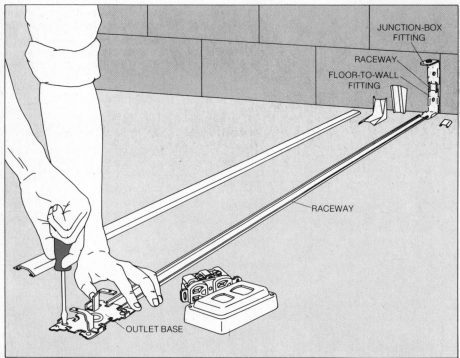

JUNCTION-BOX FITTING

RACEWAY

FLOOR-TO-WALL FITTING

RACEWAY

OUTLET BASE

A floor outlet. Place the base plate of a floor outlet in the desired location on a floor not subject to flooding, and lay out the connecting fittings leading back to and up the wall: a strip of floor raceway, a floor-to-wall fitting, another section of raceway, and a junction-box fitting. Cut the raceway with a hacksaw or, if it is prescored, simply snap it off. Fasten down all the base parts with screws and screw anchors. Lay cable inside the base parts and connect the receptacle, as on page 71. Fasten the receptacle to its base plate.

Using a hacksaw, cut cover sections for the raceway, making each section ¾ inch shorter than the length of raceway it will protect. Tap the covers with a hammer and a block of wood to snap them over the raceway and cable. Finally, connect cable in conduit at the junction box and install the cover pieces of the floor-to-wall and junction-box fittings, and the cover for the outlet, twisting out the scored part of the outlet cover to go over the raceway. More raceway can be run from the outlet base for additional outlets, if desired.

An overhead outlet. Turn a screw hook into a joist at a convenient point and hang a cord reel from it; such reels neatly store heavy-duty extension cords 50 feet long or longer. Install an outlet box on the joist within reach of the cord-reel plug and run conduit and cable from the box to a source of power. Put the cover on the outlet box and plug in the cord reel.

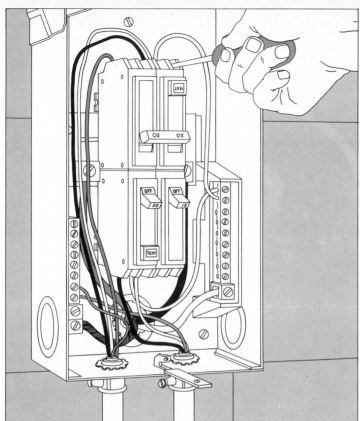

Wiring a 240-Volt Circuit

Connecting a 240-volt circuit breaker. If you are wiring to a 240-volt GFI circuit breaker, connect the bare wire of a three-conductor-with-ground cable to the grounding bus bar, the white cable wire to the terminal on the breaker marked with a white dot and labeled LOAD NEUTRAL, the black and red cable wires, one each, to the breaker terminals marked LOAD. If, instead, you are using a standard 240-volt breaker—not a GFI type—connect the bare wire to the grounding bus, the white wire to the neutral bus and the black and red wires, one each, to the breaker terminals.

If the circuit is going to be providing power to 240-volt devices exclusively, you do not need a neutral wire. Use two-conductor-with-ground cable and, instead of connecting the white cable wire to the neutral bus bar, paint the ends of the wire red, to indicate that it is not neutral, and connect it to one of the power terminals of the circuit breaker in lieu of a red wire.

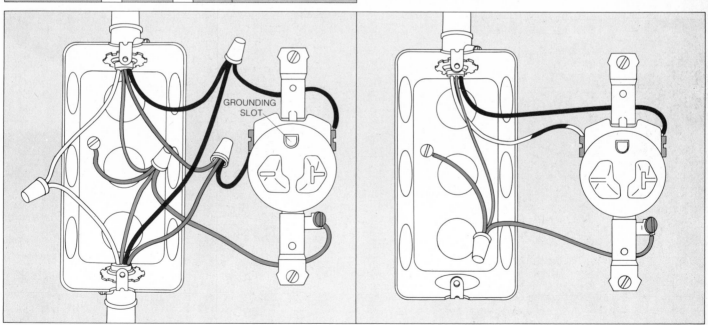

Attaching a 240-volt outlet. For an outlet box located in the middle of a 240-volt circuit—with cables both entering and leaving the box *(above, left)*—first attach short lengths of green jumper wire to the grounding screws of the receptacle and the outlet box. Next attach short black jumper wires to each of the remaining terminals on the receptacle. With a wire cap, join the bare wires of the two cables with the two green jumper wires. Then join together the white wires (if any) of the two cables, and join the two cable black wires to one of the black jumper wires on the receptacle. Finally, connect the red cable wires or white wires recoded red to the other black jumper wire, screw the receptacle in place and add a cover. Because neither terminal of the receptacle is neutral, you may install the receptacle with the grounding slot up or down, whichever is easier. For a 240-volt outlet box at the end of a run, fed by a cable with only two conducting wires *(above, right)*, connect the bare ground wire to green jumper wires on the receptacle and the outlet box, as above. Then fasten the black and white conducting wires to the two remaining terminals of the receptacle. Recode the two ends of the white wire red to indicate that it is not neutral.

Wiring a 120-volt outlet. For a 120-volt outlet in the middle of a 240-volt circuit, break off the metal connection strap between the two brass-colored screws on one side of a duplex receptacle and attach a short black jumper wire to each screw. Connect the bare ground wire of each cable to two green jumper wires, one jumper attached to a screw in the outlet box, the other to the green screw on the receptacle. Hold the receptacle in the upright position as shown and connect the two black cable wires to the black jumper wire attached to the upper brass screw, the two red cable wires to the other black jumper. Connect the two white cable wires to the two silver screws, leaving the metal connection strap between the screws intact.

If the outlet is at the end of a run, connect the bare ground wire of the cable to green jumpers on the outlet box and receptacle as above, and connect the white cable wire to one of the silver screws on the opposite side of the receptacle. Remove the metal connection strap from the side with the brass screws and connect the black cable wire to the upper brass screw, the red wire to the lower brass screw. In use, divide the loads plugged into this circuit between the upper and lower receptacle slots.

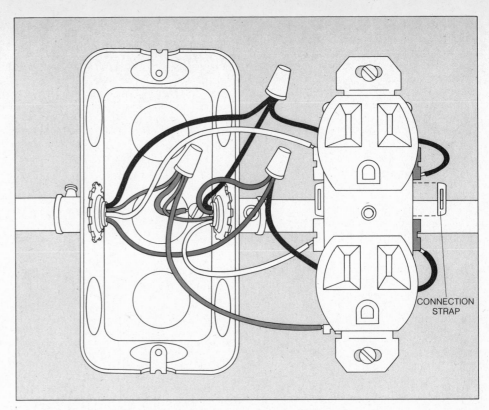

CONNECTION STRAP

Installing a Switch for a Stationary Power Tool

1 **Wiring the switch to a cord.** Mount a switch box in a convenient location on the tool stand, then wire it with a length of Type SJ No. 16 three-wire flexible cord. Strip 6 inches of sheathing from the end of the cord and thread it through a knock-out in the box; fasten with a cable clamp. Attach the green wire of the cord to a screw in the box. Attach the black wire of the cord to one of the terminals on the side of the switch.

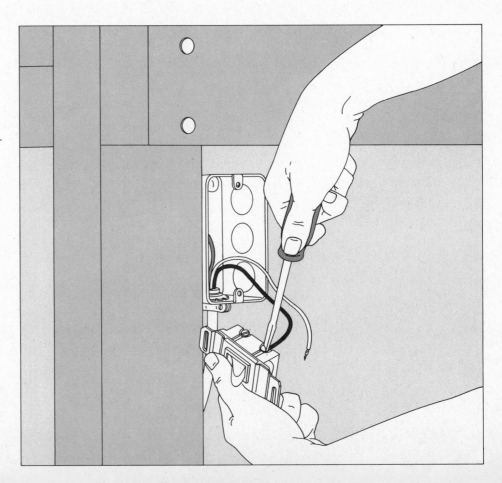

2 Connecting the motor. Cut a generous length of armored cable to fit between the switch box and the junction box of the motor. Remove the armor from the cable for 6 inches at each end by cutting the armor with a hacksaw, perpendicular to the direction of the spiral, taking care not to cut the insulated wires inside. Insert a protective bushing into each end of the cable armor; wrap the thin bond wire back around the cable armor to secure the bushing and to ensure good grounding contact when the ends of the cable are clamped in place. Fasten the cable to the switch box and the motor, using cable clamps designed for armored cable.

Connect the wires at the motor as indicated on the manufacturer's specification plate or on a diagram in the junction box. At the switch box, connect the white cable wire to the white wire of the flexible cord, and the black cable wire to the remaining screw terminal of the switch.

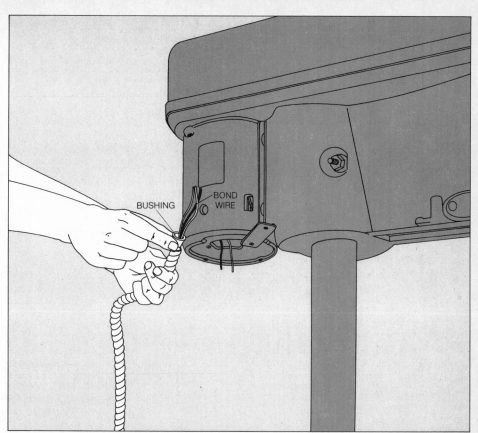

BUSHING   BOND WIRE

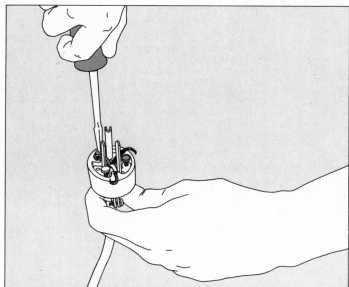

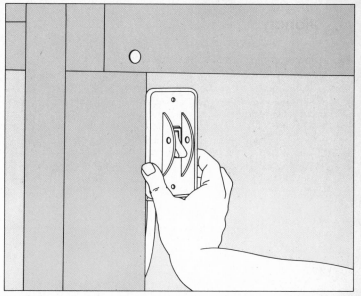

3 Attaching a grounding plug. Slip the insulating cover off the prongs of a three-prong plug and loosen its cord clamp. Slip the end of the flexible cord into the plug, remove 1½ inches of sheathing and strip ¾ inch of insulation from each wire. Make a clockwise loop at the end of each wire and attach it to the appropriate screw— green wire to green screw, white wire to silver screw, black wire to brass screw. Replace the insulating cover and tighten the clamp of the plug to hold the cord securely in place.

4 A switch lock. To prevent accidental starts, cover the front of the tool's switch box with a safety plate fitted with two semicircular flanges, one on each side of the switch. The holes in the flanges allow you to install a padlock that will prevent the switch from being used.

General and Focused Lighting

A workshop needs two kinds of light: general overhead lighting and light you can aim directly on the work at hand. The first need is met by fixtures that are wired in permanently, while the second is best served by a plug-in fixture that can be moved from place to place.

Fluorescent fixtures make the best overhead lights because, compared with incandescent bulbs, they produce large amounts of light with relatively little electricity. A standard workshop light fixture consists of two 40-watt tubes 4 feet long mounted in a metal box incorporating a reflector, a ballast transformer, the wiring and four lamp holders. The lighting unit can be mounted directly to low ceilings, or hung on chains from higher ceilings. By repositioning the fixture on different links of the chains, you can lift it out of the way of large objects or move it closer to small ones.

Overhead fixtures can be controlled by switches mounted directly on the units, by wall switches, or by both. For instance, you may want a workbench light to go on whenever a wall switch is flipped, but prefer to have the same wall switch operate the light above a table saw only when a pull chain, mounted on the lighting unit, is pulled on.

Wall switches for overhead lights are wired in one of two ways. In middle-of-the-run wiring, the switch is put between the power source and the light fixture and the power goes from source to fixture in a direct line. But a fixture that lies between source and switch is wired with a switch loop, the power going from source to switch and then doubling back to the fixture between them.

Lamps that put light right where you need it come in any number of designs. Most are incandescent, but some are fluorescent and a few are both. Some models have special features, such as a built-in magnifying glass, and one commonly found feature is a jointed arm that allows the light to be swiveled and extended. The extension-arm light (*inset, page 79*) clamps onto almost any bench and has a mounting shaft that can be fitted into a hole drilled in the workbench or a tool stand, so the fixture can be moved quickly from one work site to another.

Other popular styles of on-the-spot

lighting include gooseneck fixtures, optionally mounted on a spring clip that can be clamped directly to the work; and a "trouble light" that is attached to the end of a cord reel. Some tools are also available with built-in lights.

A Fluorescent Fixture with Switch

1 Connecting the fluorescent fixture. Strip 6 inches of sheathing from the end of a No. 16 three-wire flexible cord and clamp the end of the cord into a knockout hole in the top of the fluorescent fixture. Drill a hole in the fixture housing and screw the cord's green wire to it.

With wire caps, join the white cord wire to the white fixture wire. Connect the black cord wire to the black fixture wire, unless you are adding a separate switch on the fixture itself (*Step 2*). Assemble the rest of the fixture following the manufacturer's instructions.

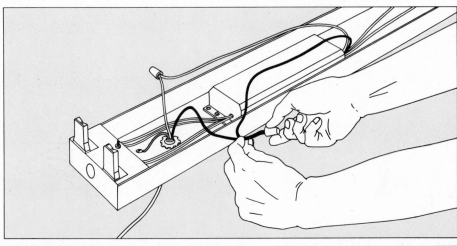

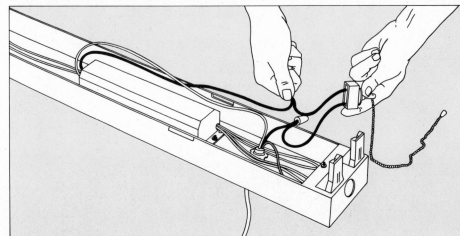

2 A switch in a light. To control the fixture with an additional pull-chain switch mounted on the fixture, fasten the black wire from the three-wire flexible cord to one of the wires of the switch. Fasten the other switch wire to the black wire of the fixture. Insert the switch into a knockout hole in the fixture's end plate and secure the switch with its retaining nut.

3 Hanging the fixture. Prepare four equal lengths of lightweight chain and use an S hook to attach one end of each chain to the openings provided in the top of the fixture. Twist eye screws in place above the work area, slip an S hook into the free end of each chain and hang the fixture by slipping the upper S hooks onto the eye screws. To change the height of the fixture, adjust the chain links on the upper S hooks.

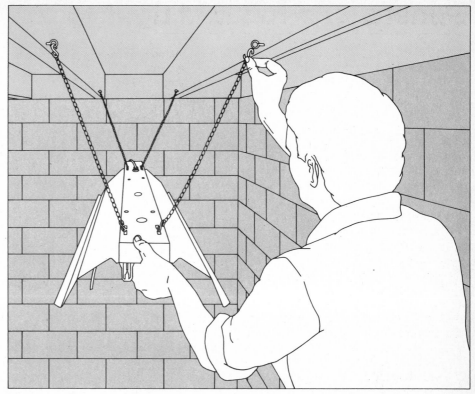

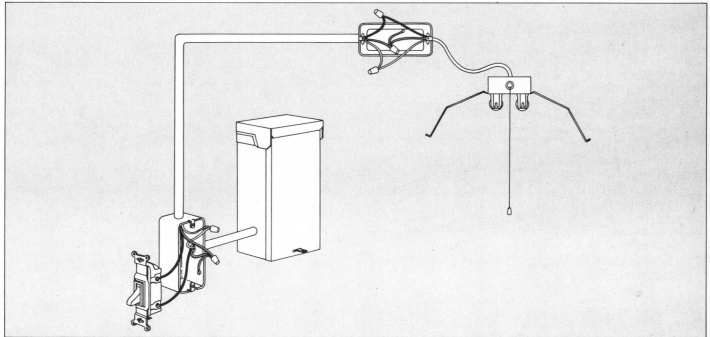

4 Running power to the fixture. Install an outlet box for the light switch in a convenient location near an entranceway and run conduit and two-conductor-with-ground cable from a power source, as described on pages 69-71. Then run conduit and cable up to a second outlet box near the light fixture. To wire the switch box, connect the bare wires of the two cables to a green jumper wire fastened to the switch box. Connect the white wires of the two cables to each other, and the two black cable wires to separate terminals on the switch. Mount the switch in the box so that the word OFF appears when the toggle is down, and add a cover. To wire the outlet box near the fixture, remove 6 inches of sheathing from the free end of the three-wire flexible cord and fasten the cord to the fixture outlet box with a cable clamp. Fasten a green jumper wire to the box and join the wire to the bare cable wire and green wire of the flexible cord. Connect the white cable wire to the white cord wire and the black cable wire to the black cord wire.

To add another fixture to the same switch circuit, run cable and conduit from the first fixture box to a second box, mounted near the added fixture. Connect the new fixture to its box, as you did above. Then connect the new cable at the first fixture box as you would if you were tapping into a junction box (*page 68*).

A Switch Loop for Any Light

1 **Connecting the fixture box.** Run conduit and two-conductor-with-ground cable from the power source to an outlet box at the light-fixture location, and then on to a second box for a light switch in a convenient location. Wire the fixture with No. 16 three-wire flexible cord, as in Step 1, page 76, and clamp the fixture cord into the fixture box. Connect the bare wires of the two cables to the green wire of the cord and to a green jumper wire fastened to the fixture box. Connect the white wire of the power-source cable to the cord's white wire. Connect the two black cable wires to each other, then connect the white wire of the switch-box cable to the black wire of the cord, and paint the end of the white wire black, to indicate it is not neutral.

2 **Wiring the light switch.** At the switch box, connect the bare cable wire to a screw in the box. Then connect the white cable wire and the black cable wire to separate terminals on the switch. Paint the end of the white wire black, to indicate that it is not neutral. Mount the light switch in the switch box and add a cover.

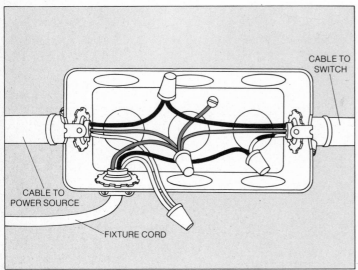

CABLE TO SWITCH

CABLE TO POWER SOURCE

FIXTURE CORD

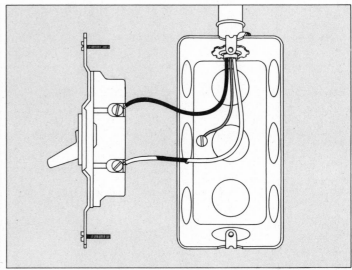

A Switch Loop that Runs through Two Fixtures

1 **Wiring the first fixture box.** When two fixtures fall between the power source and the switch, join each with flexible cord to a nearby outlet box (*pages 76-77*), and install conduit and cable as for a simple one-fixture switch loop (*above*), but use three-conductor-with-ground cable between the two fixture boxes. At the first fixture box, connect the bare wires of the two cables to a green jumper wire mounted on the box and to the green wire of the fixture cord. Connect the white wire of the cable from the second fixture box to the white wire of the fixture cord, and connect the black wires of the two cables to each other. Then connect the white wire of the switch-box cable to the black wire of the fixture cord and to the red wire of the cable from the second fixture box. Paint the end of the white wire of the switch box black. Wire the switch as you did the light switch in Step 2, above.

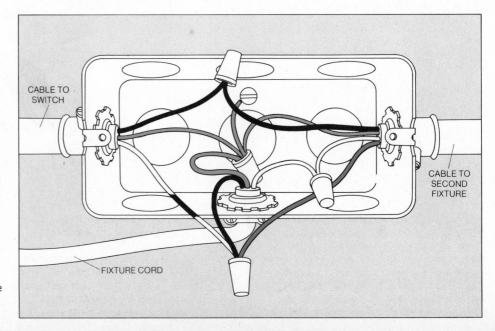

CABLE TO SWITCH

CABLE TO SECOND FIXTURE

FIXTURE CORD

2 **Wiring the second fixture box.** Connect the bare wires of the two cables to a green jumper wire mounted on the box and to the green wire of the fixture cord. Connect the white wires of the two cables to each other, and to the white wire of the fixture cord. Connect the black wires of the two cables to each other, then connect the red wire of the cable from the first fixture box to the black wire of the fixture cord.

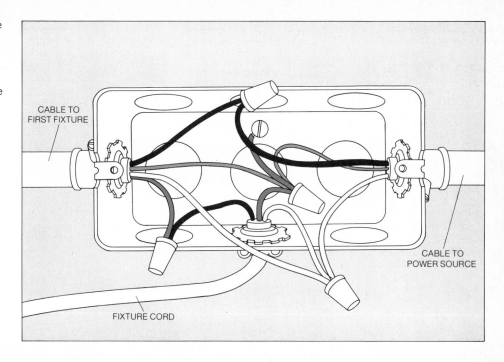

CABLE TO
FIRST FIXTURE

CABLE TO
POWER SOURCE

FIXTURE CORD

Spotlighting Work with a Movable Lamp

Mounting the fixture holder. Screw a 2-by-2 strip of wood onto the wall behind the workbench, preferably above a strip receptacle. To position the fixture at the correct light level, clamp it to the strip and hold the strip against the wall, marking along its underside with a pencil. Measure up ¾ inch and draw a second line, then drill holes at 1-foot intervals along the second line,

and install screw anchors. Caution: If you are drilling in a masonry wall, wear eye protectors.

Hold the 2-by-2 just below the screw anchors and mark their positions on the strip. Drill a hole through the center of the strip at each mark. Drive screws through the holes into the anchors. Clamp the lamp anywhere along the strip (*inset*).

3 Jigs, Benches and Accessories

Getting a grasp on the situation. Braced against a metal peg in the arm of an L-shaped corner vise, a length of pine board is held securely for planing. The vise and its peg, commonly called a bench dog, are integral parts of this finely crafted woodworking bench. Here they function in tandem as a jig: a device for maintaining the correct relationship between a tool and a piece of work. Both jigs and workbenches are in many cases homemade to fit the requirements of a particular kind of hobby or craft.

Probably the ultimate attainment in the world of do-it-yourself is a workshop whose working components are themselves homemade. Although it is perfectly possible to outfit a shop with ready-made benches, tool stands, jigs and extension tables, there are many good reasons for constructing your own. One is suitability: A workbench tailored to your own specifications will, for example, exactly fit the space you have, the kind of work you do and the tools you use. It will also fit your own height, a comfort especially welcome to people who are unusually short or tall.

Workshop components you build yourself can also be made to work together, greatly expanding their range of usefulness. When a tool stand plus a table saw matches the height of a workbench, for example, the top of the saw becomes a support for long boards resting on the bench and the bench returns the favor by supporting long boards moving through the saw. Jigs perform a similar function: Besides enlarging the scope of your tools, speeding up the work and assuring repeatable accuracy, they often act as a crucial third hand. In a home workshop, this kind of interaction between components is especially welcome, for there are often no handy helpers around, as there are in a professional shop, to hold up the ends of boards and brace them for tricky operations.

Building your own workshop accessories can be one of the most satisfying of workshop projects. You are improving your skills with tools even as you make things that will make your tools more useful. In building a simple workbench, for example, a novice learns the principles of sound construction. Then, as his expertise grows, he uses his new skills to fashion a finer, more complex bench, worthy of his craftsmanship. At the same time he will also have the satisfaction of saving money, for a truly fine workbench is expensive.

Economies of another sort come from using whatever resources are at hand. In building a tool stand for a lathe, you can, for example, power the lathe with the recycled motor of an old washing machine. And you can work your tables and jigs and benches hard, in the reassuring knowledge that they are expendable. A homemade jig constructed of scrap lumber and leftover hardware costs nothing but your labor. If you scar the top of a workbench with too many nail holes and cuts from a saw or drill, you can replace it with a new top.

Finally, since these workshop accessories are built for your own exclusive use and convenience, you can change the standard configurations shown in the projects on the following pages to suit yourself. One of the best things about having a home workshop is the opportunity it gives you to put your own ideas into practice, and sometimes to improve on the classic models.

Building the Best Workbench for Your Workshop

Whether you are tinkering with the innards of a clock or ripping a sheet of plywood, a sturdy workbench is essential for your comfort, accuracy and safety. In fact, a good workbench is probably the most useful—and the most used—tool in any workshop.

The focus of almost all shop activity, a workbench should be designed to suit both the size of the shop and the nature of the work most often performed. Although some pursuits, such as metalworking or intricate model building, require highly specialized benches *(pages 107-109)*, one or more of the five benches shown opposite will satisfy the needs of most workshop activities.

The backboard bench can be assembled quickly, easily and at modest cost to make a worktable serviceable for an amateur craftsman, while the broad, unshakable surface of the big freestanding bench is better suited to larger shops and more complex work. A small fold-down bench is the ideal solution when space is scarce, and a portable bench for work that must be done on site is sturdy enough to support a variety of tasks but light enough to carry with one hand. Finally, a tall bench resembling a bar stool is for those jobs requiring precision, time and patience; it saves you from having to bend over the work for long periods.

All of these designs can of course be modified to suit individual needs. Typically a full-sized bench should be between 5 and 7 feet long and between 25 and 35 inches wide; to find the dimensions best suited to your shop, plan your shop layout on graph paper. It is also helpful to position pieces of scrap wood on the shop floor to simulate the bench area. You should have room to work from at least three sides of the bench.

In addition to meeting the demands of the available space and the work to be done, a bench design should also be adapted to the proportions of the individual owner. Traditionally, the benchtop is as high as an owner's hip joint, but arm and torso lengths can alter this dimension. You can experiment to find the height most comfortable for you by stacking cardboard boxes and standing in front of them.

At the same time, make sure the width of the bench allows a comfortable reach from front to back so that you can work over the entire benchtop without losing your balance. You should also leave about 3 inches of space, the toe room, beneath the lowest horizontal member of any bench, so you can work close to the bench without leaning forward.

Regardless of the size and shape of the workbench, stability is vital. A bench with loose joints will wobble, not only impairing the accuracy of the work but presenting a safety hazard, especially when power tools are used. Tools slipping off unsteady work materials cause many shop accidents.

In most cases, combining glue with galvanized common nails provides a solid joint, especially when the nail holes are predrilled with a bit half the diameter of the nail shaft. This prevents the nails from splitting the wood fibers as you drive them; splitting weakens the joints. A simpler but slightly less effective means of preventing the wood from splitting is to blunt, or dub, the tip of each nail before you drive it, so that it compresses the wood. Dubbing is best suited to simpler, less expensive benches.

You should not, of course, glue together the leg joints of a big bench that you may in the future wish to disassemble and move. Carriage bolts or lag bolts, which are removable, will generally provide adequate stability without glue; for extra-strong legs, you can make notched joints, taking care that the notched pieces fit together snugly.

In addition to having strong joints, a big freestanding bench must be heavy enough to stay in place when a job requires the application of force. Massive framing members—4-by-4s, 2-by-4s and 2-by-10s—ensure this stability if you select these framing members carefully, making sure there are no pronounced twists or bows in the wood. To stabilize a lightweight bench, you can place weights such as bricks or cement blocks (or extra lumber) on the lower shelf to hold it down. You may want to fasten the tall bench to the floor with lag bolts and lead anchors, since its height makes it relatively unstable.

Generally, the top of a workbench should be kept free of clutter. When a bench is positioned against a wall, you can store tools above it. But the design for the big freestanding bench includes a benchtop trough for temporary storage of small tools and materials while work is in progress. Its purpose is to localize the clutter. You can also brush wood shavings or sawdust into it to keep the rest of the benchtop clean.

Like any good tool, the bench will be subject to wear. Gouge marks and hammer dents may eventually create irregularities in the work surface that threaten the accuracy and safety of your work. To prevent such dents, you may want to cover the top of the bench with a smooth sheet of ½-inch medium-density overlay plywood, or with ¼-inch tempered hardboard. Nailed to the top with fourpenny finishing nails, either surface can be removed and replaced if it is damaged. Or you may want to clamp such a surface on your bench temporarily, whenever you need to do heavy pounding.

Besides requiring a sturdy work surface, many jobs demand a reliable device to hold the work in place. In some cases—and especially with lightweight benches—clamps perform this function. But for a full-sized freestanding bench, you need a woodworking vise, preferably one with jaws at least 7 inches wide. Such a vise is expensive but, properly installed, it becomes an indispensable and integral part of the bench. In planning your bench, allow for the necessary overhang of the benchtop where you want the vise to be.

Most vises come with manufacturer's installation instructions, but some general rules apply. Mount the vise so the tops of the jaws are even with or slightly below the surface of the benchtop. Most vises are designed for a benchtop about 2 inches thick. If your top is considerably thicker than this, notch the underside of the top to mount the vise; if the top is too thin, you can add a mounting block to the underside.

For woodworking, line the inner faces of the metal vise jaws with wood to protect your material. Vises generally have screw holes for this wood facing, but if your vise does not, you can use yellow glue to secure the wood to the jaws, after first cleaning the jaws with a solvent.

Anatomies of five basic workbenches. Built with standard construction materials and techniques, these five workbenches are designed to meet the specifications of different shop layouts, as well as the individual needs of craftsmen. The plain but practical backboard bench consists of a simple assembly of 2-by-4 legs and frames. Three 2-by-10s constitute the benchtop, along with a 1-by-12 backboard on which you can hang small tools. Near the bottom of the bench a plywood shelf provides storage space for tools and materials.

The larger, freestanding bench requires more time and materials to build, but it provides a superior work surface, can be disassembled for moving, and should last a lifetime. The basic design is similar to that of the backboard bench,

except that 4-by-4s are used for the notched legs, and an assembly of 2-by-4s, glued and nailed together with their edges up, makes a heavy, handsome butcher-block top. A trough along the back of the benchtop can be used for temporary tool storage, to keep the surface from getting cluttered as you work.

For tight quarters, the fold-down bench offers about 16 square feet of work surface when open. When you close the bench, the 2-by-4 legs fold under the front of the plywood-covered top, against the frame, and the whole assembly pivots down into its wall frame. Shelves above are useful for storage.

The portable bench, constructed of 1-by-12 lumber, is sturdy enough to stand on, and pro-

vides a functional work surface away from the shop. An oval handhold cut out of its top makes the bench easy to carry, and the fenced lower shelf can be used to hold tools. A notch in one end of the top and parallel runners beneath it are handy for steadying vertical boards.

The tall bench is excellent for crafts, such as wood carving, that require painstaking, precise work. Built to stand about elbow height, the simple 2-by-4 leg assemblies are reinforced with trapezoids of plywood. The space between the two halves of the hardwood top and the notch on the inner edge of each half allow room for you to clamp materials in the center of the work surface. The dowels protruding from one side of the bench are for supporting boards clamped against the side of the bench, edge up.

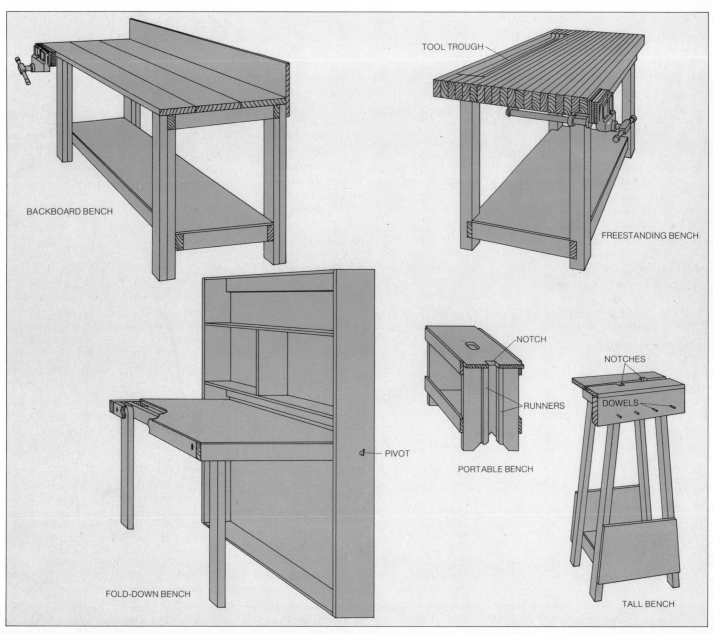

BACKBOARD BENCH

TOOL TROUGH

FREESTANDING BENCH

FOLD-DOWN BENCH

PIVOT

NOTCH

RUNNERS

PORTABLE BENCH

NOTCHES

DOWELS

TALL BENCH

The Basic Backboard Bench

1 **Making the frame parts.** To assemble a bench leg, align two 2-by-4s cut to different lengths; make one 5 inches shorter than the planned height of the workbench, the other 1½ inches shorter than the planned height. Position the two leg sections so that their bottoms are flush and a notch is created at the top. Drill pilot holes for eightpenny common nails all the way through the shorter 2-by-4 and partway through the longer one, staggering the holes in a zig-zag pattern and about 4 inches apart. Separate the two leg sections, spread glue on the adjoining faces, then realign them and drive eight-penny nails into the pilot holes. Assemble three more bench legs in the same way.

For the benchtop, assemble a frame (*inset*) consisting of two 2-by-4s cut 8 inches shorter than the planned length of the benchtop, and three 2-by-4 crosspieces cut 6 inches shorter than the combined widths of the top pieces, in this case three 2-by-10s. Fasten the frame together with glue and tenpenny nails driven into predrilled pilot holes, putting one crosspiece in the center and one at each end. Assemble a second frame for the bottom shelf in the same way, but make each crosspiece 3 inches shorter.

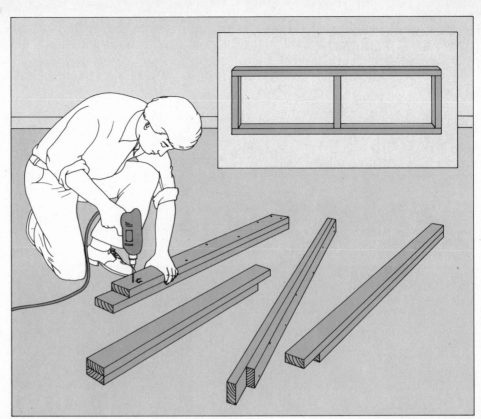

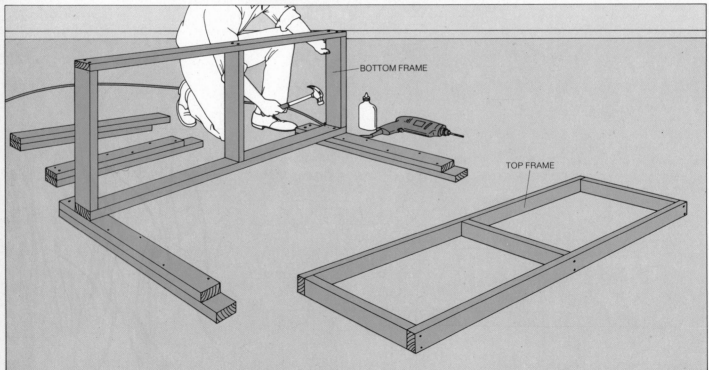

BOTTOM FRAME

TOP FRAME

2 **Assembling the frame parts.** Lay two bench legs on the floor, with their notched faces up, and rest the bottom frame against them. Position the frame upright, 3 inches up from the bottoms of the legs and flush with the legs' outer edges. Spread glue on the adjoining surfaces of legs and frame and drive 16-penny nails into pilot holes predrilled through the inside face of the frame into each leg. Turn the assembly over, propping up the free ends of the legs, and join the other side of the frame to the other two bench legs in the same way.

Fit the top frame into the notches at the opposite ends of the legs, making sure the frame is flush with the ends and outer edges of the legs. Fasten the top frame to the legs with glue and 16-penny nails driven into predrilled pilot holes, as you did the bottom frame.

3 **Attaching the benchtop.** Cut three 2-by-10s long enough to create a 7-inch overhang for a vise at one end of the work surface and a 1-inch overhang at the other. Place the 2-by-10s across the top frame so the back of the work surface is flush with the outer face of the back legs. Drill pilot holes for 16-penny nails through the 2-by-10s into the edges of the top frame, then spread glue and nail the 2-by-10s in place. For the lower shelf on the bench, cut a piece of ½-inch plywood to fit over the bottom frame and secure it with glue and fourpenny nails.

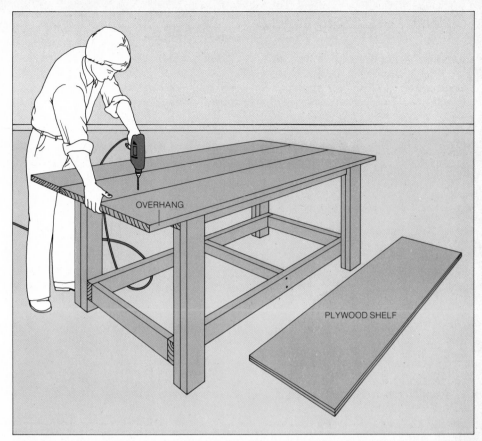

4 **Completing the workbench.** Glue and nail a 2-by-4 to the back of the top frame, filling the space between the back legs. Then glue and nail a 1-by-12 backboard against the back of the bench, positioning it so that its bottom edge is flush with the bottom edge of the filler 2-by-4. Position a woodworking vise at the end of the bench that has the wide overhang, and mark the locations of vise-mounting holes. Drill holes at the marks and fasten the vise in place with carriage bolts (inset); if necessary add blocking as shown to keep the vise jaw flush with or slightly below the benchtop.

Sand the surfaces and edges of the benchtop and backboard to smooth any irregularities and to round sharp corners slightly. Fill the cracks between the 2-by-10s with a mixture of sanding dust and white glue, allow to dry overnight, then once again sand the top smooth. To cover the top for especially rough work, cut a piece of ¼-inch tempered hardboard to fit the top and nail it in place with fourpenny finishing nails, recessing the nail heads about ⅙ inch with a nail set.

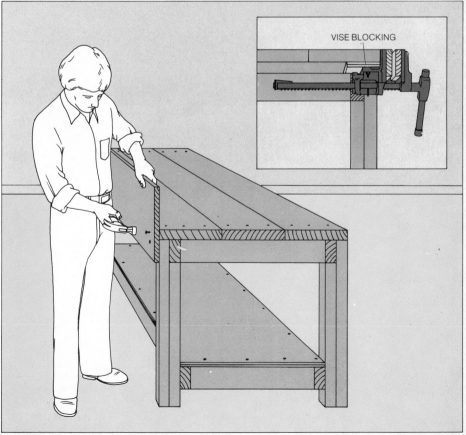

The Craftsman's Super Bench

1 Preparing legs and frames. Chisel two notches in each of four 4-by-4 legs, cut 3½ inches shorter than the desired height of the benchtop. Outline the notches on one face of each leg, locating one notch at the end of the leg, for the benchtop, and the other notch 3 inches in from the opposite end of the leg, for the shelf. Make the notches 3½ inches long and 1½ inches deep. Divide each notch into thin segments of wood by making about a dozen saw cuts and then, using a mallet and a chisel held with the bevel facing the cuts, shave out the waste wood.

From 2-by-4 lumber, assemble two identical frames (*inset*) with four evenly spaced crosspieces. Cut the front and back frame pieces 1 foot shorter than the planned overall length of the benchtop, to allow for an 11-inch overhang at one end that will hold a vise; cut the crosspieces 7 inches shorter than the planned width of the top, to provide a 1½-inch overhang front and back for clamping work to the benchtop. Join the framing pieces with glue and 12-penny nails driven into predrilled nail holes.

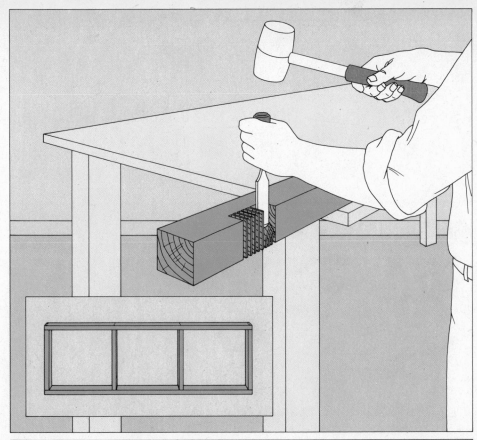

2 Attaching the legs to the frames. Lay two bench legs on the floor, notched faces up, and set one frame into the notches for the shelf, aligning the ends of the frame with the outer faces of the legs. At each notch, drill two ½-inch holes through the frame and about ½ inch into the leg. With a wrench, tighten a 3-inch-long ½-inch lag bolt into each hole, securing the frame to the legs. Do not glue these joints. Turn this assembly over and have a helper steady it while you attach the two remaining legs to the other side of the frame in the same way.

Similarly secure the top frame in the other notches, making sure the frame fits flush with the outer faces and ends of the legs. Stand the bench upright; then measure and cut a piece of ½-inch plywood for the shelf, notching it at the corners to fit around the legs. Glue and nail the shelf in place with sixpenny nails.

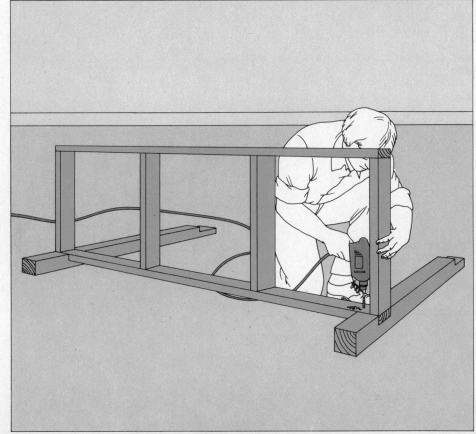

3 Adding diagonal braces to the top frame. Cut 12 diagonal 2-by-4 braces to fit into the corners of the top frame, and fasten the braces to the frame with glue and tenpenny nails driven into predrilled holes; be sure to keep the braces flush with the top of the frame. To cut the braces to size, mark the frame 8 inches out from one corner, along both a crosspiece and a side, and lay a 2-by-4 across this corner, lining up its outer edge with the marks. Mark angles on the underside of the 2-by-4 where it meets the frame. Cut along the angled lines, check the brace for fit, and then use this brace as a pattern for cutting all of the others.

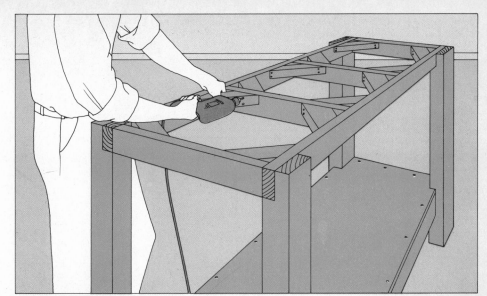

4 Cutting the top pieces. Square the ends of one 2-by-4 to the planned length of the benchtop, cutting off any unsightly lumberyard markings at either end. Nail a small piece of scrap wood against one end, as a stop block, and use the assembly as a jig to mark and cut uniform-length 2-by-4s for the rest of the top. Remove any lumberyard markings at the ends of these as well. To calculate the number of 2-by-4s you will need, divide the planned width of the bench, in inches, by 1½ and round the result up or down to the nearest whole number.

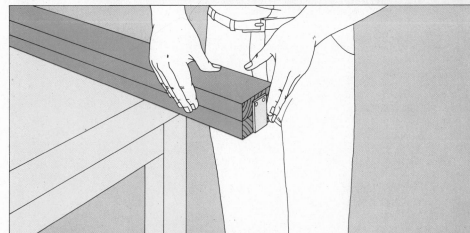

5 Notching the top pieces. Construct a cutting guide for the trough in the benchtop by drawing a line on the face of one top piece, 2 inches in from one edge; connect this line at a 45° angle to points on the edge 8 inches in from each end. Use a saber saw to cut along the marked lines, creating a long notch. Then use this board as a pattern to notch three additional top pieces; assembled, these will form the trough.

To notch the front edge of the benchtop to hold a vise, align two top pieces and clamp them together (inset). Then measure the size of the vise mounting and transfer its measurements to one end of the clamped 2-by-4s. Notch the 2-by-4s along the marked lines. Be sure the notch is cut deeply enough into the underside of the benchtop so that the vise will be flush with or slightly below the surface of the bench. Test-fit the vise and mark its bolthole locations.

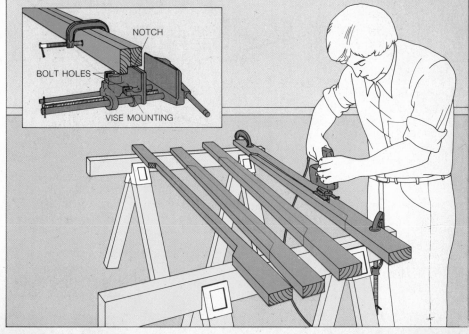

BOLT HOLES   NOTCH

VISE MOUNTING

6 **Assembling the benchtop.** Starting with the two top pieces notched for the vise, spread a wavy bead of glue on the face of the first board, place the second on top of it, and then lightly tack eightpenny nails into the second board in a zigzag pattern, 1 inch from the edges and 1 foot apart. Starting at one end, drive the nails in sequence, aligning the edges of the boards with your fingers as you go. Keep the first two boards free of nails at the end notched for the vise, except for one nail placed ¾ inch in from the end. Add the remaining boards one at a time in the same manner, but stagger the nailing pattern from row to row to avoid hitting the underlying nails. When only one unnotched 2-by-4 remains, add the four pieces notched for the tool trough, staggering the nail positions from row to row (*inset*). Then attach the final unnotched piece, to complete the benchtop.

With a helper, lift the assembled top into place on top of the bench frame. Align the top so that it overhangs the frame 1½ inches front and back, 1 inch at one end, and about 11 inches at the other end—the end for the vise.

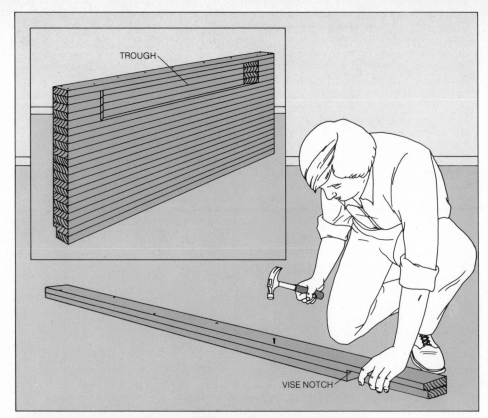

TROUGH

VISE NOTCH

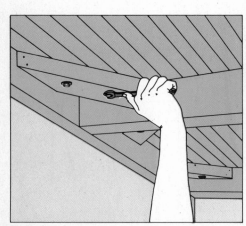

7 **Bolting the top on.** Drill two ½-inch holes for lag bolts through each diagonal brace except those under the tool trough, drilling up through the braces. Then continue with a ⅜-inch pilot hole, 2 inches up into the benchtop. Drive a 3½-inch-long ½-inch lag bolt with a washer into each hole, tightening it securely to pull the top snugly down against the frame. Then drill two ½-inch holes through each brace beneath the tool trough, with ⅜-inch pilot holes continuing ½ inch into the top. Tighten 2-inch-long ½-inch lag bolts with washers into these holes; the bolts will penetrate the top about ½ inch, anchoring the trough area against the frame.

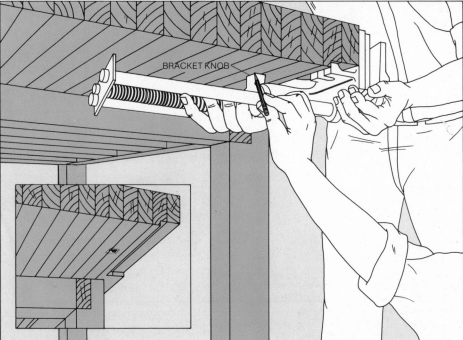

BRACKET KNOB

8 **Installing the vise.** Have a helper hold the vise in place in its notch while you mark the position of its projecting bracket knob on the underside of the benchtop. Cut out a rough indentation to make room for the knob by drilling several ½-inch holes within the marked area to the same depth as the vise notch (*inset*); then clear out the area with a chisel.

Drill boltholes through the benchtop at the marked locations, for mounting the vise, and insert 5-inch carriage bolts through the holes from the top, tightening the nuts on the underside of the bench until the boltheads sink about ¼ inch below the top surface. Then secure the inner jaw of the vise to the side of the benchtop, using 3-inch screws.

A Fold-down Bench

Constructing the wall frame. Using 1-by-8
boards, assemble the frame that holds the fold-
down bench against the wall. Glue and nail the
boards together to form a simple box about 6 feet
high. An interior width of 46½ inches makes it
easy to attach the 4-foot-wide sheet of ¼-inch plywood backing and to anchor the frame to wall
studs. Glue and nail two 1-by-8 storage shelves
into the upper half of the frame, with the lower
shelf positioned about 6 inches above the planned
height of the work surface. Glue and nail a vertical 1-by-8 between the shelves at their midpoint
to act as a shelf support.

Fasten horizontal 2-by-4s beneath the lower
shelf and beneath the top of the frame, and drive
two 4-inch lag bolts through these 2-by-4s at
each stud, to fasten the frame to the wall. In a
masonry wall, drive screws into lead anchors.
For the bolts on which the bench will fold, drill
½-inch pivot holes through the frame on both
sides, 1 inch out from the wall and 2 inches below
the planned height of the work surface.

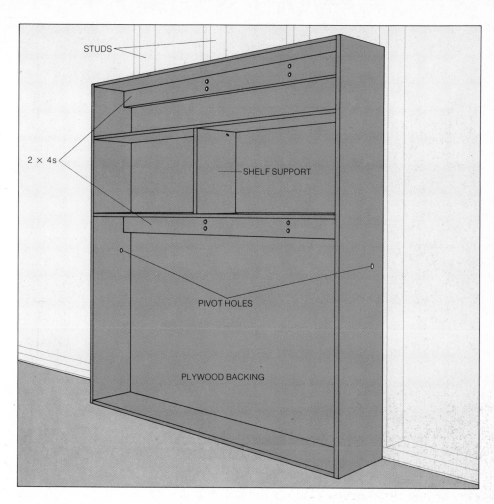

Assembling the Folding Bench

1 **Shaping the pivoting supports.** Cut two 2-by-4s
long enough to reach from the inner surface
of the bottom of the wall frame to a point 1 inch
above the top of the pivot hole. Draw a 1½-inch
square in one corner of each 2-by-4, and drill a
½-inch pivot hole at the inside corner of each
square. Cut a third 2-by-4, making it 7½ inches
shorter than the first two, and draw a 1½-inch
square at both corners of one end. Cut out
one of these squares to make a 1½-inch notch.

Set a compass for a 2-inch span and swing an
arc rounding off the outside corner of the marked
square on all three 2-by-4s. Use a saber saw
to round the three corners, following the arcs.

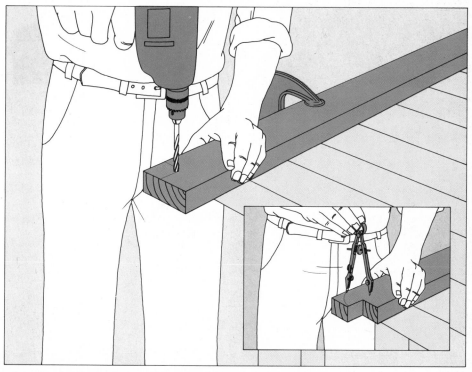

2 **Adding crosspieces.** Subtract 3¼ inches from the interior measure between the two sides of the wall frame and cut four crosspieces to this length, three from 2-by-4 stock, a fourth from 2-by-2 stock. Lay the three previously shaped pivoting supports on edge, rounded corners down and the notched support midway between the other two. Glue and nail the 2-by-2 crosspiece to the rounded end of all three supports, setting it into the notch in the center support. Then glue and nail a 2-by-4 crosspiece, edge up, between the two side supports and flush against the end of the short center support.

Add two 2-by-4 braces midway between the two long crosspieces. Reserve the two remaining 2-by-4 crosspieces for Step 3.

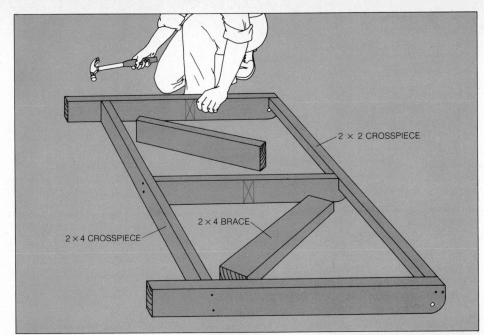

2 × 2 CROSSPIECE

2 × 4 BRACE

2 × 4 CROSSPIECE

3 **Constructing the folding-leg assembly.** Cut two spacer blocks 3½ inches long, from 2-by-4 stock, and drill ½-inch holes in their centers. Use them as patterns to drill matching holes in the ends of the two remaining 2-by-4 crosspieces. To drill these holes, use spacer blocks positioned 1 inch in from the end of each crosspiece and held in place with clamps.

Cut two legs from 2-by-4 stock, making them ½ inch shorter than the planned height of the work surface. Again using the spacer blocks as patterns, drill a ½-inch hole through one end of each leg, but this time position the spacer block flush with the end of each leg. Round the inside top corner *(page 89, Step 1, inset)*, so the leg will clear the benchtop when it is folded up.

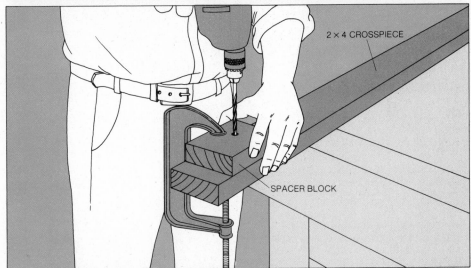

2 × 4 CROSSPIECE

SPACER BLOCK

4 **Fitting together the folding legs.** Glue and nail a spacer block to one end of each crosspiece, aligning their holes. Then insert an 8-inch length of ½-inch threaded rod through the holes at both ends of one crosspiece and slide a leg onto the rod at the end opposite the spacer block, adding a washer on each side of the leg so that it swings easily. Slide the other crosspiece onto the rods, with the spacer block on the opposite end and facing away from the leg. To complete the leg assembly, slide the second leg onto the rod opposite the second spacer block, again with a washer on each side, and temporarily tighten nuts over the projecting ends of the rods to hold them in the assembly.

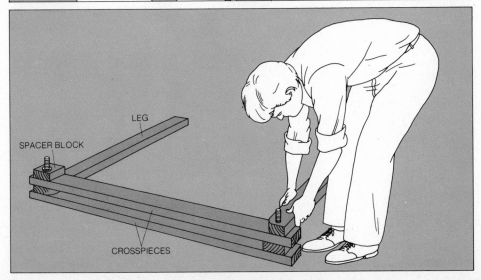

LEG

SPACER BLOCK

CROSSPIECES

5 **Attaching legs to the frame.** Position the entire leg assembly in front of the 2-by-4 crosspiece of the bench frame and, holding the upper edges of both elements flush, mark where the leg-assembly rods touch the frame crosspiece. At the marks, drill ½-inch holes and slide the rods through the holes to snug the leg assembly against the frame crosspiece. Hand-tighten nuts with washers on both ends of the rods to hold the assembly in place while you glue and nail the ends of the leg-assembly crosspieces to the sides of the frame.

Remove the front nuts and washers, retract the rods, and drill ½-inch-deep counterbored wells for the nuts and washers to fit into. Replace the nuts and washers and tighten them until the legs swing down with only slight resistance.

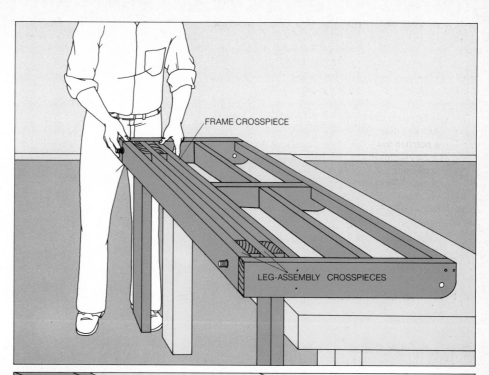

FRAME CROSSPIECE

LEG-ASSEMBLY CROSSPIECES

6 **Installing the bench frame.** With the bench legs down and the bench frame right side up, align the pivot holes in the sides of the bench frame with the matching holes in the sides of the wall frame. On each side, place a washer between the two frames, and thread 2½-inch carriage bolts through the holes to secure the bench to the wall frame. Place the head of the carriage bolt on the inside of the bench frame, and use a wing nut with a washer to tighten the bolt on the outside of the wall frame. Tighten the wing nuts firmly when the bench is in use, and loosen them slightly when you pivot the entire bench assembly, with legs folded, back into the wall frame.

Complete the benchtop by covering the entire work surface with a piece of ½-inch plywood, secured with glue and fourpenny nails.

A Portable Workbench

1 Assembling the bench. Cut two 18-inch-high legs from 1-by-12 lumber and notch each at the bottom with a triangular cutout, 4 inches high and 8 inches wide at its base. Then attach a 25-inch-long 1-by-12 shelf between the two legs, using glue and sixpenny nails. Position the shelf so that the bottom of the shelf just touches the top of each triangular cutout.

For the top, center a 30-inch length of 1-by-12 lumber over the legs, using a combination square to make sure the legs are vertical before gluing and nailing the top in place. Add two pairs of 1-by-3 braces, called aprons, to the sides of the bench (*inset*). Position one set flush with the top and the other set so the bottom edge of each apron is flush with the shelf bottom. Glue and nail the aprons in place.

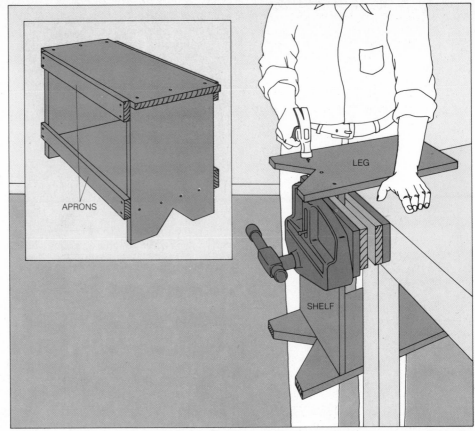

2 Finishing the bench. Mark the center of the bench top for an oval handgrip 4 inches long and 1½ inches wide. Drill a ⅜-inch starting hole inside the oval and insert the blade of a saber saw or a keyhole saw to cut out the oval.

To support vertical work—for instance, the edge of a door—cut a notch 1¾ inches square at the center of one end of the top (*inset*). Then nail two vertical 1-by-1 runners to the face of the bench leg at that end with fourpenny nails, aligning the runners with the sides of the notch.

To support work thinner than the space between the runners, you can add shims, or wedges, to hold the work in place, or remove the fourpenny nails and reposition the runners.

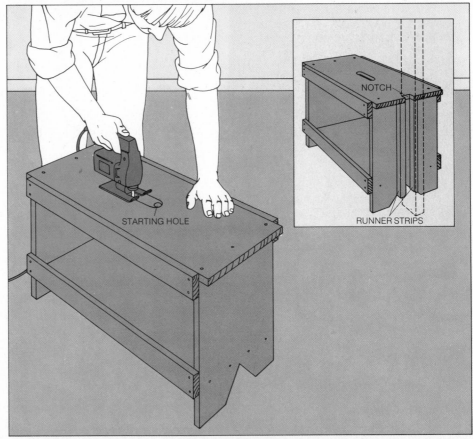

A Tall Bench for Small Jobs

1 **Making the leg frames.** Measure and cut four 2-by-4 legs to a length equal to the height of your waist, and four 2-by-4 cross braces 17 inches long. Using glue and tenpenny nails, fasten one brace across the top of each set of legs, positioning the brace flush with the ends and the outer edges of the legs. Flip this assembly over and install a second 2-by-4 brace at a point 4½ inches above the bottom of each set of legs.

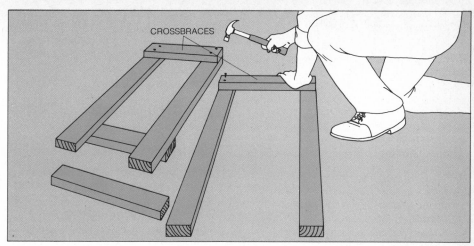

CROSSBRACES

2 **Assembling the leg frames and top.** Cut two trapezoid panels from ¾-inch plywood, making them 12 inches high with top and bottom measurements of 15 and 17 inches respectively. Clamp one panel between the leg frames, lining up the bottom of the panel with the bottoms of the lower cross braces, and lining up the sides of the panel with the outer edges of the legs. Glue and nail this assembly together, then flip it over and attach the second panel to the two legs on the other side.

For the benchtop, cut two pieces of 1-inch-thick hardwood—such as maple or oak—8¾ inches wide and 18 inches long. Clamp the pieces in a vise, edge-up and edges aligned, and cut a 1-inch-square notch in their edges, 6 inches from one end (*inset*). To make the notch, use a saw and a chisel as described on page 86, Step 1.

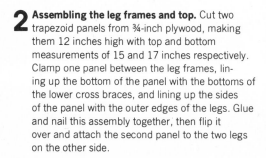

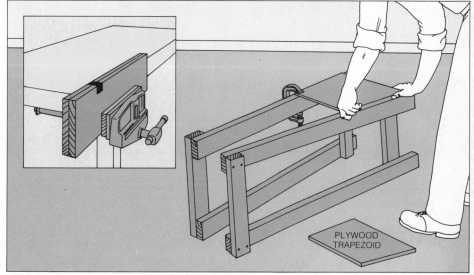

PLYWOOD TRAPEZOID

3 **Finishing the bench.** Lay the top pieces across the leg assembly and at right angles to the cross braces, trimming the braces slightly if necessary so the top pieces sit squarely. Position one top piece so that its outer edge lies flush with the outer edge of a cross brace, and the other top piece so that it overhangs a cross brace by 1½ inches. Leave a 1-inch gap between the top pieces, and place them so that the notches open into this gap on opposite ends of the benchtop, to allow for fitting clamps into the top. Secure each top piece in place with four 3-inch flathead wood screws driven through predrilled pilot holes with ¼-inch-deep counterbored walls. Trim the bottoms of the legs to eliminate any wobble in the bench, and glue and nail a shelf of ½-inch plywood over the lower cross braces.

To support long boards clamped to the side of the bench (*inset*), glue and nail an 18-inch apron of 2-by-6 lumber beneath the overhanging benchtop, setting the apron flush with the edge of the bench. Drill four ½-inch dowel holes 1 inch deep into the apron at evenly spaced intervals, and insert and glue 2½-inch dowels in them.

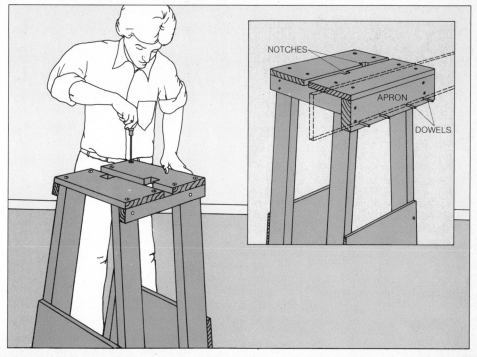

NOTCHES

APRON

DOWELS

"Third Hand" Devices to Use with Big Power Tools

Most stationary power tools are incomplete—and for some jobs, useless—without special accessories that add to their efficiency and versatility. Many saws and drill presses require side and end tables that provide a "third hand" to help support large pieces of wood, and special devices called jigs *(pages 102-103)* for guiding smaller work with safety and pin-point accuracy. Although it is possible to buy tables and jigs for these tools, you can save money and tailor the accessories to your own requirements by building them yourself.

Many stationary power tools, such as a table saw or bench grinder, require a stand similar to the workbench on pages 84-85 but fitted with a plywood top and, in some instances, metal casters. If the

machine requires a separate motor, you can enlarge the stand's top and hinge a motor-mounting board to it.

With most stationary power saws, extension tables that have rails or rollers (to minimize friction between lumber and table) are essential to help support panels and long boards. A table saw or band saw needs extension tables at both sides of the saw. For a radial-arm saw, the table may be on an independent stand or screwed to the wall and supported by legs at the outer corners.

The size of your projects will determine how large you should make the support tables. For a table saw, a pair of tables that extends the working surface to 2 feet on both sides of the saw blade will make it possible to cut 4-by-8-foot

plywood sheets easily. If you crosscut long boards frequently, you may want an even wider extension. Work-support tables for a radial-arm saw can be as long as the available space. Roller-topped tables 12 inches wide are adequate for use with table and band saws. For cutting a plywood sheet on a table saw, use two such roller tables; position them behind the saw, one on each side of the blade.

The top of a stand supporting a tool should be about 1 inch larger all around than the base of that tool, with space added for a motor if necessary or for any other tools you want to keep near the machine. The stand should hold the machine at a height that lets you work comfortably standing up; for most people, this is between 32 and 42 inches.

A Supporting Cast for Shop Machines

Added tables to steady the work. Shop-built accessory tables extend the top of this saw and are adaptable for use with other machines. For example, a wooden stand like the one supporting the saw can instead hold a bench grinder or a jointer at a convenient working height; its short back legs are fitted with metal casters so the machine on it can be wheeled to a new location. The extension table bolted to the left side of the saw can be used with any power saw to support a sheet of plywood or a long board held broadside for crosscutting. The freestanding, roller-topped table behind the saw supports the end of a long board being cut lengthwise.

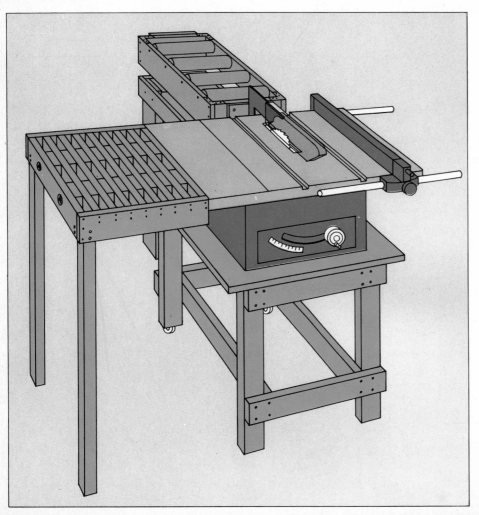

Setting Up a Machine Stand

1 Mounting casters. Build the base of the stand (*pages 84-85*), shortening the back legs by an amount equal to the height of a pair of casters. On the bottoms of the back legs, mark positions for the screw holes in the caster plates, drill pilot holes the full length of the mounting screws, and screw the casters to the legs. Since the screws are driven into the legs' end grain, be careful not to strip the insides of the pilot holes by overtightening the screws. If your shop floor is unusually slick, or you want added stability, use locking casters (*inset*).

Turn the stand right side up and attach a ¾-inch plywood top to the frame with 2-inch flat-head screws. Position the machine on the stand, mark and drill holes through the top, and secure the machine with stove bolts and nuts.

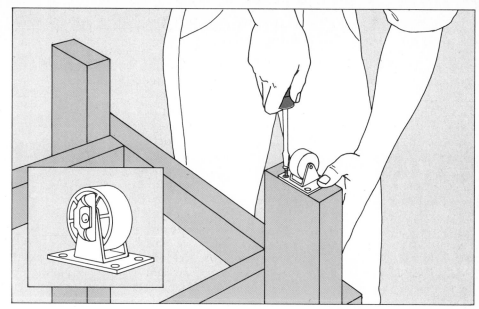

2 Hinging a motor mount. To mount a motor not attached to the machine it drives, cut a ¾-inch plywood mounting board and attach it to the top of the machine table; the motor board should be 3 inches wider and longer than the motor base plate. Screw two 2-inch butt hinges to the edge of the mounting board and to the top of the stand behind the machine, so the board drops down and away from the machine. The hinged edge of the board should be parallel with the pulley shaft of the machine. The distance between the mounting board and the machine will depend on the length of the drive belt.

To hold the board and motor firmly at any angle up to 45°, screw the lower end of a casement-window sliding stay (*inset*) to the top of the stand and screw the slide to the board.

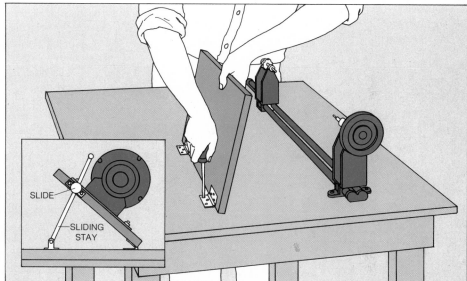

SLIDE

SLIDING STAY

3 Mounting the motor. With the mounting board propped up at about a 30° angle, set the motor on the board and slip the drive belt into the grooves of the motor and the machine pulleys. Take the slack out of the belt by pulling the motor away from the machine, then align the pulleys by sight. Mark the location of mounting holes in the motor base, remove the motor, and drill holes in the mounting board. Attach the motor to the board with 1¼-inch stove bolts and nuts, using lock washers between the nuts and the base plate. Replace the drive belt and adjust its tension with the sliding stay.

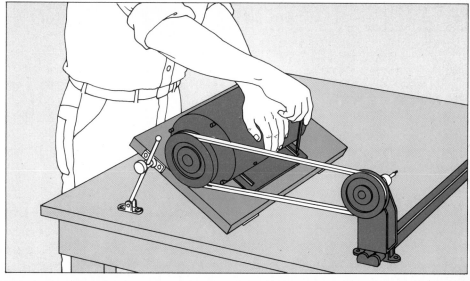

Assembling an Open-Top Extension Table

1 **Establishing hole locations.** For the side rail of an extension table that will be attached to a table saw, cut a 1-by-2 rail 1½ inches shorter than the depth of the saw table, front to back. Clamp it to the side of the saw table, centered, with its top edge flush with the top of the table. Reaching under the table, find the two holes in the side edge and mark through these holes onto the side rail behind. Unclamp the side rail and make counterbored holes at both marks, first drilling the counterbored cavities 1 inch wide and ⅜ inch deep with a 1-inch spade bit, then finishing the holes with a ⁵/₁₆-inch twist bit.

For every 1½ inches of width that you want the extension table to add, cut one 1-by-2 rail to the same length as the counterbored side rail. For each of these rails, cut two 4-inch 1-by-2 spacer blocks. Finally, cut one 1-by-4 frame piece to the same length as the rails.

2 **Drilling the top pieces.** Center a spacer block under one of the counterbored holes in the side rail and line up the edges of the two pieces. Using the ⁵/₁₆-inch hole in the side rail as a guide, drill a matching hole through the spacer block. Then use the drilled spacer block as a guide for drilling the other blocks. Use the side rail as a guide for drilling ⁵/₁₆-inch holes through the other rails and the frame piece, counterboring the 1-by-4 frame piece as you did the inside rail. Mark the top of each piece after drilling so that you can quickly line up the drilled holes later.

With a hacksaw, cut two ¼-inch threaded rods 1 inch longer than the extension-table width; put a flat washer and a nut on one end of each rod.

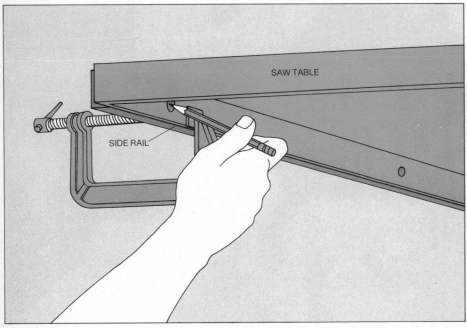

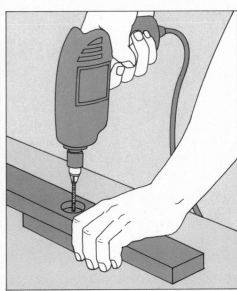

3 **Assembling the top.** Set the top edge of the 1-by-4 frame piece on a flat surface and slide the rods through the holes. Spread a thin coat of wood glue on both sides of two spacer blocks, slide them onto the rods with their top edges down, and press them against the frame piece. Except for the side rail, slide the rest of the pieces onto the rods, alternating rails with pairs of glued spacer blocks. Then slide the side rail onto the rods, with the counterbored side facing out. Put a flat washer and a nut onto the outer ends of both rods, seat them in the counterbored cavities, and tighten the nuts until some of the glue has been squeezed out.

Top edges of rails and spacer blocks should still rest firmly on the flat surface and about 1 inch of threaded rod should extend from the counterbored holes in the inside rail.

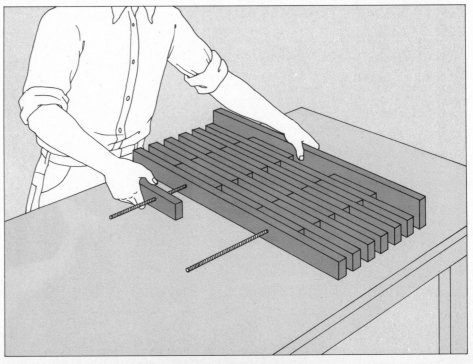

4 Attaching table ends. Cut two 1-by-4 frame pieces for the ends, as long as the width of the extension table. Brush glue onto the rail ends and fasten the two frame pieces to them with sixpenny coated box nails, keeping the top edges of the frame flush with the extension-table top.

Slide the protruding ends of the threaded rods through the holes in the side of the saw table and prop up the outer end of the extension table with scrap wood so the tabletop is level. Cut two 2-by-2 legs 1½ inches shorter than the height of the tabletop.

5 Attaching the legs. Holding a 2-by-2 leg inside one outer corner of the extension table, drill four staggered $^3/_{32}$-inch pilot holes through the frame pieces and into the leg, and attach the leg with 2-inch wood screws. Attach the other leg in the same way. Under the saw table, thread a lock washer and a nut onto each of the threaded rods and firmly tighten the nuts.

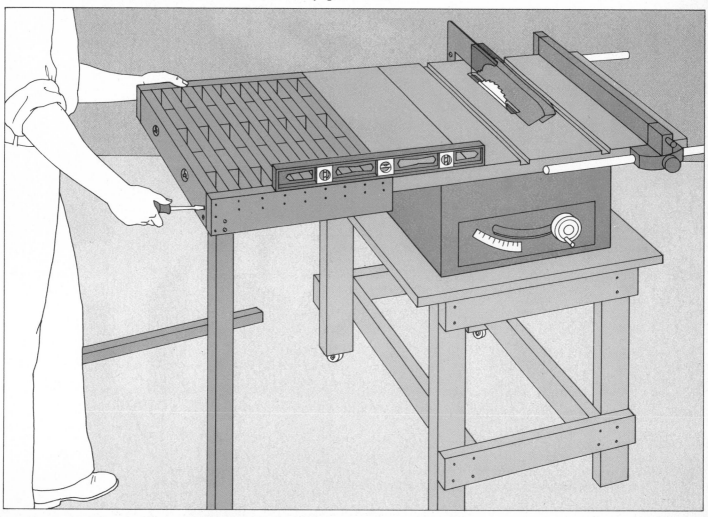

A Table Topped with Rollers

1 **Drilling the sides of the roller frame.** To make the sides for the frame that will hold the rollers, cut two 1-by-4s to the planned length of the roller-topped table. Line up the two frame sides, clamp them in a vise and, on a line ⅝ inch below the top edge, drill ⅛-inch holes through both boards at once. Space the end holes about 2 inches in from the ends and the intermediate holes about 6 inches apart.

Cut two 1-by-4 ends for the roller frame, 1½ inches shorter than the planned width of the table. Nail through the sidepieces into the end pieces with sixpenny box nails, and reinforce the corners with flat corner irons (*inset*).

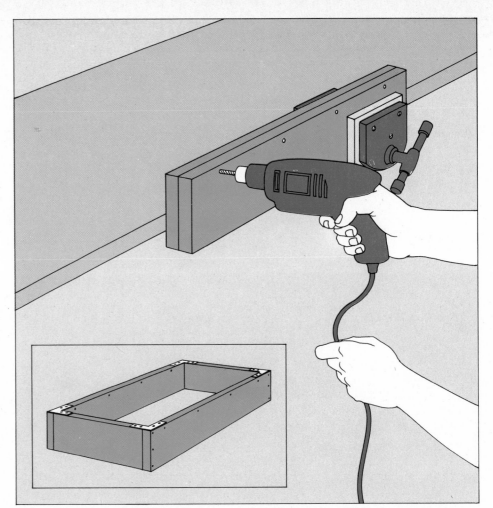

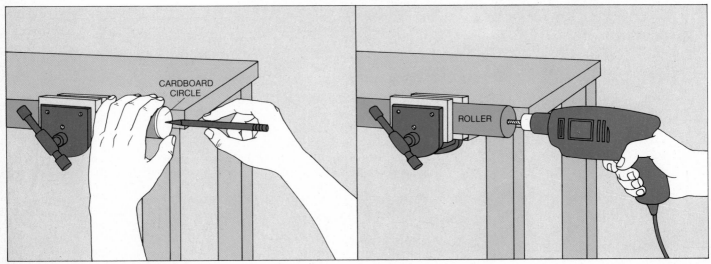

CARDBOARD CIRCLE

ROLLER

2 **Drilling the rollers.** Cut wood dowels 1½ inches in diameter ½ inch shorter than the inside of the roller frame. With a compass, draw a 1½-inch circle on cardboard, cut it out and pierce its center with a nail or sharp pencil. Use this pattern to mark the centers of the roller ends (*above, left*). Drill a ³/₁₆-inch hole about 2 inches into the center of each roller end (*above, right*).

3 **Mounting the rollers.** Drive tenpenny common nails into the holes in the roller frame until their points barely protrude on the inside. Align a roller between one pair of nails and drive the nails into the holes in the roller ends; the nails should be tight in the frame and loose in the roller. Mount the remaining rollers the same way. All the rollers should spin freely.

4 **Assembling the base.** Make two base frames of 1-by-3 lumber to match the roller frame. Cut four 1-by-4 legs 3½ inches shorter than the lowest height at which the roller-topped table will be used. Clamp the legs to the inside corners of the base frames, setting one frame with its top flush with the tops of the legs, and the bottom of the other frame about 6 inches above the bottoms of the legs. Drill pilot holes through the frames and the legs and assemble them with two 1½-inch wood screws at each leg.

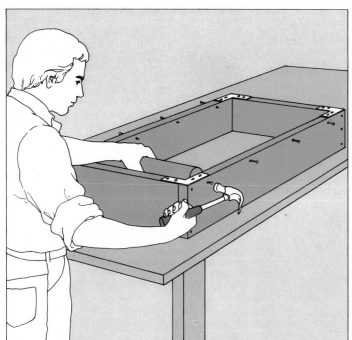

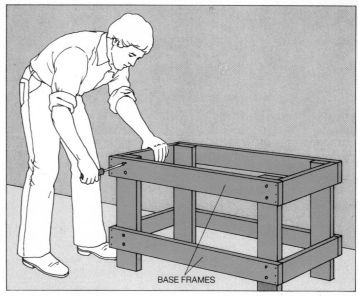

BASE FRAMES

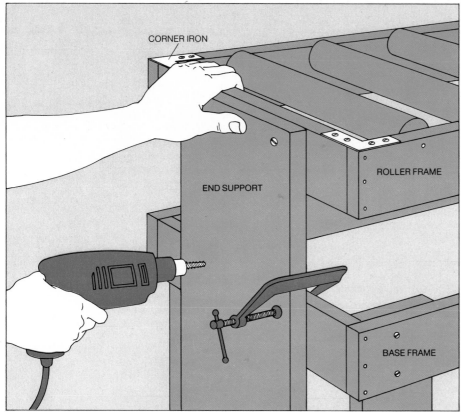

CORNER IRON

END SUPPORT

ROLLER FRAME

BASE FRAME

5 **Making the table adjustable.** To support the roller frame above the base, screw an 18-inch 1-by-12 to each end of the roller frame so the tops of these supports are flush with the top of the roller frame. Clamp the supports to the base, setting the roller frame at the working level desired, and drill two ¼-inch holes through the supports and the base frame.

For each tool with which you will use the roller-topped table, clamp the roller frame to the base so that the rollers will be level with the tool table, and drill another pair of holes through each end support. Use the holes in the base frame as guides. To secure the roller frame, insert ¼-inch stove bolts through the appropriate pair of holes and secure them with wing nuts.

Handy Helpers for Extra Accuracy

A few special accessories, such as jigs and platforms, can greatly increase the variety and quality of the work you do with your stationary power tools. They make it easier to cut and drill precisely at any angle and they provide support for work that is difficult or dangerous to hold by hand.

A sliding platform for a table saw, for example, is fitted with miter guides that let you make a succession of miter cuts without having to reset and test the machine as you would with a standard miter gauge. Guided by rails that ride through slots in the tabletop, the entire platform moves past the blade, carrying the work. Similarly, a tilting platform clamped to the post of a drill press lets you drill holes at an angle in mitered edges.

Because these platforms and the other accessories shown here are designed to ensure accuracy, accuracy must be built into them. Use clear, dry hardwoods whenever possible, for durability and resistance to warping and shrinking. Make sure all boards and plywood are perfectly straight and flat. Take particular care to make all angles exact, laying them out with precision measuring devices such as protractors, drafting triangles and rulers.

A Miter-cutting Platform for a Table Saw

1 **Assembling the platform.** Cut two hardwood guide rails, each the same width, depth and length as the miter-gauge grooves in the tabletop, and insert the rails in the grooves. Lower the saw blade below the table and place a ¾-inch plywood platform, the size of the tabletop, over the hardwood rails, aligning the platform with the table edges. Mark the position of the rail center lines on the face of the plat-

form, and drive 1-inch wire nails through the platform into each rail at 2-inch intervals.

Turn on the motor and slowly raise the blade to its full height, holding the platform firmly down on the table. When the blade has fully penetrated the platform, move the platform forward and backward, lengthening the slot to within 2 inches of each end of the platform.

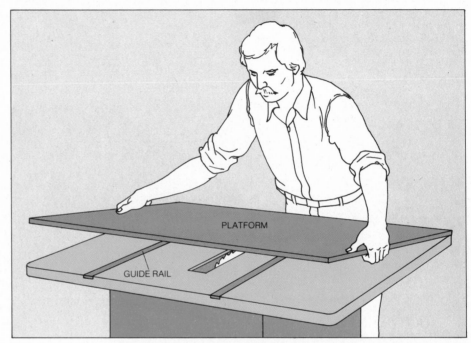

PLATFORM

GUIDE RAIL

2 **Attaching miter guides.** Draw two lines at 45° angles to the blade slot, one on each side of the slot, perpendicular to each other. To make the miter guides, cut a 45° miter on one end of two 1-by-2s and nail them to the platform, each with one edge along the pencil line and the mitered end flush with the slot.

To make a platform that will cut a miter at any point on a board, position the point of the miter guide near the middle of the platform and place the work against the outside of the angle (*inset, top*). But to make a platform to cut a miter at the end of a board, position the point of the miter guide near one edge of the platform, and place the work inside the angle (*inset, bottom*). Always feed either platform across the saw table so that the blade cuts the work before passing through the miter guide.

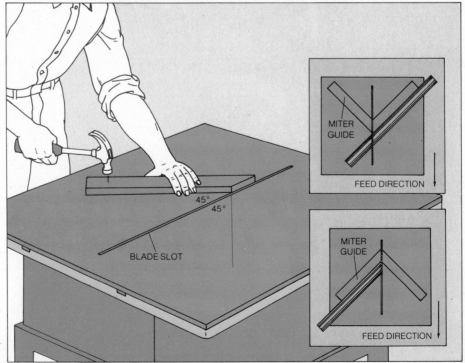

45°
45°

BLADE SLOT

MITER GUIDE

FEED DIRECTION

MITER GUIDE

FEED DIRECTION

A Tilting Platform for a Drill Press

1 **Notching the supporting arm.** Cut a 2-by-4 supporting arm to go under the platform, making it 4 inches longer than the distance from the center of the drill-press column to the front of the table. With a table saw, cut a V groove into one 4-inch face of the arm, about 4 inches from one end. First set the saw blade for a 45° bevel, raise the blade ¾ inch above the table, and use the miter gauge, set at 90°, to guide the arm across the blade. Then put the miter guide on the other side of the blade and cut the other side of the V.

To clamp the arm, cut a 2-by-4 block 8 inches long and make an identical V groove across one face. Mark for the groove by lining up the end of the block with the end of the arm.

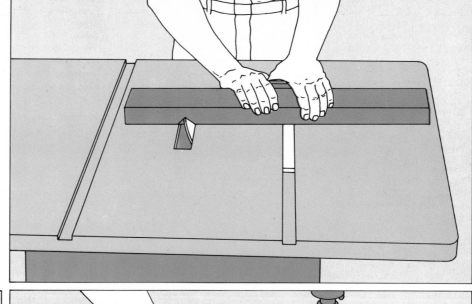

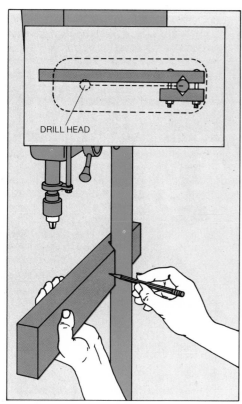

DRILL HEAD

2 **Assembling the arm.** Hold the V groove of the arm against the drill-press column and mark the arm for boltholes, placed to bridge the widest part of the column. Drill ¼-inch holes at both marks, then, using the arm as a template, mark and drill identical holes in the clamp block.

Adjust the existing drill-press platform to its lowest height. Fasten the arm and clamp block around the column with ¼-inch carriage bolts, nuts and washers, aligning the arm by eye to lie parallel to an imaginary line between the centers of the column and the drill head (*inset*).

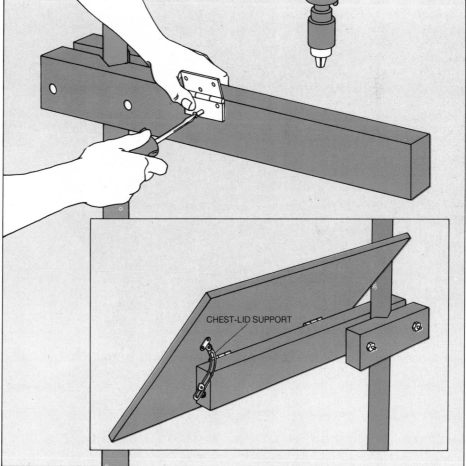

CHEST-LID SUPPORT

3 **Adding the hinged platform.** Screw two 2-inch fixed-pin butt hinges to the outside face of the arm, with the pivoting edges of the hinges flush with the top edge of the arm. Cut a ¾-inch plywood platform to the same dimensions as the drill-press table. Place the platform on the arm, centering it under the drill head, and screw the remaining leaf of each hinge to the underside of the platform. To control the platform tilt, screw a sliding chest-lid support to the underside of the platform and to the end of the arm (*inset*). Adjust the height of the platform by loosening the nuts on the clamp block, repositioning the platform, and tightening the nuts.

Jigs for Greater Accuracy with Less Danger

A tenoning jig. Straddling the rip fence of a table saw, this device enables you to cut tenons and grooves on the ends of a narrow board, keeping your hands safely clear of the blade. You clamp the board, or hold it firmly, against the face of the jig, one edge against the work guide, then push the jig past the blade.

The two legs of the jig, made from ¾-inch boards or from plywood, are separated by a ¾-inch-thick spacer whose width matches the thickness of the rip fence (*inset*). Screws driven through the two legs and into the spacer hold the assembly together. The work guide, a ¼-inch strip, is glued and nailed to the face of the tall leg, perpendicular to the bottom edge of the leg.

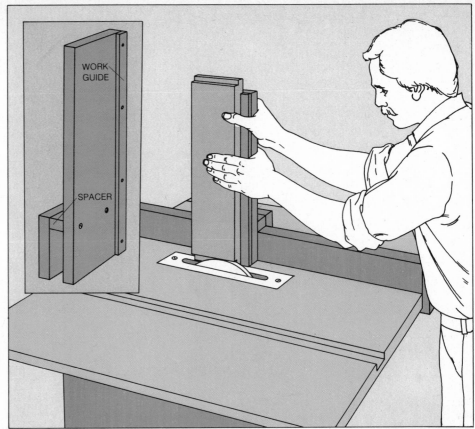

A tapering jig. Sliding against the rip fence of a power saw, this adjustable jig allows you to re-peat identical tapered cuts along the lengths of boards. The board to be tapered faces the saw blade, with its end butted against the stop on the jig. The jig is then held against the rip fence and pushed past the blade.

The two legs of the tapering jig are made of 1-by-3s, about 30 inches long, connected by a 2½-inch fixed-pin butt hinge screwed into one end of each leg (*inset*). A 1-by-3 stop is nailed to the unhinged end of one leg, and a sliding chest-lid support near the unhinged end locks to set the legs at the desired taper. Reference lines marked on the edge of each leg, 12 inches from the hinge end, allow you to measure the amount of taper in terms of inches per foot.

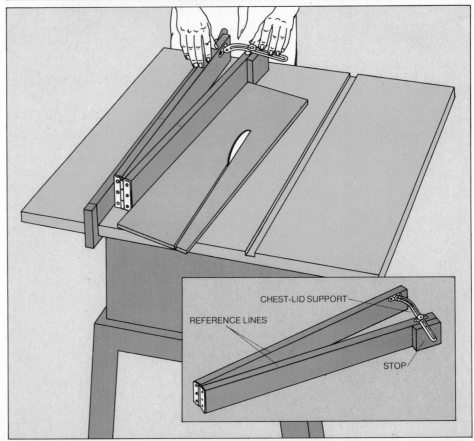

A featherboard. With its springlike fingers, this slotted board holds the work firmly against the rip fence while permitting the work to feed smoothly past the blade. Cut from a ¾-inch piece of hardwood or clear fir, the featherboard is about 6 inches wide and 16 inches long. The feathered end of the board is mitered at an angle of 45° and then cut lengthwise at ⅛-inch intervals, each cut 5 inches long.

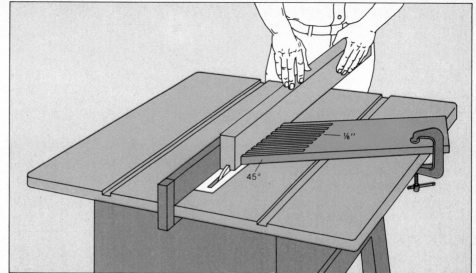

A stopblock. Clamped to a rip fence by means of a thumbscrew, a stopblock is useful for limiting the length of a rip cut or dado. Used on the fence of a radial-arm saw, such a stopblock enables you to crosscut several pieces of work to identical lengths.

Make the stopblock of ¾-inch hardwood in the shape of an inverted U. Cut the vertical legs ¾ inch higher than the fence that the block will straddle, to allow for the depth of the spacer; make the spacer $\frac{1}{16}$ inch wider than the thickness of the fence. Glue and screw the legs to the spacer; drill a hole for the steel thumbscrew slightly smaller than its thread diameter.

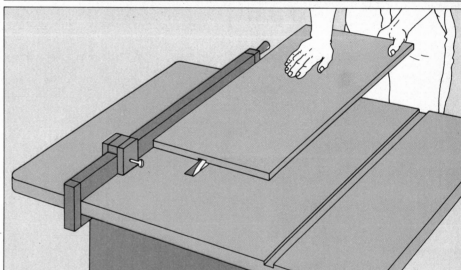

Hold-down and push stick. These two safety devices hold a board against the work surface and guide it toward the blade of a tool while keeping your hands well away from the cutting edge. The hold-down straddles the rip fence of a table saw, holding down the back end of the work while you are pushing it forward. The push stick, used with any machine, lets you hold work against the table or fence while pushing it.

The ¾-inch-thick legs of the hold-down are about 6 inches wide and ¾ inch higher than the rip fence. They are screwed to a 6-inch-wide handle slightly thicker than the width of the fence. A 45° bevel about 1¾ inches high is cut across the bottom front corner of each leg and the handle is shaped to your hand with two additional 45° bevels at the front and the back. The push stick, a 1-by-2 about 12 inches long, is notched at a right angle to grip the corner of the work. The angle should be slightly off-center from the end of the stick, so that the stick can be used at about a 45° angle to the work surface.

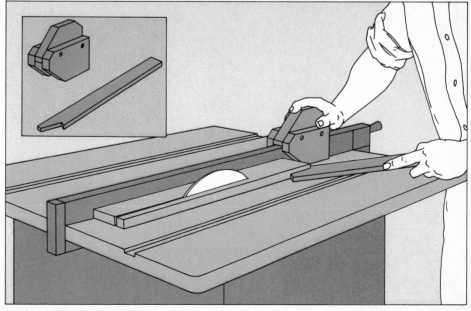

Workshops that Go to the Job

Like a tow truck, a home workshop ought to be ready to move at a moment's notice to meet emergencies. If a faucet leaks or a hole is punched in a wall, you may not be able to make repairs in the workshop—but you should be able to take your workshop to the problem. Armed with an assortment of portable tools and custom-made tool carriers, you will be able to cope with emergencies the way a professional does.

The first of these devices to make is the portable toolbox *(right),* which you can build in any size to organize and tote anything from a nail set and hammer to a full-length crosscut saw. You can design the toolbox and its scaled-down companion, the hardware carrier, to fit your own collection, and if you have a chronic home-repair problem, such as plumbing that leaks repeatedly, build a separate toolbox to hold just the specialized tools needed for that job.

In addition to carrying tools through the house, you may sometimes need to carry cumbersome materials such as 4-by-8 sheets of plywood or wallboard. One simple way to maneuver these panels through doorways and around corners is to transport them in a rope-handled carrier *(opposite, top)* that puts the weight of the panel in a sling. Finally, when the repair job calls for a temporary workbench, two folding sawhorses to support a work surface provide an ingenious answer; they pass easily through doorways and, when not in use, hang almost flat against a workshop wall.

Keeping nuts and bolts orderly. An open tray made of ½-inch plywood is partitioned into sections to contain, organize and carry those small items of hardware that are so essential and so easily misplaced—nails, screws, washers, nuts, bolts—and even to carry the screwdrivers, wrenches and pliers used with them. The slotted handle, itself a divider, is fastened to the bottom and ends of the tray with wood glue and 1-inch wood screws; the number and placement of other dividers, similarly fastened to the tray, are a matter of personal preference.

Homemade Carriers for Tools and Materials

The basic toolbox. Constructed of ½-inch plywood fastened together with wood glue and 1¼-inch wood screws, this simple open toolbox can be custom-designed to fit any tool collection. Typically the sides of the toolbox are at least 14 inches high and the end panels are high enough to raise the carrying handle about 6 inches above the top of the tools. Several tool-holding accessories are possible, such as the slotted saw holder and the tool rack screwed to the sides of the box shown here; the slots are cut with the saws to be carried, the holes in the rack are drilled to the appropriate sizes. For the handle, a ⅞-inch wood dowel is inserted through holes drilled through the ends panels of the toolbox and is held in place with cotter pins.

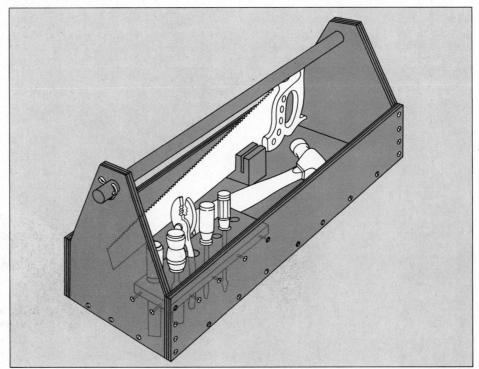

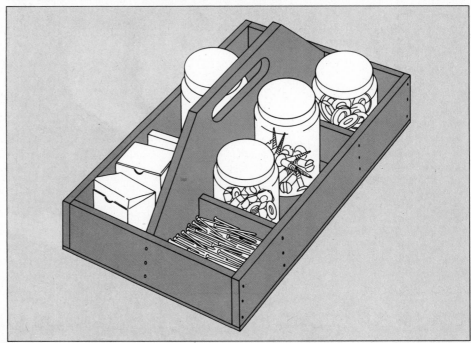

Carrying panels comfortably. A rope-handled panel carrier, constructed of two pieces of ½-inch plywood, 16 inches wide, sandwiched around a spacer block, is bolted together with machine screws. One side of the carrier is higher than the other, to tip the panel onto your shoulder. The rope handle is knotted against the carrier, and may be untied and adjusted to suit the height of anyone carrying the panel. The handgrip is a short length of plastic pipe or garden hose that has been threaded over the rope.

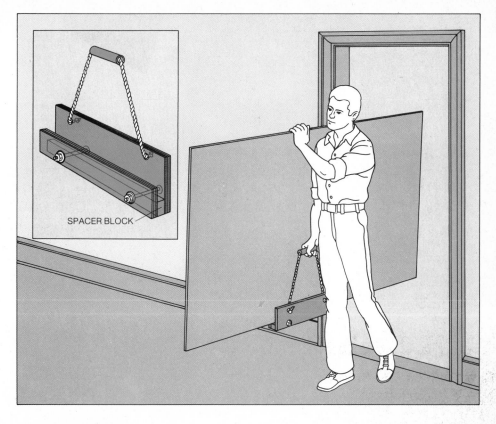

SPACER BLOCK

Building a Space-saving Sawhorse that Folds

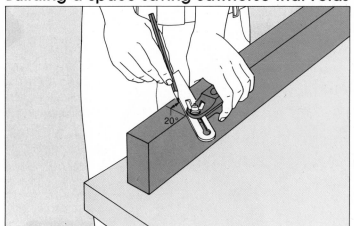

20°

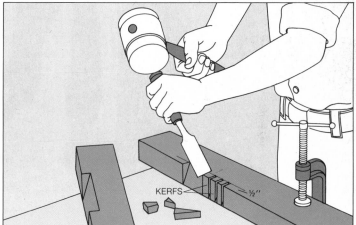

KERFS
½"

1 Cutting the sawhorse legs. Using a protractor, set the blade of a sliding T bevel at an angle of 20° and hold the blade against one 2-by-4 sawhorse leg, to mark an angled cut; measure and mark a parallel angled cut 24 inches away, for the other end of the leg. To guide the saw blade, extend both lines completely around the leg, with lines straight across the faces of the 2-by-4 and a matching angled line on the opposite edge. Cut the first leg and use it as a pattern for cutting the other three legs.

2 Notching the top pieces. Cut two 2-by-4s of identical length for the folding top of the sawhorse and mark both top pieces for chiseled notches to receive the legs. Mark each notch 4 inches in from the end of each top piece, making it 3½ inches wide and angling it from the bottom edge to a line ½ inch in from the top edge.

With a crosscut saw, cut kerfs across the area of the notch at ¼-inch intervals. Clear out the notch with a chisel and mallet, angling the beveled face of the chisel toward the edge of the 2-by-4. Place each leg in its notch, the top of the cut end flush with the surface. Secure the leg to the top with three tenpenny nails.

3 **Hinging the sawhorse top.** Butt the top pieces together, upside down, and tack a piece of scrap wood across them to hold them temporarily while you mark and drill pilot holes for two leaf-type hinges. Locate the hinges about 6 inches in from the ends of the top pieces, and fasten them to the top pieces with 1¼-inch wood screws. Remove the scrap wood.

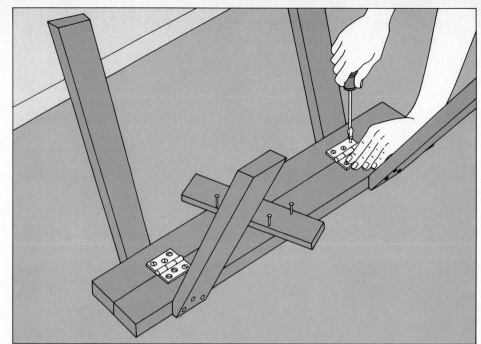

4 **Bolting braces to the sawhorse legs.** Cut two braces for each pair of legs from 1-by-3 lumber, putting one brace directly under the top of the sawhorse and the other about 10 inches down. Use the angle of the opened legs as a cutting guide for the angled ends of the braces. With the sawhorse open, upside down, nail the upper braces to the legs temporarily while you drill ⅜-inch boltholes through both brace and leg. Then remove the nails and attach the brace to the leg with 4½-inch machine bolts over flat washers, fastened with wing nuts. Drill holes in the lower braces and bolt them on in the same way.

To fold the sawhorse for transport or storage (*inset*), unfasten one bolt from each brace and let the braces hang free. The hinges under the top pieces will let the legs collapse.

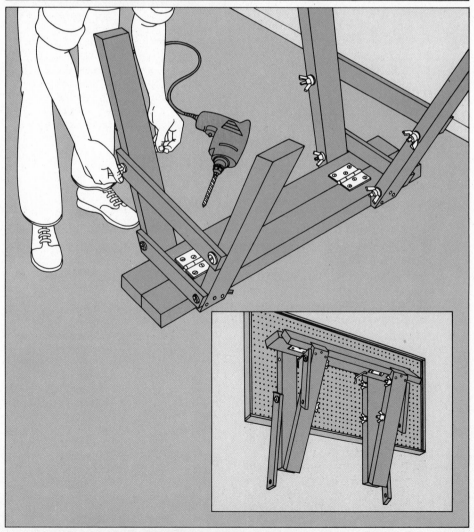

106

Specialized Work Spaces for Special Pursuits

Although most home workshops are designed to accommodate woodworking projects, they often are used for other pursuits as well. For anyone seriously interested in fine lacquering, for instance, the spray booth on page 110 is invaluable. And though you can solder or braze metal on a woodworking bench, provided you protect its top with firebricks, it is more satisfying to do metalwork on a bench especially designed for the job. The same is true of such light crafts as model-building or fly-tying, more conveniently pursued at a desk-type bench that includes storage for myriad tiny parts.

Anyone whose specialty is metalworking will appreciate the practical island-style metalworking bench at right, top. Weighted at the base like homemade benches used by generations of farmers, it is small enough to allow a worker to circle his job, approaching it from any side. Typically, the bench was made of scrap iron. This modern one has a steel-plate top that can withstand years of pounding and is absolutely flat—an advantage in aligning metal seams.

A heavy concrete base keeps the bench immobile, making it ideal for a heavy-duty metal vise. Although base and top together weigh more than 400 pounds, the bench can be tipped onto a dolly and moved fairly easily. Its weight demands a strong floor, either of concrete or of wood with sound, strong joists.

To build the bench, you will need an empty 55-gallon steel drum for the base; you can probably purchase one from a fuel-supply company. You can have a metalworking shop trim the drum down to a 16-inch height, or do the job yourself, using a hacksaw or, if you have access to one, an acetylene torch. Do not use a torch, however, if the drum ever contained flammable liquids or chemicals. Both the ¼-inch-thick steel plate you will need for the top and the 2-inch-wide, ¼-inch-thick angle irons for the legs are available at metal-products shops. The top should be of ungalvanized steel, to reduce glare.

Most metal-products shops will cut and drill the angle irons to your specifications and will shape a square steel plate into a smooth disk. Have the shop drill countersunk holes in the plate at the same time, for the screws that will attach the plate to its plywood base. You can eliminate the cost of shaping the top by building a bench with a square top, but you may find that you bump the sharp corners as you walk around the bench.

At the opposite end of the spectrum from the metalworking bench, which is designed for use with heavy-duty tools and equipment, is the hobby bench for light crafts (page 108). These activities too require a special work surface, one more like a desk, since light crafts often involve long periods of sitting. Ample storage is also needed for the small tools and delicate parts used in such pursuits, as well as for plans, instructions and hobby magazines usually kept at hand.

The hobby bench shown incorporates the features most useful for a variety of light crafts; it is a practical workbench but handsome and compact enough to be placed in almost any room in the house. Constructed of plywood fitted together with dadoes and butt joints, the bench is simple and inexpensive. By modifying the design slightly, and adding a fold-down drafting top, you can make the bench double as a planning center for all workshop activities.

Anatomy of a metalworking bench. The top of this strong bench consists of a disk of plywood, 1 inch thick and 32 inches in diameter, supporting a second disk of ¼-inch steel plate. The base of the bench, a 55-gallon oil drum cut down to a height of 16 inches, is filled with concrete—about 4 cubic feet. Two post-and-lintel assemblies of ¼-inch-thick steel angle irons act as legs supporting the benchtop; they are bolted to the underside of the plywood disk and sunk into the concrete base. A heavy-duty metalworking vise can be mounted on the benchtop. The height of such a bench is typically fist level—the height of the worker's clenched fists when he is standing and his arms are dropped by his sides.

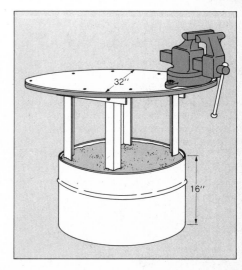

A Heavy-Duty Bench for Metalworking

1 **Assembling the benchtop.** Using a saber saw, cut a circle of 1-inch plywood, 32 inches in diameter. Fasten two 21-inch-long angle irons flat against its underside, placing them parallel, 16 inches apart, with their vertical flanges inward. Use three 1-inch lag bolts to anchor each angle iron to the plywood, driving the bolts through predrilled holes 8 inches apart into pilot holes in the plywood. Then bolt four 24-inch-long angle-iron legs through predrilled holes 14 inches apart on the vertical flanges. Use a lock washer behind each nut but, before finally tightening the assembly, check with a square to make certain that the legs are at right angles to the benchtop.

2 **Attaching the top to the base.** Use C clamps to fasten a 24-inch scrap of 2-by-4 about one third of the way up each pair of legs. Then fill the drum base with concrete and sink the legs into it, letting the 2-by-4s rest on the edges of the drum. Loosen the C clamps and adjust the position of the legs until the surface of the bench top is level and at fist height—generally about 30 inches. Then tighten the clamps again.

Allow the concrete to set for 24 to 48 hours before removing the 2-by-4s. Then attach the steel disk to the plywood top, driving 1-inch-long wood screws through eight predrilled, countersunk holes spaced evenly around the plate about 2 inches in from the edge (inset). The screwheads should lie flush with the plate surface.

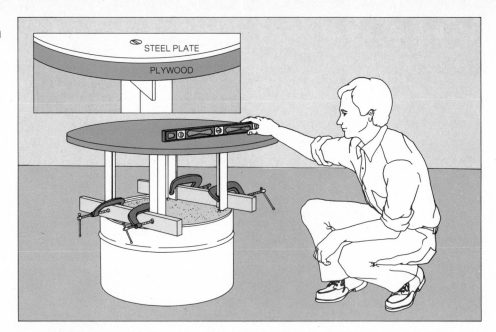

For Light Crafts, an Efficient Hobby Bench

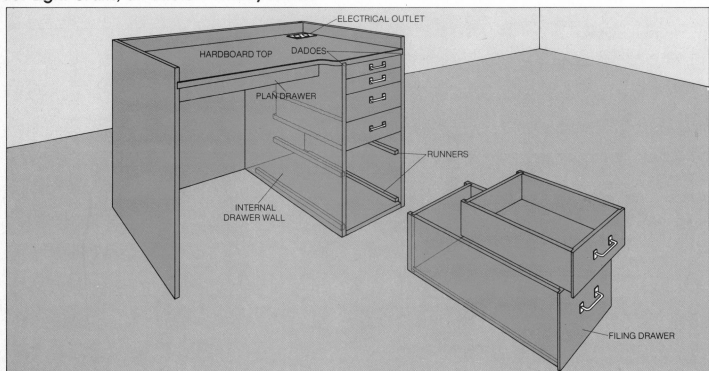

Anatomy of the bench. A combination desk and bench for light craftwork has a 2-inch-high parapet around the sides and back of the 30-inch-high desk surface to keep small parts from rolling off. It also has an electrical outlet in the surface as a power source for hobby appliances or a high-intensity lamp. Storage includes a wide, shallow drawer under the work area for holding plans, plus a stack of pedestal drawers, five for hand tools and drafting equipment and a sixth, deeper drawer for power tools or files.

A piece of ¼-inch tempered hardboard, held on the plywood top with contact cement, gives a smooth, durable work surface. The curved desk edge—in this case designed for a right-handed person—gives support for the elbow.

The desk frame is made of ¾-inch plywood, assembled with glue and finishing nails. The sides and back are joined with simple butt joints; the top fits into ⅜-inch-deep dadoes routed in the sides and back. The inside wall of the drawer

pedestal fits into ⅜-inch-deep dadoes on the underside of the top and on the back.

The drawers, built of ½-inch plywood with ¼-inch plywood bottoms, fit together as shown on page 118. However, the bottom edge of each drawer front extends ¾ inch below the drawer sides, and acts as a stop against the runners. The runners, of ¾-by-¾-inch pine, are set back ½ inch from the front of the frame so the closed drawers are flush with the frame.

Preparing the desk top. After gluing the ¼-inch tempered hardboard to the plywood top, outline a 2-by-4-inch rectangle for an electrical outlet in one corner of the top. Drill a ⅜-inch hole just inside each corner of the rectangle and, with a saber saw, cut out the rectangle, using the hole at each corner to turn the saw blade.

To cut the recessed front, draw a line 3 inches in from the front edge, starting from the left corner *(inset)*, and extending 23 inches across the front. Then draw a perpendicular line through this point, forming a 3-by-23-inch rectangle. To form the S curve, set the point of a compass 1½ inches to the left of the mid-point of the end of the rectangle, and scribe an arc with a radius of 1½ inches; repeat the process, centering the compass 1½ inches to the right of the mid-point *(inset)*. Cut along the touching arcs with a saber saw, then continue the straight cut for the recessed front. Assemble the bench, using the joining techniques specified opposite, below.

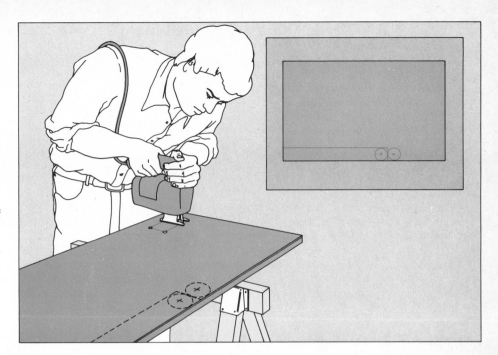

A Bench Combined with a Drafting Table

Modifying the basic design. This bench is identical with the one shown opposite, except that the parapet around the top is raised to 8 inches along the back, and the sides slope from 8 inches at the back to 2 inches at the front. The left side panel must be extended to match the width of the right side panel, to support the drafting top at the proper angle.

A rectangular piece of ¾-inch hardwood plywood—blemish-free on the top side—is hinged to the back of the bench, closing to protect work stored below and serving as a slanted drafting surface; its dimensions are ¾ inch greater than those of the bench top prior to cutting the recessed front. The back edge of this folding top and the top edge of the desk back are both beveled at a slight angle to allow the top to close completely; the top is attached to the bench with 3-inch butt hinges *(inset)*. For stability, the hinges are screwed onto the face of the plywood rather than onto its edge, which is weaker. A length of 1-inch molding nailed to the front edge of the drafting table acts as a lip for pencils, and a piece of cork glued to the underside of the top allows this area to be used as a bulletin board when the top of the table is open.

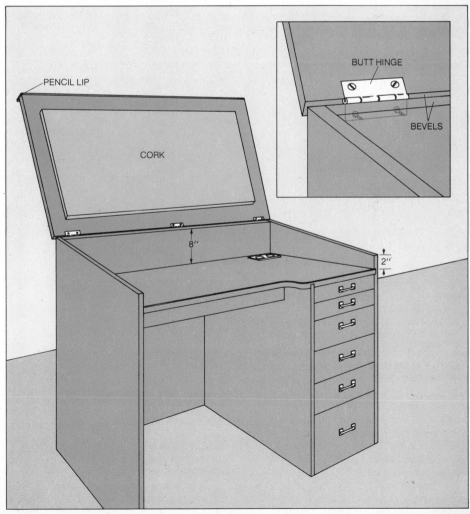

A Booth for Spray Painting

A spray-painting booth may seem a luxurious addition to a home workshop, but in fact it is very useful, providing a controlled environment for many sorts of jobs. It is ideal for painting objects that are hard to paint with a brush—such as shutters, grillwork and wicker furniture. You can also use the booth for applying mothproofing, waterproofing or other protective solutions to fabrics, and for spraying wax on furniture or pesticides on house plants. A properly constructed spray booth guards against the potential dangers of fire and poisoning that always accompany work with flammable or toxic substances, making the jobs safer as well as cleaner and faster.

The basic design for any booth is an open-ended rectangle equipped with a powerful, specially designed exhaust fan at the inner end. The fan draws fumes through a filter and ejects them outside; the filter traps drifting spray. The size of the booth and the fan may vary but they should always be at least 20 feet away from any open flame such as a furnace,

the pilot light of a water heater or, of course, a cigarette. The exhaust fan must be vented through an exterior wall, with no buildings, bushes or other barriers on the outside closer than 6 feet.

The exhaust fan and its filter—both available from manufacturers listed in classified directories under "Spraying Equipment," "Filters, Air and Gas" or "Fans, Industrial and Commercial"—are the most important components of the booth. To avoid the risk of explosion from electrical sparks in the fan motor, choose a fan designed especially for spray booths, with a motor and drive belt shielded from the air passing through the fan duct. An opening in the vent wall is fitted with a special paint-arrester filter. To connect the square filter to the round fan, you will need a round-to-square adapter duct, which you can order from a sheet-metal shop once you know the dimensions of the filter and the fan casing.

When using the booth, wear a face-mask respirator—get the heavy-duty type with activated-charcoal filters.

Anatomy of a spray booth. This spray booth consists of an L-shaped partition that isolates an open-ended spraying area in one corner of a room. The short back wall of the assembly, the vent wall, is offset from the nearby existing wall and from the window where the exhaust fan is mounted, to isolate the fan motor from the booth (inset). The fan pulls air through the booth and through a filter, carrying fumes outdoors and trapping drifting spray. The 2-by-4 partition walls and the ceiling inside the booth are covered with fire-retardant wallboard.

Explosion-proof bulbs guarded by wire baskets provide overhead lighting in the booth, and all electrical switches are mounted outside the booth. During the spray operation, the air compressor and any extra hose are kept outside the booth. In the center of the booth a piece of 1-inch-thick plywood mounted on casters serves as a revolving platform so the worker can always stay upwind of the spraying.

When an existing window is not conveniently located, an opening can be cut in the exterior wall for the exhaust fan. If you cannot put the booth in a corner of the room, build a U-shaped rather than an L-shaped partition to isolate the work area from the rest of the room.

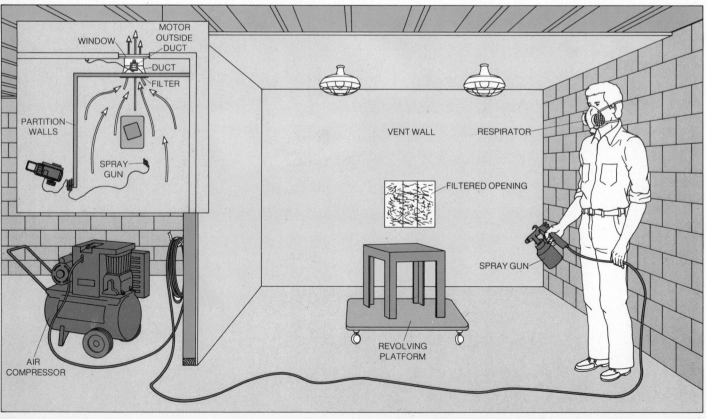

SASH

MOUNTING BLOCK

WINDOW STOOL

ADAPTER DUCT

MOUNTING FLANGE

FAN CASING

MOTOR

Building the Spray Booth

1 **Installing the exhaust fan.** Place the fan casing, flange side down, against a backer board of ¾-inch plywood cut to fit the window opening and with a casing hole in the center. To cut the casing hole, use a saber saw. Position the casing against the board so that the fan motor will be at the top, and mark for the screw holes. Then drill holes and screw the casing to the board.

To secure the fan to an opened double-hung window, as here, first nail a 2-by-4 mounting block atop the window sill, setting the block against the outside edge of the window stool. Then screw the backer board to the mounting block and to the raised window sash. Install fan shutters outside the window to keep out cold air and rain. (This fan will not fit into the frame of a basement-type awning window.)

When the fan is securely mounted, insert the round end of the custom-made round-to-square duct adapter into the fan casing.

2 **Planning the partition walls.** With the fan assembly in place in the window, drop a plumb bob from one side of the adapter duct to the floor, holding the plumb line 2 inches in from the front edge of the duct. Mark the point where the plumb bob reaches the floor. Repeat on the other side of the duct, and draw a line across the floor, connecting the two points. Then extend the line the desired length of the vent wall. Checking with a steel square, draw a second line perpendicular to the first, to mark the position of the side partition wall.

Cut two 2-by-4s the length of the vent wall, to serve as top and sole (bottom) plates of the wall. Lay them side by side along the marked floor line. With a steel square, and using the two original plumb-bob marks as reference points, mark the positions for two 2-by-4 studs to frame the fan duct *(inset)*. Then, starting at one end of the plates, mark off additional stud positions at 16-inch intervals, skipping the space between the two studs that will frame the duct.

Cut a pair of plates to length for the second wall, positioning them so their ends lie flush with the outside edge of the vent wall. Mark stud positions at 16-inch intervals along them. Then cut 2-by-4 studs for both the vent and side walls; for the stud height, measure the floor-to-ceiling height and subtract 3 inches.

PLUMB-BOB MARK

3 **Assembling the partition walls.** Set the top plate of the vent wall on edge on the floor and nail studs to it at the marked positions, using 16-penny nails, two nails per stud. Then nail the sole plate of the vent wall to the floor, placing its outer edge flush with the marked line. (If the floor is concrete, use masonry nails.) Have helpers raise the top-plate-and-stud assembly into position against the ceiling and hold it there while you nail the top plate to the ceiling joists and toenail the bottoms of the studs to the marked positions on the sole plate. Check with a level as you go, to keep the wall plumb.

Assemble the side partition wall in the same way, but before installing it, reinforce it at the end where the two walls will join. Nail a second stud to that end of the side-wall frame, inside the end stud and separated from it by 2-by-4 nailing blocks nailed to the inside face of the end stud, at the top, middle and bottom (*inset*). Nail the second stud to the blocks. When the side wall is in place, reinforce the corner by nailing the end stud of the vent wall to the nailing blocks in the corner assembly of the side wall.

SOLE PLATE

TOP PLATE

SECOND STUD

NAILING BLOCK

END STUD

4 **Finishing the booth.** Cut two 2-by-4s to frame the top and bottom of the fan duct, and nail them into place between two studs that you have added to frame the sides of the duct. Punch holes through the edges of the duct with an awl, and fasten the duct to the frame with wood screws.

Install fire-retardant wallboard on the inside of partition walls and over any other potentially flammable surface, such as exposed ceiling joists. Caulk the joints between wallboard panels to make them airtight, but do not bother to finish the walls since paint will soon splatter them. .

To install the fan's filter assembly (*inset*), first screw the metal frame for the filter into the opening in the vent wall; install it flush with the inside edges of the framing studs. Then snap the filter grid into the filter frame, insert the filter material and snap in the two retainer rods that hold the filter material in place.

FILTER FRAME

RETAINER RODS

FILTER GRID

FILTER

A Space-efficient Tool Turret

Turntables have been used for years in homes and industry to increase the accessibility of work and storage areas. Here, a round platform 3 feet in diameter is mounted on a turntable to transform a bench corner into a work center and storage site for three small power tools—a grinder, a drill stand holding a portable electric drill, and a jig saw. Other tools may be substituted, if they can be used in restricted quarters and their weight is evenly distributed around the platform. The turntable can be locked in any of three positions with a wood dowel set into a hole drilled through the platform and partway into the workbench below; a nearby outlet supplies electric power.

The turntable top is made of ¾-inch plywood outlined with a nail-and-string compass, then cut with a saber saw. This top is attached to a heavy-duty Lazy Susan mounting made to carry a tool load of up to 1,000 pounds. The mounting, available at hardware stores, consists of two interlocking and inseparable disks sandwiching a ring of ball bearings.

Such a Lazy Susan arrangement is most useful when it is positioned in the corner of either an L-shaped bench or a counter built against adjoining walls.

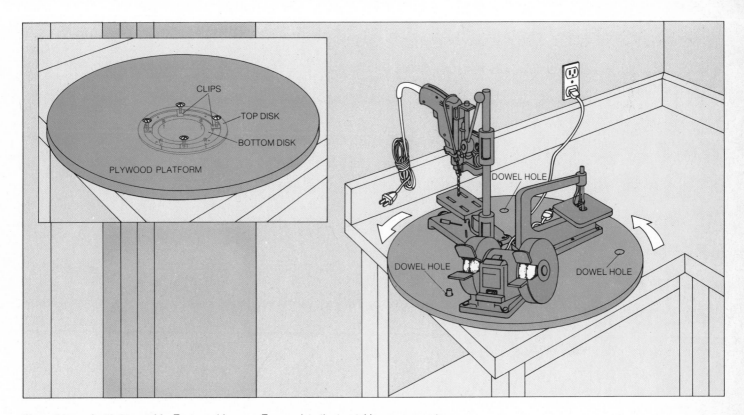

The makings of a tool turntable. To assemble this turntable, turn the plywood platform upside down, mark through the holes in the top disk of the mounting, then drill at these marks through the plywood. Fasten the bottom disk of the mounting to the workbench with wood screws. Set the plywood atop the mounting, countersink the holes in the plywood's top surface and thread flathead stove bolts through the holes to engage speed nuts—clips that act as nuts for the bolts (*inset*). Smaller mountings for a light-duty turntable require no speed nuts, and may be assembled with sheet-metal screws instead.

To complete the turntable, use screws to mount the tools where you want them. Set one tool into its position, then drill a ½-inch hole near the edge of the platform, through the plywood and into the workbench. Check with a ½-inch dowel to make sure the two holes align, sanding the dowel lightly for an easy fit. Then rotate the table to another tool, measure in from the plywood edge and drill a second hole in the plywood. Drill a third hole near the third tool. Cut the dowel so that when it is lowered all the way into any of the three turntable holes, you will be able to grip and remove it with your fingers.

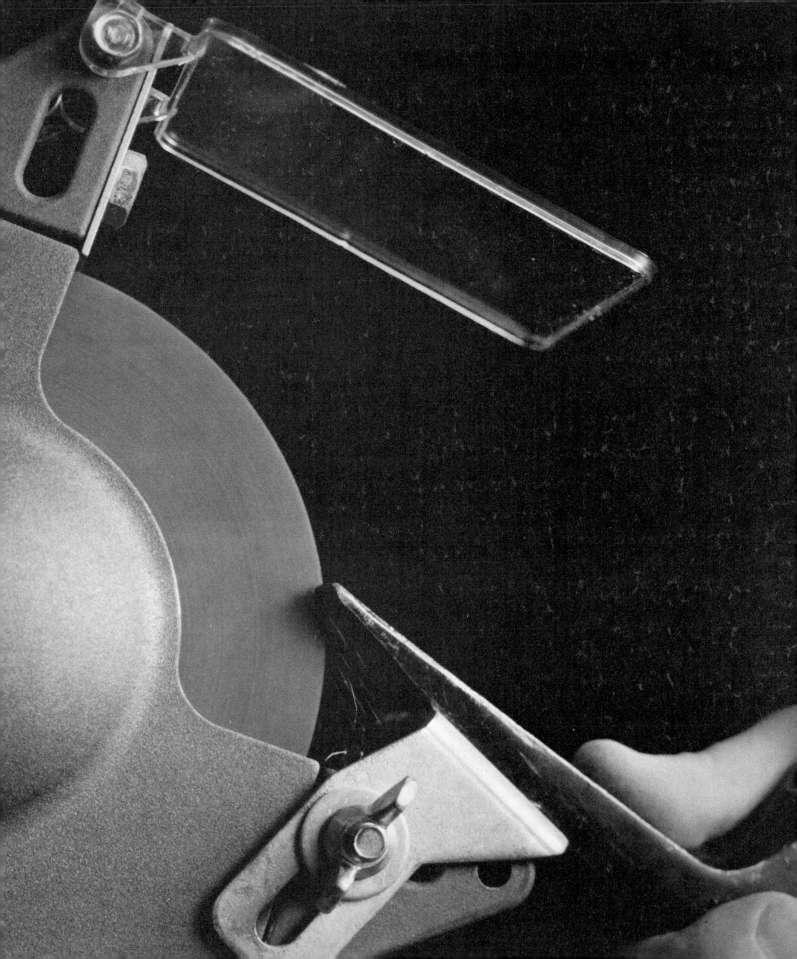

4 A Place where Neatness Counts

Rejuvenating an old edge. Whirling at a speed of 3,000 revolutions per minute, the wheel of a bench grinder removes nicks from the blade end of a bricklayer's hammer. A basic aid to the care of tools such as chisels and planes, the bench grinder does in seconds a job that would take long, patient hours of hand grinding.

In 1645 the colony of Virginia enacted a law prohibiting overzealous carpenters from burning down old buildings just to "gett the nailes." For modern home carpenters the problem lies not in acquiring nails but in finding a place to keep them: Any workshop worthy of the name accumulates all kinds of things, sometimes at an alarming rate. Many of these items—scrap lumber, leftover hardware, spare tool parts—are ultimately useful and, if neatly stored, broaden the range of home-repair possibilities. Who has not blessed the empty coffee can, and its cousins, the wide-mouthed peanut-butter jar, the diminutive baby-food jar and the cigar box, as agencies for dividing and conquering armies of odd hinges, brackets, washers, eye screws and the like? No one who has sorted through 20 pounds of miscellaneous hardware in search of a nut to match a bolt will scoff at the wisdom of having a storage system, however humble, that keeps like objects together and different objects apart.

With larger items, such as tools, good housekeeping in the workshop involves maintenance as well as storage, and often the two are one. Rust, for example, is a constant threat to tools. It is best to deal with rust before it appears, and preventing rust is as much a matter of good maintenance as of proper storage. Tools prone to rust should be kept in a moisture-free atmosphere, but they must also be periodically oiled or waxed to protect their metal surfaces.

Other forms of tool maintenance are concerned with problems that arise after the fact—with cleaning up and correcting damage after it is done. By keeping cutting tools sharp with regular touch-ups to blades and teeth, you will save the cost and down time involved in sending them out for professional sharpening. And, of course, regular cleaning improves their performance.

Two of the most common substances affecting the performance of saws, for example, are resin and pitch, for which one standard solvent is kerosene. In the 19th Century, kerosene was a great favorite of loggers, who used it lavishly. The loggers kept their kerosene in empty whiskey bottles, which they discarded when the kerosene was gone, thus requiring the logging company to order more whiskey in order to replenish the bottle supply.

Finally, there is the problem of keeping the entire workshop clean. Compared to the 150,000 pounds of sawdust produced by the average sawmill in the course of a day, the fine layer of sawdust that collects around a table saw may seem negligible. But the task of clearing it away is handled most effectively by a scaled-down version of the same central vacuum system used in a sawmill. Such a system, described on page 132, makes light, quick work of a messy job that once had to be done with dustpan and brush.

Tool Storage: Everything in Its Designated Spot

All it takes to understand the importance of efficient tool storage is the experience of reaching for a tool at a crucial point in a project, only to find that the tool is missing, out of reach or damaged. Storing tools where they are likely to be needed and under conditions where they will remain in good working order is essential for smooth shop operations. Beyond that, a carefully planned system allows you to make the most creative use of the space in your particular shop.

Generally, the best storage system uses every nook and cranny, for the one common denominator of most home workshops is that space is at a premium. The best systems also draw upon a variety of storage devices—pegboard (perforated tempered hardboard), tool racks, shelves, drawers and cabinets. Of these, the most popular is probably pegboard, especially the tempered grade with a glassy, mar-resistant surface. It transforms fragments of space above a workbench, inside a door or against the side of a table into efficient storage areas. Available in thick-

nesses of ⅛ or ¼ inch, pegboard can be fitted in an instant with any of more than 200 different varieties of metal and plastic hangers.

Practically anything can be hung on a sheet of pegboard if the pegboard is mounted with at least ½ inch of space behind it, to accommodate the hangers. The ⅛-inch thickness will hold small hand tools such as screwdrivers, pliers and small wrenches, while the ¼-inch thickness will support such weightier tools as routers and electric drills.

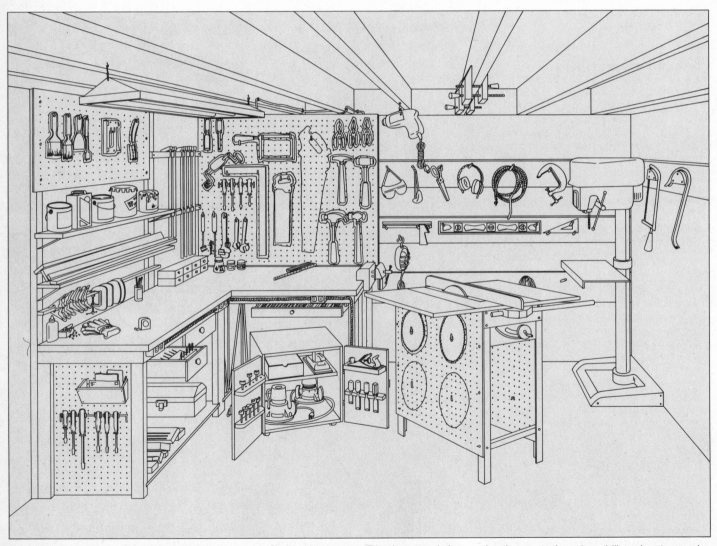

Storing tools efficiently. This well-stocked workshop combines several of the most useful tool-storage techniques. Hand tools and saw blades are stored on pegboard above the workbench and along the sides of the workbench and table saw. Shallow drawers conveniently suspended beneath the workbench provide accessible, dry, dust-free storage for drill bits, files and other small hand tools. A movable cabinet on casters— with tool racks mounted on its doors—stores hand power tools such as drills and routers, and provides a convenient extra work surface. Bar clamps hang in a notched rack against the wall, while spring clamps and C clamps are fastened onto a wooden cleat just above the workbench.

However, this is not the only solution to tool storage, and it may not be the best for you. Ordinary eightpenny finishing nails driven into a sheet of plywood will often do the job as well and at less cost—the hangers for pegboard are not inexpensive. And for gentle, mar-free storage of especially fine tools, dowel pegs inserted in holes that have been drilled at an angle in a plywood backing are even more desirable.

There are also tools that do not lend themselves to hanging. Planes, for example, are best stored on their sides in a drawer. If a plane must be stored bottom down, the blade should be retracted after each use, for its own protection—and a piece of felt provided for it to rest on in case you forget.

Some small tools are handier if they are stored in shallow drawers hung on runners directly beneath the work surface; drill bits, hex wrenches and small screwdrivers are typical examples. If you build the drawers, you can divide them into compartments tailored to the size of their intended contents. Or you can use the type of molded-plastic tray sold to hold tableware. Another alternative for small tools is the rack you build with holes or cleats fitted to the shapes of the tools in your collection. And for certain tools—those that are heavy, dangerous or valuable—a shelved cabinet that can be locked is desirable.

The most versatile enclosed storage is a simple cabinet with adjustable shelves mounted on casters that let you roll it from one work area to another. It can be built inexpensively from ¾-inch pine or interior-grade plywood *(page 120)*. Because you will frequently want to roll the cabinet out of the way, perhaps under a table, its height should be tailored to that purpose. For the same reason, allow 2 to 3 inches of toe space at the bottom of the cabinet so you can tuck your feet beneath it when you stand against it.

Perforated Panels for Quick Storage

Attaching pegboard. In this typical installation, 1-by-2 furring strips hold the pegboard ¾ inch from the wall to allow space for the backs of the hangers. The furring strips are nailed to studs in the wall with sixpenny common nails, and pilot holes are drilled through the pegboard and furring strips at 6-inch intervals for the roundhead wood screws and washers that fasten the board to the strips.

If you are attaching pegboard to a cinder-block wall, use masonry nails and high-bonding construction glue to fasten the furring strips to the blocks. Then attach the pegboard as above.

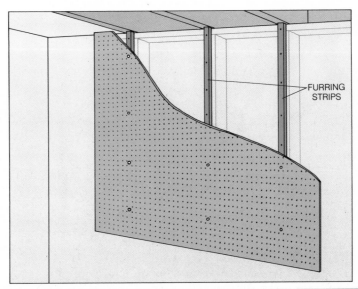

FURRING STRIPS

Hangers for pegboard. Store-bought hangers for pegboard come in a vast array of shapes, some specialized, some multipurpose. In the latter category, able to hold several different types of tools, is the standard U hook, suitable for hand tools that have straps, holes or loop-shaped handles. When you buy U hooks—or other hangers of similar shapes—get the type that has an extra tip on the back that fits into a second hole in the pegboard to keep the hook from swiveling or coming loose when a tool is removed *(inset)*.

Double hangers are used for hammers, mallets and other wide-headed tools, while multiple hangers with double rows of loops hold tools of graduated sizes such as screwdrivers and pliers. The extended arm of the single-loop hanger is convenient for supporting a hand drill, clamp, level or hand saw. Clamping holders offer especially firm support for chisels and other tools with round handles, and a flat-bottomed tool such as a sharpening stone can rest on a plate hanger, a small metal shelf that is cantilevered from the surface of the pegboard.

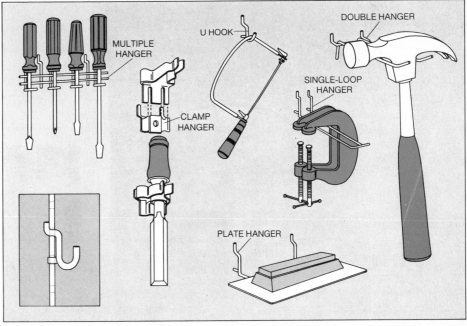

MULTIPLE HANGER

U HOOK

DOUBLE HANGER

CLAMP HANGER

SINGLE-LOOP HANGER

PLATE HANGER

A Tool Drawer Hung Underneath a Worktable

Planning the drawer. The front, back and sides of the drawer are cut from a 1-by-4 board, and the bottom from ¼-inch hardboard or plywood. The back piece is ¾ inch shorter than the front, to allow the back piece to fit into dadoes in both sides. Vertical rabbets are cut ¾ inch wide and 9/16 inch deep into both ends of the front to accommodate the sides, and dadoes of the same width and ⅜ inch deep are cut into each side, ½ inch from the end, to hold the back. The dadoes for the bottom are cut while the 1-by-4 is still in one piece; they are ⅜ inch in from the edge of the board, ¼ inch wide and ⅜ inch deep. The bottom is ⅝ inch longer and wider than the insides of the drawer.

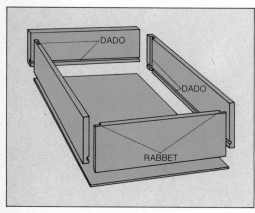

1 **Cutting the dadoes and rabbets.** Mark two guidelines for the bottom dado ⅜ and ⅝ inch from the edge of the 1-by-4 intended for the front, back and sides of the drawer. Butt a second piece of 1-inch lumber against the first, on the guideline edge, and clamp both boards in place. Center the router, fitted with a ¼-inch bit, between the guidelines and outline the curved edge of the router on both ends of the second board. Place a third board against the two curves and clamp it in place. Using the third board as a guide for the router, cut a ⅜-inch-deep dado the length of the first board.

Cut the dadoed board into four pieces as shown (*inset*). Then, using a ¾-inch router bit (or making two passes with a ⅜-inch bit if your router does not take a ¾-inch bit), cut the other rabbets and dadoes into the front and sides, using the method described above.

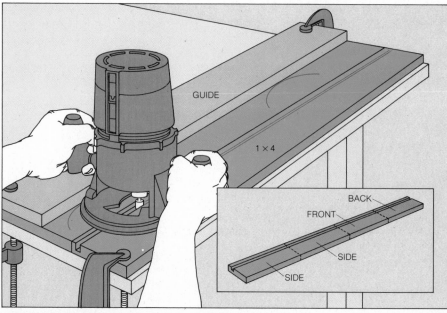

2 **Assembling the drawer sections.** Spread wood glue in the vertical dadoes in the sidepieces and set the back of the drawer into them, clamping it securely with a bar clamp. Place the drawer front over the sides without gluing it and measure the inside dimensions of the drawer, side to side and front to back. Then cut the drawer bottom ⅝ inch longer and wider than the inside measurements. Set the drawer on its back and slide the bottom into the horizontal dadoes made to hold it; do not glue the bottom in place.

Finally, spread glue in the rabbets in the drawer front, position it over the bottom and sides, and clamp it in place. To strengthen the back joints, drive fourpenny finishing nails at an angle through each side and into the back, spacing them about 2 inches apart.

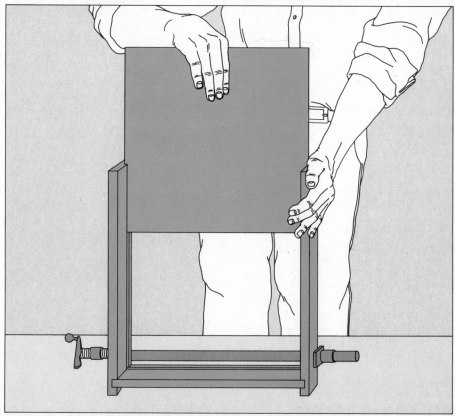

3 **Doweling the drawer front.** Using a ¼-inch bit, drill two holes at a slight angle through both sides into the rabbeted front, positioning the centers of the holes about ½ inch from the top and bottom edge of the drawer front and ½ inch in from the front edge. Make each hole the same depth, about 1¼ inch, by wrapping a piece of tape around the bit at that point; stop drilling when the tape touches the wood.

Cut four pieces of ¼-inch doweling about 1½ inches long, place glue in the holes and hammer the dowels in. Cut off the ends of the dowels with a backsaw or dovetail saw and then sand the dowels flush with the sides of the drawer.

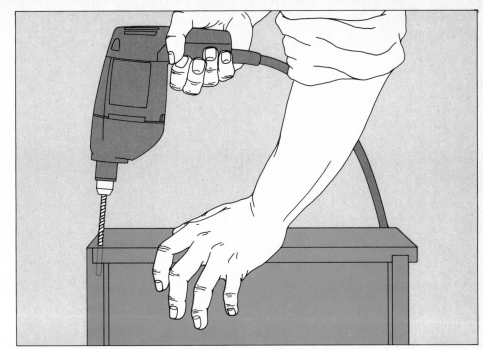

4 **Cutting the drawer guides.** Cut a pair of 2-inch-by-2-inch guides just a bit longer than the depth of the drawer and, with a table saw or circular saw, make two cuts down the length of each guide, thus removing a strip of wood about ⅝ inch square. Cut both pieces to the exact length of the drawer sides; use the square strip to make runners on the drawer, and use the remaining L-shaped strip to make tracks to mount on the underside of your work surface.

Fasten both runners flush against the top edges of the drawer with glue and 1-inch brads (*inset*). Sand the adjoining surfaces of the runners and tracks, so the drawer will slide smoothly.

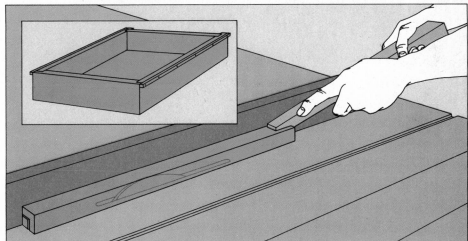

5 **Suspending the drawer from the table.** Drill and countersink screw holes at about 5-inch intervals through one leg of the L-shaped tracks and, with the drawer clamped in position under the table, slide the tracks over the runners. Mark and drill starter holes into the underside of the table through the countersunk holes. Secure the tracks to the table with flathead wood screws; be sure the screws do not penetrate the tabletop.

Screw a small block of scrap wood against the back of each guide to stop the travel of the drawer. Lubricate the guides with wax.

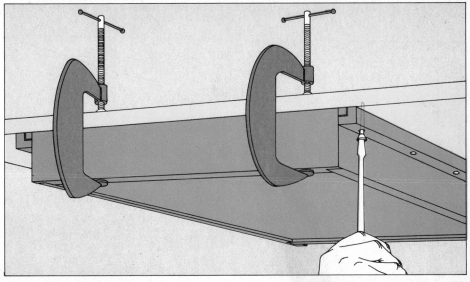

A Roll-around Tool Cabinet Built of Plywood

Planning the cabinet. Determine the dimensions of a cabinet that best suits your needs and, following the example at right, make your own sketch of its parts. The sides, top, bottom and doors of this cabinet are all made of ¾-inch interior-grade fir plywood; the back is of ¼-inch plywood or hardboard.

The top is ¾ inch shorter than the overall width of the cabinet and drops into rabbets cut in the sides. The bottom, cut to the same dimensions as the top, fits into dadoes about 2 inches above the bottom of the cabinet, allowing for toe space. (Be sure to measure the height of the casters before planning the toe space.) The back fits squarely against the top, sides and bottom. Bracket pins to hold shelves fit into holes drilled in the sides, and the two doors are hinged to the cabinet sides with offset hinges. Magnetic catches keep the doors closed. The cabinet rides on swiveling casters.

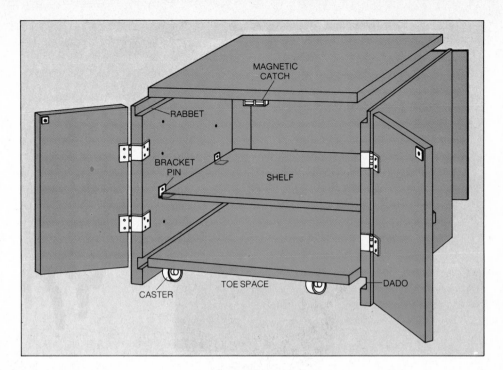

Assembling the Movable Storage Cabinet

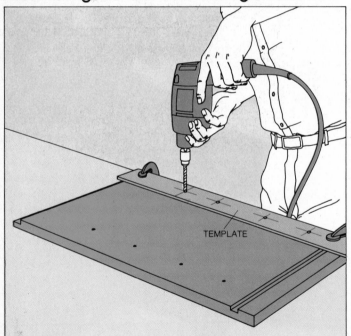

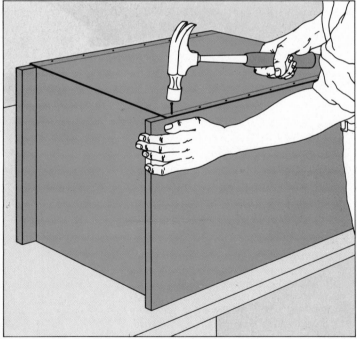

1 **Preparing cabinet parts for assembly.** Cut ¾-inch plywood into parts of the dimensions you have established, then cut rabbet and dado grooves *(page 118)* into the cabinet sides. Drill parallel rows of holes down both sides for shelf brackets, positioning the holes at least 1 inch in from the edges and spacing them at whatever distance apart you desire. Use a predrilled template to align the hole locations. Wrap a piece of tape around the drill bit to control the depth of the holes, which should be about ⅝ inch.

2 **Assembling cabinet parts.** Glue, clamp and nail together the top, bottom and sides *(page 118)*; use finishing nails on all joints. Then attach the back with glue and finishing nails.

Measure the width of your cabinet and the height from the lower edge of the bottom piece to the top and cut a piece of ¾-inch plywood to size for your doors. Cut the piece of plywood in half lengthwise—the kerf removed by the saw blade will assure enough space between the doors.

3 **Hinging the doors to the cabinet.** Prepare mortises for two ¾-inch offset hinges on the inside of the doors *(right, top)* by outlining the hinges, placing them about 3 inches from the tops and bottoms of the doors and avoiding shelf locations. Cut around each outline with a mallet and woodworking chisel to the depth of the hinge leaf. Then hold the chisel beveled side down and, in a series of small, shallow cuts, shave the recess to the exact thickness of the hinge.

Fasten the hinges into the recesses with the screws provided, first marking the screw positions with an awl. Then hold the doors flush against the cabinet sides, and mark the positions for the other leaf of the hinges on the cabinet. In the front edge of the cabinet, cut recesses for the hinges. Then mark and drill screw holes and fasten the inside leaves of the hinges to the cabinet *(right, bottom)*. Attach magnetic catches to the inside top corners of the doors and to matching positions under the cabinet top, to hold the doors of the cabinet closed.

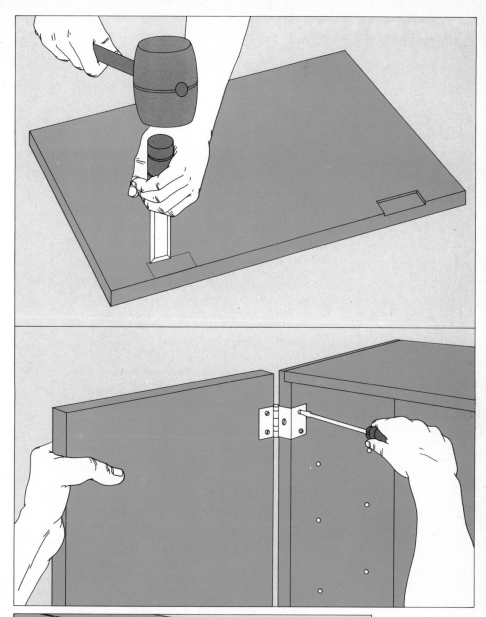

4 **Finishing the cabinet.** Screw four swivel-type plate casters to the bottom of the cabinet with the screws provided, placing them far enough in from the corners so they will not bump against the cabinet sides when they rotate. Use plastic casters for loads up to 35 pounds and metal casters for heavier loads; if you intend to use the cabinet as a work surface, use locking casters so the cabinet can be immobilized.

Cut shelves for the cabinet ⅛ inch shorter than the inside dimensions, to allow for an easy fit. Insert bracket pins in the holes provided for them and insert the shelves.

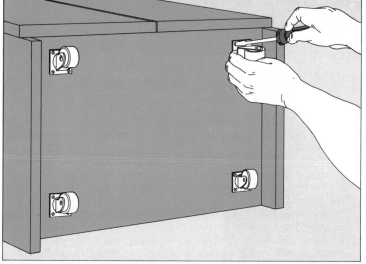

Tailored Storage Spaces for All That Miscellany

Every home workshop, no matter how well organized its tool-storage system, fights a constant battle against encroaching chaos. Bits and pieces of hardware, half-used cans of paint and varnish, leftover scraps of lumber inevitably accumulate, too valuable to throw away, yet threatening to create hopeless clutter. To find storage space for these miscellaneous materials, you may have to make appropriate accommodations in the shop layout to fit the focus of the work done there. You must also take into account the ever-changing inventory of materials that accompany various current projects. Nevertheless, though the number of possible storage systems is infinite, a few general rules apply.

The most convenient way to store coils of rope and electrical cables, for example, is to hang them on the wall. Lumber—both leftover scraps and reserve stock—can be stored on racks that keep it off the floor, neatly out of the way but still readily accessible. The best racks are firmly anchored to wall studs or ceiling joists; freestanding racks take up valuable open space and tip too readily. Plan the placement of lumber racks to suit the size of their contents. Large, heavy boards, for example, should be stored on racks against the wall and near the floor, where you can reach them without having to lift them down from overhead.

For almost all other shop materials, drawers and shelves are the preferred catchalls. They are especially useful for storing hardware, which accumulates at an alarming rate and must be sorted and stored in an assemblage of separate containers ranging in size from baby-food jars to coffee cans. (The contents of the jars, of course, will be easily visible; you should identify the cans with large, legible labels.) These myriad containers are easier to keep track of and are less apt to break or spill if they are an-

chored to shelves or collected in drawers.

Drawers can also be subdivided into small compartments for a variety of small parts. In deep drawers, you can make the maximum use of space by installing a shallow compartmentalized tray that slides back and forth in the upper half of the drawer, leaving the lower half of the drawer for larger objects. For maximum use of space in the workshop, you can suspend drawers from the underside of an existing work surface (page 119).

Shelves can also be fitted to the available space in a variety of configurations. You can install a single long shelf on L-shaped metal braces over a workbench or cover an entire wall with a network of

similarly mounted shelves. On interior partition walls that contain no insulation, you can remove a section of wallboard and install narrow shelves between the studs, making the shelves either stationary or, with the use of metal standards and shelf clips, adjustable in height.

The distance between shelves as well as the depth of the shelves themselves will depend on the materials to be stored. As a general rule there should be at least 2 inches of clearance between the tallest object and the shelf above. Ideally a shelf should hold only a single row of containers, so that all labels are visible. Remember that a gallon paint can will need a shelf 7 inches deep.

Shelves Mounted on Braces

1 Positioning shelf braces. On a stud wall, mark the center of every other stud at the desired height along the proposed shelf span. Center a brace just below the last mark at one end of the span and, with a level, plumb its vertical arm. Outline the screw holes, drill pilot holes at the marks and screw the brace to the wall.

Cut a shelf from 1-inch lumber or ¾-inch plywood; the shelf can extend beyond the arm of the brace by one third of the arm's length. Allow a 4- to 6-inch overlap past each end brace. Hold the shelf against the wall, resting one end on the installed brace, and transfer the marked intervals to the underside of the shelf; use a combination square to extend the lines across the shelf. For a shelf on a masonry wall, cut the shelf to fit and fasten braces at 32-inch intervals to its underside.

2 Fastening braces under the shelf. Skipping the line that corresponds to the brace already fastened to the wall, center braces over the remaining marked lines, squaring them at the back edge of the shelf by butting them against a combination square. Mark the screw-hole locations, drill pilot holes and fasten the braces to the shelf with ½-inch wood screws.

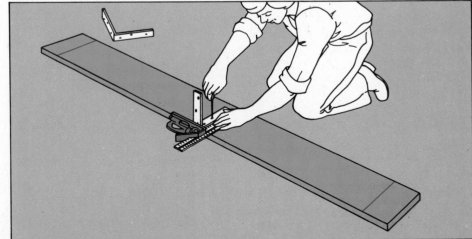

3 **Leveling and fastening the shelf.** On a stud wall, have a helper hold one end of the shelf steady over the brace that is already on the wall while you match the remaining braces with their corresponding wall marks. Check to make sure the shelf is level, then mark the screw-hole locations for each brace. Remove the shelf, drill pilot holes at the marks, put the shelf back in place and drive wood screws through the braces and into the studs. Then screw the first brace to the underside of the shelf.

On a masonry wall, have a helper hold the shelf and its attached braces level at the proposed height while you mark the screw-hole locations. Drill holes at the marks with a masonry bit and secure the shelf to the wall with bolts driven into expansion shields inserted in the holes.

Building Shelves Between Wall Studs

SOLE PLATE

1 **Backing the shelf area with hardboard.** Remove a section of wallboard from an interior partition wall to expose its studs, then cut a panel of ¼-inch hardboard to fit into each recessed area between studs. Remove any horizontal fire stops in the exposed area. Spread mastic adhesive on the back of each panel and, while a helper steadies the wallboard on the far side of the wall, gently press each panel into place, to provide protection for the far wall.

2 **Marking shelf heights.** At each proposed shelf position, hold a carpenter's level across two adjacent studs and draw level lines across the front edges. Cut two vertical 1-by-4 supports for each shelf in the lowest row, matching their height to the distance from the top of the sole plate to the first shelf level. Then cut shelves to fit between the studs at each level; generally this distance is 14½ inches. Use 1-by-4 or 1-by-6 lumber, depending on the shelf width desired.

3 **Nailing in supports and shelves.** Rest the first row of shelf supports on the sole plate, flat against the inside faces of the studs, and nail them in place. Lay the first row of shelves across their supports and drive two nails down through each shelf into the support below.

Cut the next set of supports to fit between the top of the first level of shelves and the marks for the second level. Install these supports and their shelves, as above. Continue in this fashion, alternately installing supports and shelves, until the shelf sections are complete.

Shelving on Masonry Walls

1 **Installing the frame.** In a room with exposed ceiling joists, lay a pressure-treated 2-by-6 baseboard flat on the floor against the wall, shim it level, and nail it to the floor. If the joists run perpendicular to the shelves, position the baseboard so the ends fall directly beneath joists. Cut 2-by-6 vertical supports to fit between the baseboard and every other joist, making the supports overlap the joists by at least 6 inches. Fasten the top end of each support to its joist with three eightpenny nails. Hold each support plumb and toenail the bottom to the baseboard.

If the joists run parallel to the shelves, toenail 2-by-6 blocking between the joists at 32-inch intervals *(inset)*. Line up the baseboard with the blocking and nail the vertical supports to the blocking and the baseboard.

In a room with concealed ceiling joists, build the shelf framing as you would a partition wall *(pages 111-112, Steps 2 and 3),* but use 2-by-6s and space the vertical members 72 inches apart.

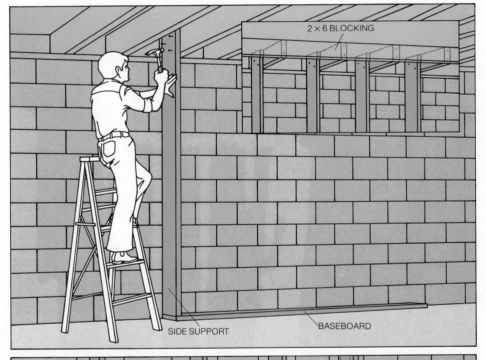

2 **Installing standards to hold shelves.** Mark the inside faces of the first and last vertical supports with pencil lines, top and bottom, 1 inch in from the front and back edges. Then mark both faces of each subsequent support, top and bottom, but, to prevent the screws from hitting each other, stagger the marks on opposite faces of each support. Make them 1 inch from the front edge and 1½ inches from the back edge on one side, and 1 inch from the back edge and 1½ inches from the front edge on the other side. Set metal shelf standards just inside each pair of top-and-bottom marks, with the bottoms of the standards resting on the baseboard. Drill pilot holes and drive the screws.

Snap shelf clips into the standards *(inset);* then use 1-by-6 lumber to make shelves that lie on the standards, flush with the supports.

Anchoring Containers on and under Shelves

Using jar lids as hanging fixtures. Plot a series of circles on the underside of a shelf, using a jar lid as a pattern and leaving about 2 inches between circles; if you plan to install two rows of jars, stagger the positions of the circles so all the jars will be visible. Punch two holes through each jar lid with an awl, then drive a roundhead screw through each hole to fasten the tops in the outlined circles. Install the shelf and screw the jars into their lids.

Create a protective guardrail for the objects that are stored on top of the shelf by nailing a 1-by-2 lip to the front edge of the shelf *(inset)*.

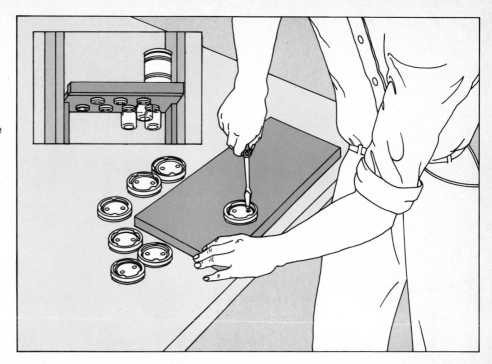

Egg-Crate Compartments to Organize a Drawer

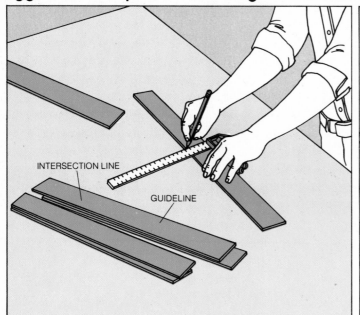

INTERSECTION LINE

GUIDELINE

1 Cutting and marking divider strips. After planning the size and number of drawer compartments needed, cut two sets of divider strips from ⅛-inch hardboard, one set for each dimension. Make each strip ½ inch narrower than the height of the drawer, and ⅛ inch shorter than the drawer dimension it must span. Draw a guideline ¼ inch off-center down the length of one strip from each set, then use a combination square to mark intersection lines perpendicular to the guideline across the wider portion of the strip, at each point of intersection.

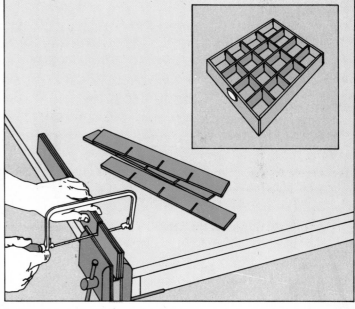

2 Cutting slots in the divider strips. Stack together each set of parallel divider strips, with the marked strip on top. Clamp a set of strips on edge in a vise, then use a coping saw to make a pair of cuts at each intersection line; space the cuts ⅛ inch apart, one on each side of every intersection line. Push out the waste wood from between each pair of cuts on each strip. Assemble the strips by sliding the slots in one set over the slots in the other. Place the assembled divider unit in the drawer *(inset)*.

A Sliding Tray that Fits in a Drawer

1 Assembling the tray. Cut four lengths of ¼-inch plywood for the sides of the tray, making them half as wide as the inside height of the drawer. Cut the front and back pieces ⅛ inch shorter than the width of the drawer, and the side pieces half the depth of the drawer from front to back. Butt-nail the plywood pieces together with brads so the pieces form a rectangular frame. Then cut a base from ⅛-inch hardboard to fit over the frame and glue and nail it to the bottom edges of the four sides. Make egg-crate dividers for the tray (*page 125*).

A Drawer Divider for Jars

Cutting holes in a plywood inset. Cut a rectangle of ½-inch plywood to fit flat into the bottom of the drawer, and draw circles on it, outlining the bottoms of jars to be stored; with a compass, enlarge the radius of each circle by ¼ inch. Clamp the plywood over the edge of a worktable and use a sabre saw to cut out the circles, drilling a hole just inside the circle to start the saw blade. Slip the plywood into the drawer and stand jars in the cutout holes (*inset*).

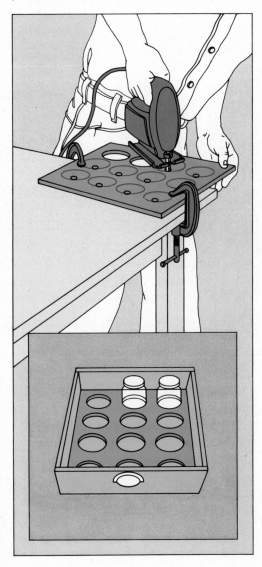

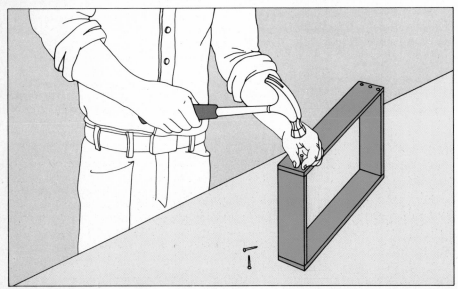

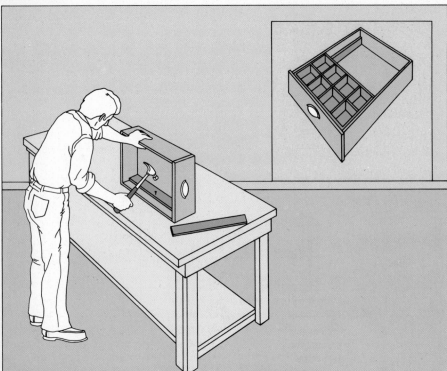

2 Installing tray glides. Cut two strips of ½-inch plywood as long as the depth of the drawer from front to back and ½ inch narrower than half the inside height of the drawer. Position each tray glide flat against the inside face of a drawer side, one edge butted against the bottom, and nail it in place. Then set the tray in position on the glides so that it slides back and forth, allowing easy access to larger items stored in the bottom of the drawer (*inset*).

Keeping Wood High and Dry

Storing lumber on wall racks. Multilevel storage racks keep a large amount of lumber stacked neatly against the wall. The basic framework for this unit is identical to the framework for the 2-by-6 shelf unit (*page 124*), except that these 2-by-6s are fastened to joists or overhead blocking with machine bolts instead of nails. Each of the three brackets that support the lumber at each level consists of a horizontal 2-by-4, 3 feet long, bolted at one end to the vertical 2-by-6 and at the other to a diagonal 2-by-4, 5¼ feet long, that extends upward from the vertical support at a 45° angle. Each diagonal brace is bolted to its vertical support through a 2-by-4 spacer block and overlaps the end of the horizontal 2-by-4 by 1 foot, to prevent lumber from slipping off the rack.

In workshops that have exposed studs, these racks can be installed directly on the studs instead of on a specially built framework. You can also nail plywood strips across the front of exposed studs to create shallow compartments that are useful for upright storage of dowels, moldings and other thin scraps (*inset*).

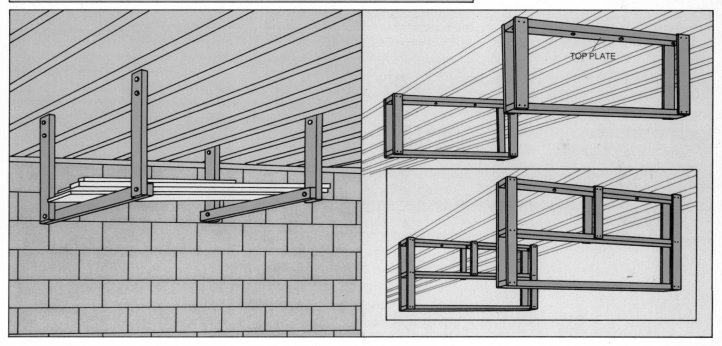

SPACER BLOCK

TOP PLATE

Storing lumber overhead. In areas where ceiling joists are exposed, lumber can be stored on an overhead rack (*left*) consisting of two U-shaped slings spaced approximately 4 feet apart. Each sling is constructed of 2-by-4s that are joined by bolts. The two 2-foot-long vertical pieces are fastened with lag bolts against the face of a joist. The verticals are 3 to 4 feet apart and are joined at the bottom by a horizontal piece, which is secured by machine bolts.

When ceiling joists are hidden, lumber can be stored in a frame (*right*) that has a 2-by-4 top plate, 4½ feet long, set flat against the ceiling, perpendicular to the joists, and lag-bolted to each joist it crosses. For maximum strength, the ends of the top plate should not extend more than 3 inches beyond a joist. Two strips of ½-inch plywood, each 2 feet long and 3 inches wide, are glued and screwed to the ends of the top plate. A second horizontal 2-by-4, cut to match

the top plate, is then glued and screwed between the lower ends of the plywood strips. If the shop layout makes positioning the top 2-by-4 perpendicular to the ceiling joists impossible, install the rack at left, cutting away enough ceiling covering to expose the face of the joists.

Either rack can be widened or divided into compartments with additional vertical and horizontal pieces (*inset, right*).

Organizing the Workshop's Housekeeping Chores

Whether you are building furniture or simply mending a leaky hose, nothing takes the joy out of a project faster than a messy work space or badly maintained tools. Keeping the work area clean and conditioning tools are peripheral activities, and they take time. But the time spent is more than compensated for by the time saved in a clutter-free shop with tools that work like new.

First of all, taking care of tools means keeping them clean. Remove resin from any blade used to cut wood by rubbing it with kerosene or ammonia applied with steel wool or a stiff brush.

Light rust can usually be removed with pumice or an ink eraser. But it is better to protect blades before rust attacks by wiping them with machine oil. For such metal surfaces as the tables of power tools, the best rust inhibiter is a thin coat of paste wax; rubbing with wax paper will do the job. You can also discourage rust by using a shop dehumidifier (page 12) or by storing tools in tight-fitting drawers and cabinets with uncovered containers of silica gel. When the gel mixture has absorbed all the moisture it can hold and has changed color, you can renew it by placing it in a 250° oven until it dries out.

Tools should also be checked periodically for wear. Wood handles may need sanding to keep them splinter-free, and wood handles of hammers, hatchets, axes and mallets may become loose as the wood dries and shrinks. To correct looseness, pound a small metal wedge, obtainable at a hardware store, into the top of the loose handle.

Examine saw blades for kinks or bends by sighting down the line of teeth. Sometimes unevenness can be straightened by hand; if not, lay the blade flat on a wooden surface and tap it with a wooden mallet. Check the sawteeth for set too, making sure they are cocked slightly to the sides, with alternate teeth set in opposite directions. If the teeth are out of line, you can realign them yourself, with the proper tools, but a professional will do it quickly and inexpensively. If the teeth are dull and need only touching up, that is easily done at home with a triangular taper file. You can sharpen the teeth of a circular saw with a larger triangular file or a mill bastard file unless the teeth are carbide-tipped; in that case, the blade must be sharpened professionally.

To keep chisels and plane blades razor-sharp, hone them often on a whetstone. Natural stones, made of a fine-grained rock called novaculite, are effective but expensive. Man-made stones of silicon carbide or aluminum oxide are more common and work faster to produce a sharp edge; the best of them have a medium-grit surface on one side, a fine-grit surface on the other. Both kinds of stones should be soaked in mineral oil or light machine oil so the surface offers less friction; some come this way from the factory. Before using a stone, apply a new film of oil; wipe off excess oil before storing. If the stone becomes gummy, warm it in an oven, then wipe away the beads of oil that appear.

When a chisel or plane blade needs more than honing—when it has encountered a nail, for instance, or fallen off the workbench—you will have to grind a new edge on it. The coarse side of a whetstone will suffice, but a bench grinder (page 56) is the best tool to use for this job; it gives the blade a hollow-ground edge that will hold its sharpness through many honings.

Grinding is made easier by such accessories as tool holders and special guides, but it is possible to do an excellent job with only the tool rest that comes with the bench grinder, carefully adjusted to match the original angle of the edge of the blade. While you are using the grinder, you must cool the blade frequently in water to avoid burning out its temper; a burned blade, which turns blue, will not hold a sharp edge.

To establish a prescribed angle for grinding—for example, 59° for the cutting lips of most twist bits—use a sliding T bevel and a pencil to transfer the angle to the grinder's tool rest.

To maintain power tools, lubricate and adjust them according to the manufacturer's instructions. Most motors are sealed and need little care, although they should be kept free of oily sawdust. For this, periodically wipe away the dust with a tack rag—a cloth dampened with turpentine and shellac.

To keep the shop itself clean, equip the room with a push broom, a wide dustpan, a bench brush, cleaning rags, paper towels and perhaps a rolling bin or two for debris. If your small power tools are equipped with dust-bag attachments, make use of them. To clean up the mess that is created by large power tools, the most effective agent is a central vacuum system (page 132).

Sharpening Handsaw Teeth

Sharpening at the correct angle. Clamp the saw in a woodworking vise with the saw handle to the right, and with the bottoms of the tooth valleys, called gullets, ⅛ to ¼ inch above the vise. Starting at the handle end, place a triangular taper file in the gullet to the left of the first tooth set toward you. On a crosscut saw, point the file to the right and at an angle of approximately 60° to the blade, and tilt the file 15° from horizontal, tip up and handle down. Rotate the file 15° counterclockwise and stroke forward. Remove the file from the gullet, return it to its original position and again stroke forward at the same angle as before. Repeat until the edges of the gullet are shiny. File every other gullet in this way, using the same number of strokes and the same amount of pressure each time.

Reverse the saw position in the vise so that the handle is to the left. Angling the file 60° to the blade with the file pointed toward the left, repeat the procedure, filing the tooth edges that were skipped the first time.

To file a ripsaw, change the angle of the file: Keep it horizontal, position it so that it is perpendicular to the blade, and rotate it counterclockwise 30° (inset) before you stroke. Otherwise, proceed in the same manner as you did for a crosscut saw, stroking alternate gullets until the edges become shiny.

A 4½-inch slim taper file can be used to sharpen any handsaw, including one that has 11 to 15 teeth (points) to the inch. For handsaws that have coarser teeth, however, larger files are more efficient—a 5-inch file for 9 or 10 points, a 6-inch file for 7 or 8 points, and a 7-inch file for a saw with 4½ to 6 points per inch.

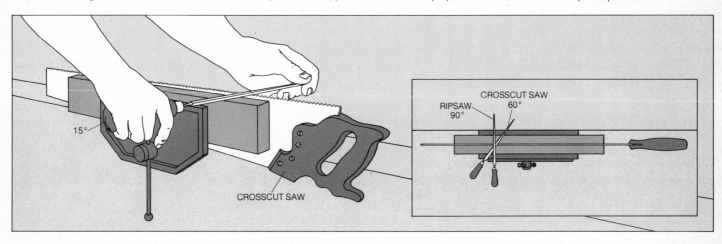

15°

CROSSCUT SAW

RIPSAW
90°

CROSSCUT SAW
60°

Touching Up the Blades of a Circular Saw

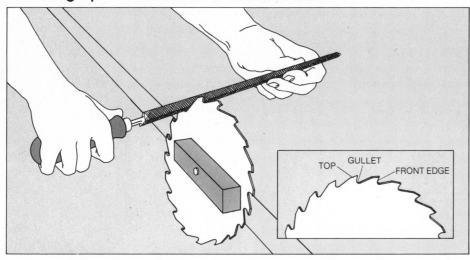

TOP GULLET FRONT EDGE

1 **Filing the front edges.** Clamp the blade in a special blade vise, teeth pointing clockwise, or clamp the blade to the side of the workbench with a wood block, nailed or screwed through the blade hole to the bench edge. Starting at the nine o'clock position, place a triangular file against the front, or under, edge of the first tooth pointing away from you, angling the file so it lies flat against the bevel of that edge. (For a ripsaw blade, you can use a larger, more efficient mill bastard file with rounded edges.) Push the file forward, maintaining the angle and being careful to keep the file off the bottom of the gullet. Repeat until the bevel is shiny, noting the number of strokes this takes. Then use the same number of strokes on alternate teeth, all pointing away from you, around the top of the blade, ending at the three o'clock position.

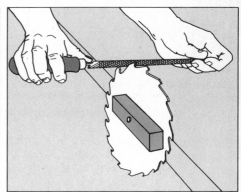

2 **Filing the back edges.** Go back to the first tooth you filed and sharpen its back, or top, edge by aligning the file face with the bevel and stroking forward. Again, working only on the teeth set away from you, bring the top of every other tooth to a shine.

Rotate the blade clockwise in the vise, exposing new teeth to be filed, and continue to sharpen the teeth set away from you. Then unclamp the blade, turn it over and reclamp it in the vise, teeth pointing counterclockwise. Working on the unshined teeth, now pointing away from you, file the front and back cutting edges as before.

Grinding a Twist-Bit Tip

Anatomy of a twist bit. A twist bit consists of two raised spirals, or lands, that slope inward at the top, forming two point surfaces. These meet at the apex along a line called the chisel edge. The point surfaces usually lie at an angle of 118° to each other, and each has a straight leading edge, called a cutting lip, from which it gradually slopes downward to curved back edge, the heel. With use, the cutting·lips become rounded and the point surfaces lose their downward slope; to cut smoothly through wood, both must be remachined with a grinder.

Grinding a twist bit. Clamp a wood guide against the tool rest of the grinder, setting the guide at an angle of 59° to the edge of the grinding wheel; the most comfortable angle for the rest itself is usually between 20° and 30°. Hold the bit against the wood guide, one hand on the shank of the bit, the other near its tip, and rotate the bit until one cutting lip is exactly horizontal. With the grinder on, move the bit forward until this lip barely touches the wheel, then slowly rotate the bit clockwise, simultaneously swinging it a little to the left until, when you reach the heel, the bit lies at an angle of 47° to the

grinding wheel. (For guidance, use a pencil to rule off these 59° and 47° angles on the face of the tool rest, as shown in the inset.)

Grind the other cutting lip in the same manner, alternating passes from one lip to the other. Cool the bit in water between passes and wear safety goggles during the entire operation.

Inexpensive jigs are available to hold twist bits during grinding, and you can also buy a self-powered bit sharpener that works something like an electric pencil sharpener.

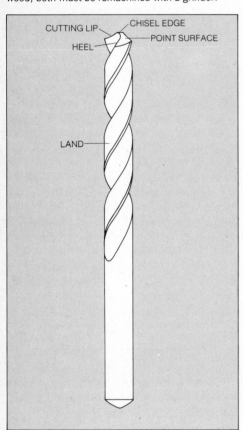

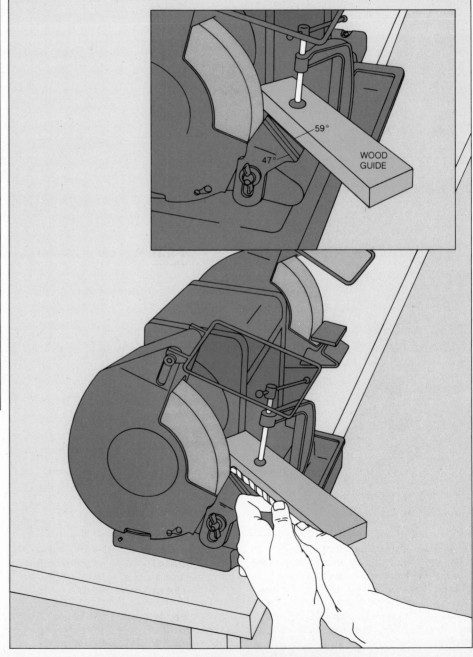

Reclaiming a Dull Spade Bit

Grinding the edges. Set the tool rest at an angle of 8° down from horizontal and position the bit on the tool rest with the left-side cutting lip, bevel down, touching the wheel. Slide a drill stop up the shank of the bit until it is 1/64 inch from the edge of the rest; tighten it at that position. Turn the machine on and apply the bevel to the grinding wheel; then turn the bit over and grind the other lip.

To grind the edges of the spur, the bit's pointed tip, swing the bit to the right so the right beveled edge of the spur is flat against the face of the wheel *(inset)*. To grind the left side of the spur, move the bit to the left at the same angle.

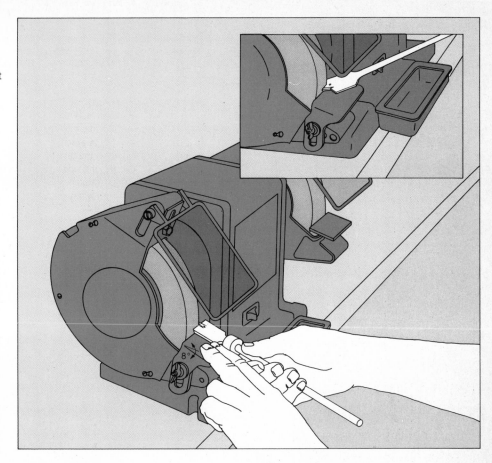

Grinding and Honing a Plane Blade or Chisel

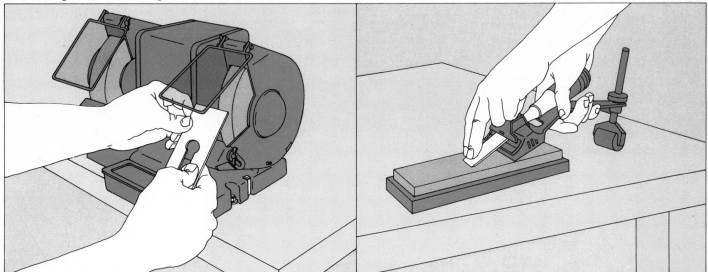

Grinding and honing. To grind off nicks or sharpen the edge of a badly dulled blade, hold the bevel face against the revolving grinder wheel and move the blade from side to side *(left)*. Position the blade so the width of the bevel is twice the thickness of the blade, a bevel angle of approximately 25° to 30°; use a special grinding attachment to secure the blade at this angle, or simply support it freehand on the adjustable tool rest. Dipping the blade frequently in cool water, grind it until a wire edge, called a burr, appears along the back of the very tip.

To hone the blade, clamp it, bevel down, in a honing jig and push and pull it in a straight line along a whetstone *(right)*; exert pressure only on the pull stroke. If no jig is available, rest the bevel flat against the stone and move the blade in a circle or figure-8 pattern, pressing when drawing the blade toward you. To remove the burr, turn the blade over and, holding it flat against the whetstone, move it lightly a few times across the stone in a sideways direction. To finish, stroke both sides of the blade on a leather strop.

Putting Refuse in Its Place

Few people look forward to cleanup time at the end of a day in the workshop, but sawdust and shavings cannot be ignored. Luckily, there are ways to ease this final chore. The wood waste can either be collected in a bin or an ordinary shop vacuum cleaner, or it can be sucked through a central vacuum system into a large waste container. While the first method is simpler, the second, by drawing waste from all parts of the shop to a central point, makes the cleanup faster.

Such a central vacuum system, modeled on industrial ones, can be installed in a home workshop at about twice the cost of a single ordinary household vacuum cleaner. Its main components are PVC, or plastic, pipe, sold at plumbing-supply stores, and a 2½-horsepower shop vacuum with a 30- to 55-gallon canister. For the system shown here 3-inch PVC pipe is used, with Ts of the type called straight, meaning there is no curve to the bottom leg of the T, and 90° elbows of the type called long radius.

Special fittings called 3-to-2 reducers connect the 3-inch pipe to a standard 2½-inch vacuum hose. The inside diameter of the narrow end of the reducer is still a fraction larger than the outside diameter of the stiff cuff at the end of the hose, allowing air leakage, so a rubber gasket is needed for a leakproof junction.

A central vacuum system works best if turns are kept to a minimum and vertical runs are short. For easy waste disposal, mount the canister on a wheeled dolly and empty it when it is two-thirds full.

Trapping Sawdust at the Tool

The dust catchers. An open-end plywood box (*below, left*) encloses all but the working face of a radial-arm saw. The box, bolted to the saw table, stops sawdust blown toward the back wall and drops it to the bottom, where an opening accommodates the cuff of a vacuum hose connected to a shop vacuum and canister.

An enclosed chute of ¾-inch lumber (*below, right*), built into an opening in a workbench, funnels shavings into a movable bin. The chute is attached to the underside of the bench with cleats on three sides of the opening. A whisk broom is handy for sweeping debris into the chute.

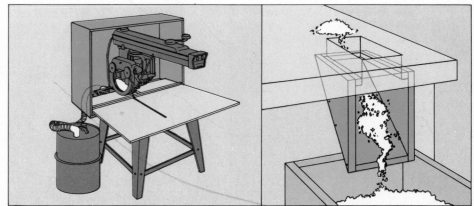

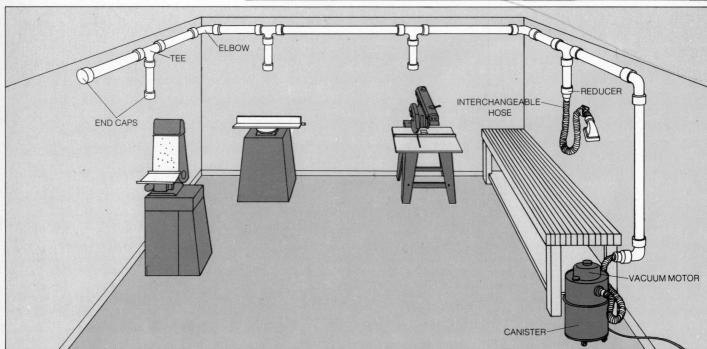

Layout of a central vacuum system. In this workshop, 3-inch PVC pipe runs above major tools and ends at a powerful vacuum motor with a large canister. Pipe elbows turn the corners, and Ts direct short lengths of pipe to locations where a movable vacuum hose might be needed. Short pipes that are not in use are plugged with friction-fitted end caps, as is the end of the pipe farthest from the vacuum machine. Since the vacuum hose is smaller than the PVC pipe, the end of the pipe near the vacuum is fitted with a special street elbow, collarless at one end to accept a 3-to-2 reducer. A second reducer connects the movable vacuum hose to the 3-inch pipe at the various tool locations.

Installing a Vacuum System

1 **Attaching the hanger straps.** Mold 12-inch lengths of perforated metal strapping around a section of 3-inch PVC pipe to form U-shaped hangers. For a pipe running perpendicular to joists, bend the ends of the hangers in opposite directions, forming fastening strips at least 4 inches long, and nail through the strip ends into a joist with 1½-inch roofing nails. For a pipe running parallel to a joist under a finished ceiling, bend the ends of the hanger in the same direction and nail to a joist through both ends at once; then bend the loop down *(inset)*. For a pipe running parallel to joists in an unfinished ceiling, simply nail the straps to the sides of a joist.

Cut and shape a pair of straps for each elbow and a pair for each T. Cut one strap for every 4-foot run of straight pipe.

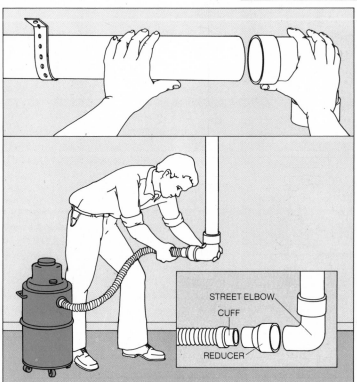

2 **Joining pipe sections.** Measure and cut pipe, then, starting in a corner, slide the pipe through the straps, slipping Ts or elbows onto the pipe as planned *(above, top)*. There is no need to use glue. Connect all the pipe for the system, including vertical runs to tools and the vacuum.

At the end of the pipe leading to the vacuum *(above, bottom)*, slip the collar end of a street elbow onto the pipe. Then slip a 3-to-2 reducer over the collarless end of the street elbow and insert the vacuum-hose cuff into the narrow end of the reducer *(inset)*, adding a rubber gasket to the cuff if necessary for a tight fit.

STREET ELBOW
CUFF
REDUCER

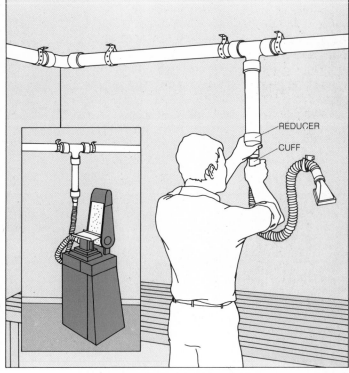

REDUCER
CUFF

3 **Attaching hoses at tool locations.** Uncap an intake pipe to which you want to attach the movable vacuum hose, and slip a 3-to-2 reducer into it. Then insert the hose cuff into the reducer and hang the hose on a hook until it is needed. If a tool has a fitting for a vacuum hose, remove the nozzle end of the hose and connect the hose directly to the fitting *(inset)*. Make certain that you keep all other pipe ends capped when the system is in operation.

Picture Credits

The sources for the illustrations in this book are shown below. The drawings were created by Jack Arthur, Laszlo Bodrogi, Roger C. Essley, Charles Forsythe, Dick Lee, John Martinez and Joan S. McGurren. Credits for the illustrations from left to right are separated by semicolons, from top to bottom by dashes. Cover: Fil Hunter. 6: Fil Hunter. 11: Forte, Inc. 13-17: Terry Atkinson. 19-26: Frederic F. Bigio from B-C Graphics. 29-31: Elsie Hennig. 32-40: Photographed by Henry Groskinsky, courtesy Henry Francis du Pont Winterthur Museum and Gardens. 41: Forte, Inc. 42: Fil Hunter. 49-60: Frederic F. Bigio from B-C Graphics. 61-63: Walter Hilmers Jr. from HJ Commercial Art. 64-71: John Massey. 72-79: Eduino J. Pereira. 80: Fil Hunter. 83-93: John Massey. 94-99: Ray Skibinski. 100-103: Gerry Gallagher. 104-106: Terry Atkinson. 107-113: Walter Hilmers Jr. from HJ Commercial Art. 114: Fil Hunter. 116-121: Walter Hilmers Jr. from HJ Commercial Art. 122-125: Melissa B. Pooré. 126, 127: William J. Hennessy Jr. 129-133: Snowden Associates, Inc.

Acknowledgments

The index/glossary for this book was prepared by Louise Hedberg. For their help in the preparation of this book, the editors also wish to thank the following: John Ascosi, Schaeffer's Piano Co., Silver Spring, Md.; Henry Barrow, Glen Echo, Md.; Edward C. Benfield, The Stanley Works, New Britain, Conn; The Bilco Company, New Haven, Conn.; Jerry G. Butcher, Arlington Career Center, Arlington, Va.; Harold Cohan, The Big Tool Box, Aurora, Colo.; Brad Coolidge, Washington, D.C.; Ronald V. Croy, Bethesda, Md.; Dennis Defliger, Greenlee Tools, Rockford, Ill.; J. C. Deliso, Toolkraft Corporation, Enfield, Conn.; David Draves, Woodcraft Supply Corporation, Woburn, Mass.; Ernest Maier, Inc., Bladensburg, Md.; William Everard, Fire Prevention Engineer, City of Alexandria, Va.; T. J. Fannon, Fannon Fuel Oil Co., Alexandria, Va.; Rich Fleming, Shop Vac Corporation, Williamsport, Pa.; Sheldon M. Gallager, Executive Editor, *Popular Mechanics*, New York, N.Y.; The Gordon Corporation, Farmington, Conn.; Dr. Lee Grant, Agricultural Engineering Extension Specialist, University of Maryland, College Park, Md.; John Greguric, Rockwell International, Pittsburgh, Pa.; Harrison Brothers Plumbing Supply, Alexandria, Va.; R. Bruce Hoadley, Professor, Wood Science and Technology, University of Massachusetts, Amherst, Mass.; Charles F. Hummel, Deputy Director for Collections, Winterthur Museum and Gardens, Winterthur, Del.; Erskin Jenkins, Thomas Jefferson High School, Alexandria, Va.; David A. Kolb, Torit Division, Donaldson Co., Inc., St. Paul, Minn.; Jim Palmisani, Merrifield, Va.; John W. Pollock, Brookeville, Md.; Martin M. Simon, Detect-a-Tronics, Inc., Arlington, Va.; Daniel Smith, Arlington, Va.; Terence P. Smith, Office of Fire Protection and Engineering Safety Standards, Washington, D.C.; Bart Spano, Polysonics, Washington, D.C.; Star for Parts, Inc., Denver, Colo.; Jim Surane, McCulloch Corporation, Los Angeles, Calif.; Thomas N. Tully, Hand Tool Specialist, National Museum of History and Technology, Washington, D.C.; Harold J. Tyson, Manager, Wood Hobby Shop, Bolling Air Force Base, Washington, D.C.; Claxton Walker, Potomac, Md.; Lee Yake, Virginia Vacuum and Sewing Machine Center, Arlington, Va.; The editors also wish to express their appreciation to Wendy Murphy, writer, for her help with this book.

Index/Glossary

Included in this index are definitions of many of the technical terms used in this book. Page references in italics indicate an illustration of the subject mentioned.

Access to shop: adding a basement entrance, 18, *19, 21-26;* cutting pass-through in wall, 18, *19, 20;* doors, 8, 10, *11;* providing, 8, 18, *19-26;* stairs, 10, *11*
Areaway (outside basement entrance), 18, *19;* excavating, 18, *21-22;* steps in, *26;* wall, *22-23;* waterproofing, 18
Attic: shop in, *9;* soundproofing, 30, *31*
Automatic sprinkler system, 28, *29*
Auxiliary work surfaces: extension table, *94, 96-97;* machine stand, *94, 95;* roller-topped table, *94, 98-99;* supporting stationary power tools, 61, 81, *94. See also* Jig; Platforms

Band saw: accessories, 52; auxiliary table, 94; space for, 52, *61, 62;* uses, 48, *52*
Basement: access to, 8, 18, *19, 21-26;* adding entrance, *21-26;* controlling dampness in, 8, 12, *13;* cutting through wall, *24-25;* humidity in, *13;* and shop, 8; sump pump, 12; waterproofing walls, 8, 12. *See also* Areaway
Belt sander, *55, 61, 62;* safety, *60*
Bench grinder, *114;* grinding spade bit, *131;* grinding twist bit, 128, *130;* restoring blades, 128, *131;* space for, 56, *61, 62;* using, 48, *56*

Cabinet, storage, *120-121*
Ceiling, soundproofing, 30, *31*
Central vacuum system, installing, *132-133*
Chisels: buying, 44, 46; grinding and sharpening blade, 128, *131*
Circuit breaker: *safety device that stops excess flow of current.* GFI, 64, 67, *71;* in 120-volt circuit, *71;* standard, 67, *71;* in subpanel, 64, 67; for 240-volt circuit, *73. See also* Wiring
Concrete: cap for cellar door, 18, *19, 23-24;* flooring, 27; footing and slab in areaway, 18, *19, 22;* patching and replacing, 27
Condensation, controlling in basement, 12
Conduit: *protective pipe.* Running wire through, *69-71*

Dampness: controlling in basement, 8, 12, *13;* testing for cause, 12

Dehumidifier, 12, 128
Disk sander, *55*
Door: cellar, 18, *19, 23-24;* prehung, in basement wall, *24-26;* to shop, 8, 10, *11*
Drawer: assembling, *118-119;* dividers for, 122, *125, 126;* sliding tray, *126;* storing hardware, 122; storing tools, 116, 117; suspending from worktable, *119,* 122
Drill press: attachments, *53;* safety measures, *59;* space for, 61, 62; tilting platform for, *101;* uses, 42, 48, *53*
Dubbing: *blunting tip of nail to keep wood from splitting.* In bench joint, 82
Dusting: *crumbling of improperly mixed concrete.* Stopping, 27

Eighteenth Century shops, 32, *33-40*
Electrical system: adding circuits, 64, 69, 73-74; computing power capacity of existing circuits, 64; distributing power in shop, 10, *11,* 69; extending cables, 65; planning for, 10, 61, 64, 69; running 120-volt circuit through conduit, *69-71;* in spray booth, 110; tapping into existing circuit, 64, *68;* voltages, 69
Exhaust fan: mounting in window, *111-112;* in spray booth, *110-112;* in stud wall, *16-17;* using kitchen-type fan for ventilation, 10, *11,* 12, *16-17;* wiring, *17*
Extension table: building, *96-97;* and table saw, 94

Featherboard: *slotted board used with table saw to hold and feed work.* Cutting, *103*
Fire hazards: in electrical system, 28; in shop, 14, 28; of spray booth, 110; of wood-burning stove, 14, *15*
Fireproofing: automatic sprinkler system, 28, *29;* extinguishers, *11,* 28, *29;* fire stops, 28; fire-retardant wallboard, 10, *11,* 28, 110, 112; prevention, 10, 28; smoke detector, *11,* 28, *29*
Floors, 27; shoring up floor joists, *9,* 27
Floor plans, *6, 61-63*
Foundation: patching cracks in, 12, *13;* waterproofing, 12, *13*
Furring strips: *thin strips of wood or other material attached to wall, ceiling or floor.* Mounting pegboard on, 117; for soundproofing, 30, *31*

Garage, and shop, *6, 9*
Gasoline, storing, 28
Ground-fault interrupter (GFI): *very sen-*

sitive circuit breaker that detects leakage of tiny amounts of current from circuit. Wiring breaker, 10, 64, 67, *71,* 73; wiring receptacle, 64, *68, 71*

Hand tools: selecting, 43, 44-45, *chart* 46-47; storing, *116-117*
Heating: electric baseboard heater, 14, *15;* extending forced-air system, *14;* wood-burning stove, 14, *15*
Hobby bench, 107, *108-109*
Honing: blades, *131;* jig, *131*
Humidity, measuring, 12, *13*

Insulation: fiberglass batts, 30, *31;* lining ducts, 30, *31*

Jig: *device that guides tool or holds wood in position.* Featherboard, *103;* hold-down and push stick, *60, 103;* honing, *131;* for stationary power tools, *80,* 81, 94, *102-103;* stopblock, *103;* tapering, *102;* tenoning, *102*
Jig saw: space for, *61, 62;* uses, 48, *52*
Jointer-planer, *54;* safety precautions, *60;* space for, 54, *61, 62;* uses, 48, *54*
Junction box: *metal enclosure where circuits are joined.* With multi-outlet strip, *72;* for power-tool motor, *75;* tapping power at, 68

Lathe: safety in using, *59;* space for, *61, 62;* using, *55;* wheel, 32, *36-37*
Layout: floor plans, *6, 61-63;* shop in alcove, *62;* shop in closet, *63;* shop in small space, 62
Lighting, 10; explosion-proof bulbs, 10, *110;* extension-arm light, 76, *79;* fluorescent fixtures, *76-77;* wiring wall switches, 76, *77-79*
Lumber, storing, 122, *127*

Machine stand, *94, 95;* mounting motor on, *95*
Maintenance: cleaning shop, 8, 128, *132-133;* cleaning tools, 115, 128; filing saw blades, 128, *129;* grinding bits, 128, *130-131;* removing rust, 128; restoring blades, 128, *131;* rust inhibitors, 115, 128; using whetstone, 128, *131*
Mechanical principles of simple machines, *41*
Metalworking: building bench for, *107-108;* tools for, *chart* 46-47
Multipurpose power tool, 48, *56-57*

Neoprene antivibration pads, *30*

Outlets: adding, *11, 69, 72;* extending wiring between, *71;* GFI receptacle, *68;* grounding, 10; grounding in Canada, 69; multi-outlet strips, *64, 69, 72;* for 240-volt circuit, *73-74;* wiring, *69, 71;* wiring for wall switches, 76, *77*

Painting: concrete floor, 27; removing oil-based paint from concrete, 27

Pegboard: attaching to cinder-block wall, 117; hangers for, *117;* mounting, 116, *117;* storing tools, *116, 117*

Plane: buying, 45, 47; grinding and honing blade, 128, *131;* storing, *116, 117*

Planning: access to shop, 8, 10, *11,* 18, *19-26;* arranging space, 8, 43, 48, 61; climate control, 12, *13-17;* evaluating site, 7, *8-9;* fireproofing, 28, 29; floor, 27; floor plans, 6, *61-63;* safety measures, 10, *11;* soundproofing, *30-31;* tools, 43, 44-47, 48

Platforms: for drill press, *101;* for table saw, *100;* wood for, 100

Pliers, buying, 45, 47

Power tools: adapting, 48; attaching and wiring switch, *74-75;* auxiliary work surfaces, 61, *94, 95, 96-99;* buying secondhand, 48; jigs, 100, *102-103;* machine stand, *94, 95;* maintenance, 115, 128; multipurpose, 48, *56-57;* platforms for, *100-101;* portable, 45, *chart 47;* power for, *64, 69;* reducing vibration, *30;* safety precautions, *58-60;* selecting, 43, 48, *49-56;* space for, 48, 61

Raceway: *channels and outlets to carry electrical wires along surfaces.* Using, *11, 15, 69, 72*

Radial-arm saw: accessories, 50, *51;* auxiliary table, 94; space for, 51, *62;* stopblock, 103; using, 48, *50-51*

Resilient channels: *metal strips attached to framing members of wall or ceiling.* Soundproofing, 30, *31*

Roller-topped table (auxiliary work surface): building, *98-99;* and table saw, *94*

Rust: inhibiting, 115, 128; removing from tools, 128

Safety considerations: of exhaust fan, 16; of floor, 27; hand tools, 58; handling power tools, *58-60;* of heating systems, 14, *15;* storing tools and supplies, 10, *11,* 28. *See also* Fireproofing

Saw (hand): buying, 44, 46; checking blades, 128; cleaning, 115; filing circular saw blade, *129;* filing teeth of, 128, *129;* realigning teeth, 128

Sawdust: clearing with central vacuum system, 115, *132-133;* collecting in boxes and chutes, *132*

Sawhorse, folding, *105-106*

Screwdrivers, buying, 45, 47

Shaper, *54*

Shelves: anchoring jars on, *125;* building between studs, 122, *123-124;* individual, supported by braces, *122-123;* wall of, *124*

Smoke detector, *11,* 28; types of, 28; mounting, 28, *29*

Soundproofing, *30-31*

Spade bit, grinding, *131*

Spray booth: building, *111-112;* design, *110;* exhaust-fan assembly, *111, 112;* placement of, 110

Stairs: in areaway, 18, *19, 26;* to shop, 10, *11*

Storage: cabinet, *116,* 117, *120-121;* devising a system, 115, *116-117;* drawer dividers, *125, 126;* of flammable liquids, 10, 28; of hardware, *122-126;* in hobby benches, *108, 109;* of lumber, 122, *127;* of materials, 28, *122-127;* safety measures, 10, *11,* 28; shelving, *122-125;* tool turret, *113;* of tools, 7, 10, *11,* 61, 62, 63, 115, *116-121,* 128; in workbenches, 82, *89*

Subpanel: *auxiliary service panel connected to main panel.* Connecting 120-volt circuit to, *70-71;* GFI breaker in, *67;* mounting on damp basement wall, 66; standard circuit breaker in, *67;* wiring, *64, 66-67*

Table saw (bench saw): auxiliary tables, *94-99;* blades, *49;* featherboard, *103;* hold-down and push stick, *103;* platform with miter guides, *100;* safety, *49, 58;* space for, 50, *61, 62;* stand, *94, 95;*

stopblock, *103;* tapering jig, *102;* tenoning jig, *102;* using, 48, 49, *50*

Tiles: laying over concrete, 27

Tool turret, *62, 113;* mounting for, 113

Tools: maintenance, 115, 128, *129-131;* mechanical principles, *41;* portable toolbox, *63, 104;* selecting hand, 43, 44-45, *chart 46-47;* selecting power, 48, *49-56;* storage, 115, *116-121. See also* Hand tools; Maintenance; Power tools; Storage

Twist bit: in drill press, *53;* grinding, 128, *130*

Ventilation, 8, 12; *See* Exhaust fan

Voltages, described, *69*

Wallboard, fire-retardant, 10, *11,* 28, 110, 112

Whetstone, honing blades on, 128, *131*

Wiring: adding switch to power tools, *74-75;* adding 240-volt circuit, *69, 73-74;* additional outlets, *69, 72;* connecting electric baseboard heater, 14, *15;* connecting subpanel, 64, *66-67;* extending cables in house, *65;* fluorescent lights, *76-77;* GFI breaker, 64, 67, *73;* GFI receptacle, 64, *68, 71;* kitchen-type exhaust fan, *17;* middle-of-the-run, *76-77;* multi-outlet strip, *72;* overhead outlet, *72;* planning, *64;* protecting wires, *69;* running cables through concrete, *65;* running 120-volt circuit through conduit, *69-71;* standard circuit breaker, 64, *67;* switch loop, 76, *78-79;* tapping existing circuits, 64, *68;* tapping power at junction box, *68;* voltages, *69;* wall switches, *76-79;* wiring cables in a wall, *65*

Woodworking vise, mounting on workbench, *80, 82, 83, 85, 86, 87, 88*

Workbench: backboard, 82, *83, 84-85;* bench and drafting table, *109;* designs, 82, *83;* desk-and-bench combination, *108-109;* dimensions, 82; fold-down, 82, *83, 89-91;* freestanding, 82, *83, 86-88;* for metalworking, *107-108;* placing in shop, 61, *62, 63;* portable, 82, *83, 92;* tall, 82, *83, 93;* using natural light, 32, *34-35, 61*